Helen Redina

W9-DEC-358

FROMMER'S

1985-86 GUIDE TO
ATHENS

by Ian Keown

Published by Frommer/Pasmantier Publishers
A Division of Simon & Schuster, Inc.
1230 Avenue of the Americas
New York, NY 10020

ISBN 0–671–52467–4

Manufactured in the United States of America

Cover Design by Steve Jenkins
Motif drawings by Paul Berkow

CONTENTS

MAPS

INFLATION ALERT: It is hardly a secret that a wave of inflation has battered the countries of Europe, and Greece has not escaped. The author of this book has made every effort to ensure the accuracy of prices appearing in this guide. As we go to press, we believe we have obtained the most reliable data possible. However, we cannot offer guarantees for the tariffs quoted, and so in the lifetime of this edition the wise traveler will add 10% to 15% to the prices quoted.

The Dollar and the Drachma

Where currency conversions from drachmas to dollars appear in parentheses on these pages, they were prepared on the basis of 100 drachmas = $1. That rate may not be accurate by the time you travel, as it varies from day to day, depending on the relative values of both currencies on world markets. Use these currency conversions, therefore, only as a gauge for what you'll be spending and check with a banker before you leave for Greece to determine what the actual rate of exchange is at that time.

THE GREEK IN ALL OF US

GREECE IS THE CRADLE of civilization, the origin of the West, the birthplace of democracy . . . etcetera, etcetera. That gets the clichés out of the way. Nevertheless, it's hard to imagine what civilized life would be like today without the influence of Ancient Greece. The Greeks invented drama, and amphitheaters to perform it in. They invented the Olympic Games. Euclid and Pythagoras formulated the theories geometry students slave over to this day. And there isn't a computer programmer who hasn't studied the logic of Aristotle. Ancient Greece created a style of architecture that was the model for the White House, the Lincoln Memorial, and state capitols all across the land. Doctors still take the Hippocratic Oath, named for the father of medicine, a Greek, of course. Children learn about the ant and the grasshopper and other characters from the fables of Aesop. And Greek myths have become so interwoven with our civilized consciousness that we sometimes forget where they came from. Oedipus, after all, was a Greek, not a character living in Freud's Vienna.

And then there's the Greek language. It doesn't exactly sound like poetry when spoken in the streets of Athens, but what a debt we owe to it! Sophisticated, metropolitan, aristocratic, philanthropy, gymnastics, pornographic—are all from the Greek. Even ecology, our newest "in" word, comes from the Greek words *oikos,* meaning house, and *logos,* meaning word or thought.

The mighty Romans, conquerors of almost the entire ancient world, were so awed by the accomplishments of Ancient Greece that they copied its art, its architecture, and in general acted as if they had been conquered by the Greeks rather than the other way around. Perhaps in a way they were. Perhaps in a way we *all* were.

In fact, the Greek influence has been so strong throughout our heritage, so ubiquitous in our everyday lives, that a visit to

Greece is like a prodigal's return. So as the Greeks tell their visitors, "Welcome home. You've been away too long!"

Erechtheum

A REFRESHER COURSE IN GREEK HISTORY

ANCIENT GREECE, rather than modern Greece, is what brings most visitors to Athens (the Greek islands are something else again), and since you're going to be looking at quite a lot of ruins you might as well take a quick refresher course in Minoans, Mycenaeans, and Macedonians. After all, the more you remember, the more you'll enjoy.

THE BULL DANCERS: Around 3000 B.C., the most ancient civilization of Greece began to flourish. The **Minoan** civilization of Crete is one of the oldest civilizations in Greek history, and this civilization, with Crete at its center, lasted almost 2000 years.

The Minoans were generally peace-loving people. They lived in cities without protective walls, and they were never invaded. They were an artistic people, but didn't develop a script until some time around 1700 B.C. Their art, which you can still see in some of the ruins at Knossos in Crete, was colorful and sunny—red columns and sky-blue temple walls.

One of their favorite pastimes was bull jumping (the bull dancers would grab the bull's horns and flip themselves over its back, etc.), a sport that makes today's bullfighting look like a sheepdog trial. Bulls, in fact, were a key part of the culture, and were worshipped by the Minoans. The most famous bull of all, the Minotaur, was a creature with a bull's head and a human body, the mythological offspring of a bull sent from the sea as a sign to prove King Minos's right to the throne of Crete. Unfortunately, when the king refused to sacrifice the bull to the god Poseidon, his queen was cursed with a passion for it. Her child, the Minotaur, was then imprisoned by King Minos in the center of the Labyrinth, a maze so convoluted no one could reach the center to kill it and thus free the people from the influence of the monster. Except the great Theseus, of course, but even he couldn't kill the Minotaur without the help of Minos's daughter, Ariadne. We'll come back to Theseus in a minute.

THE FAMILY THAT SLAYS TOGETHER . . . On mainland Greece the first civilization you have to contend with is the Mycenaean, which started to make its presence felt about 1400 B.C. It was focused on the city of Mycenae, about 25 miles from Corinth in the region known as the Peloponnese. Mycenae was the home of that happy family headed by Agamemnon, who was put to death by his wife Clytemnestra and her lover, who in turn were wiped out by her son Orestes at the instigation of her daughter Electra. The Trojan War was launched from here.

Then about 1100 B.C., a people called the Dorians invaded Mycenae and other cities of Greece and crushed them. Almost overnight, the great "palace bureaucracies" disappeared, and the Greeks were reduced to small, illiterate communities. This was the Dark Age of Greece.

THE YARN SPINNERS: Throughout history the Greeks have been nothing if not hardy, and at this time they began to develop the *polis* that was to become the central political unit in the upcoming classical period. The polis was a cluster of houses around a "palace" that stood on a safe hill, called an *akropolis*, and its inhabitants usually had a common family relationship. Apart from that, they had nothing—no culture, no literature, only memories of past glories. So they got together on their akropolis and consoled themselves by singing songs and reciting poetry extolling the heroism of their ancestors. Two of these songs were the *Iliad* and the *Odyssey*. No one knows for sure in what form Homer learned the legends he wrote about in the *Iliad*, but no matter how he received them he handed the legends along in a great new art form that excites scholars to this day.

Around this time, 800 B.C., the Greeks came into contact with the Phoenicians, who did have an alphabet and knew how to put things in writing; so the Greeks adapted it, just in time for Homer to polish up his spoken poetry and get it down on stone.

THE SPARTANS: Slowly, aristocracy began replacing monarchy (except in Sparta and Macedonia); trade was flourishing, slavery increasing, and coined money was introduced to simplify trading throughout the entire Mediterranean. Revolutionaries came along, roused the slaves, and overthrew governments—except in Sparta, where two kings ruled, and reared their people to live frugally (hence the word "spartan") and to cultivate physical discipline. From the age of seven, Spartan youths were given military training. All men of military age lived in barracks and were not allowed to live with their wives until they were 30. Thus, when any revolutionary tried to start anything in Sparta he was quickly put down by the militaristic establishment.

THESEUS RIDES AGAIN: The scene now shifts to Attica, which is the part of mainland Greece where Athens, and several other small independent cities, were located. These city-states were being united by King Theseus (this is the same Theseus who penetrated the Labyrinth and killed the Minotaur—the Minoan civilization was still there all this time). No sooner had Theseus finished with the Minotaur than he was off battling the Centaurs. Somewhere along the way he became king of Athens, married an Amazon, conquered Thebes, and united Attica.

Sometime around 621 B.C. a legislator named Draco appeared on the Athenian scene and codified laws that substituted public justice for personal revenge, and thus outlawed the feuds that were a popular Greek pastime. His laws were so severe that the legislator has been immortalized by the word "draconian." The laws were said to be written in blood rather than ink, because he rewarded many types of crime (such as stealing a cabbage!) with the death penalty. These laws held for only a quarter of a century until Solon, who came to be called the founder of Athenian democracy, abolished the death penalty for everything but murder. Solon also instituted constitutional reforms that set up free elections and brought all classes (except slaves) into the process of government. And so democracy began.

MARATHON AND SALAMIS: A hundred years later democracy and everything else Greece had built up were threatened by Persia. The first of Persia's expeditions took place in 490 B.C., when its army arrived at Marathon. This was the event where a Greek soldier ran the 26 miles back to Athens, managed to gasp "We have won," then collapsed and died. In their second expedition the Persians were matched by the genius of Themistocles, an Athenian leader who made his people nervous by going out and building a huge fleet rather than an army. However, he turned out to be right: the Persians were blasted off the sea at the battle of Salamis. When the Greeks, and their Spartan allies, turned to the attack on land at the pass of Thermopylae, they trapped the Persians for four days. But the Persians eventually gained the upper hand, and rather than retreat, the Spartans remained and died to the last man. A Greek poet composed one of history's most famous epitaphs for them: "Stranger, go tell the Spartans that here we lie in obedience to their wishes."

THE GOLDEN AGE: Athens, now a naval power, was headed for its golden age. Its ruler at this time (the middle of the fifth century B.C.) was **Pericles,** the most dazzling orator in a city of dazzling orators. He practiced democracy at home, imperialism abroad. One of his wisest decisions was to pay jurors, so that even the poorest citizens could sit on juries. One of his not-so-smart decisions was to restrict Athenian citizenship to people whose mother and father were both Athenians. This would have been fine if he hadn't at that time fallen under the spell of Aspasia. Aspasia had been born in Mileta but had migrated to Athens because that was where the action was in those days; she quickly established herself as a beautiful and intelligent courtesan, who taught rhetoric on the side. One of her students was Socrates, and another was Pericles. Pericles took her as his mistress, promptly divorced his wife, but he couldn't marry Aspasia because of the new law he himself had brought into being. So they lived together. Aspasia became the uncrowned queen of Athens, and their son was later honored with citizenship by a special act of the Athenians. Aspasia was later condemned to death for impiety, a trumped-up charge, and Pericles had to muster all his dazzling oratory to save her. It was Pericles who built the Parthenon, the Propylaea, the long walls to Piraeus, and many of the temples you'll see on your strolls around town. This was quite a time in Athens. Aspasia was right—Athens was *the* place. While Pericles was building his Parthenon, Aeschylus, Sophocles, and Euripides were writing their plays, and Socrates and Plato were teaching. But Sparta was smoldering with jealousy, and became increasingly worried about Athens's imperialistic policies.

Now we get involved with another series of wars. Or rather one long, lingering, 27-year war—the **Peloponnesian War.** Pericles led Athens, avoiding battles on land, attacking the Peloponnese from the sea, because Athens ruled the waves. Pericles, unfortunately, saw only two years of the war—he died of a plague which struck Athens in 429 B.C. A host of demagogues and lesser leaders followed, who eventually brought Athens to defeat in 404 B.C. But victorious Sparta's influence lasted only 30 years after; it was then superseded by Macedonia, a kingdom in the north of Greece.

THE PRINCE AND THE HORSE: Philip of Macedon's ambition was to unify all of Greece, restore Greek culture to Macedon, and eliminate Persia as a lingering threat. But before he could do that, he too divorced his wife, who thereupon hatched a plot and had him assassinated because she was jealous of his new consort. His nephew was next in line to the throne, but the crown went instead to his first wife's son, Alexander. One of the first legends about Alexander began when he fulfilled an oracle's prediction by succeeding in mounting a high-spirited horse named Bucephalus. Philip had intended to destroy this horse because he was unmountable, but the clever Alexander noticed that the problem with Bucephalus was that he was literally afraid of his own shadow; so Alexander turned the horse's eyes into the sun and mounted. At the age of 20, Alexander became king, and Bucephalus would soon carry him across an empire.

ALEXANDER THE GREAT: Alexander, as you know, conquered Greece, united it against Persia, then marched his armies across continents, conquering Asia, Syria, Egypt, Babylon, Susa, Persepolis. He was on his way to conquer India when his troops finally became so exhausted they compelled him to return to Macedon. He was a humane man (he had studied under Aristotle), who maintained the civil liberties of all the peoples he conquered, honored their gods and their customs. He even went so far as to adopt one Oriental custom for himself, and married several Eastern princesses. In 323 B.C. Alexander the Great caught a fever and died. He had lived an extraordinary life, and died when only in his early thirties.

Alexander's death marked the end of the great classical period of Greece—in literature, philosophy, and art. The city-states withered, the upper classes took over, and there was constant bickering and battling until 146 B.C. when Greece was conquered by the powerful and indomitable armies of Rome.

CENTURIONS AND CHRISTIANS: Although the Romans, as we noted earlier, admired the art and culture of Greece, they had no respect at all for its countryside. Rather than fight all their battles on Roman soil they tended to move them to neutral territory. Mark Antony and Octavius fought it out with Brutus and Cassius in Greece, at Philippi; Octavian then routed Antony and turned back Cleopatra's ships in Greek waters.

For 500 years, right through the early era of Christianity, Greece was subject to the power of Rome. It also became a stronghold of Christianity. Saint Paul preached in Greek, and his famous epistles were written to the Greek communities of Corinth, Thessaloniki, and Ephesus.

For most practical purposes the history of classical Greece ends at this point. Tourists come to Greece mainly to see the remains of the classical ruins, and to relive the days of glory of Pericles and the Athenians. That's what Greece is all about. Obviously, though, its history continues, and there are many people who want to see the country's examples of Byzantine art and culture (which you'll read about next)—but that's not the essential Greece. From the time of Saint Paul and the Apostles, the history of Greece is a chronicle of sieges, battles, and struggles to regain independence. The struggle was heroic enough but it lacked the grandeur of Ancient Greece. Or maybe they just didn't have a Homer to glorify it.

BYZANTIUM: In A.D. 330 the Roman emperor Constantine chose a fishing village on the Bosporus, the channel leading to the Black Sea, to be his eastern capital. He named it Constantinople. Eventually it became the capital of its own empire, the Byzantine, and managed to resist invasions and maintain its hold on the Balkan Peninsula, Asia Minor, Cyprus, the Middle East, and Egypt. Rome at the time was slowly succumbing to invasions of barbarians. Greece was a mere province.

For many hundreds of years, Byzantium was the only civilized part of Europe. Art, especially religious art, flourished, and churches, monasteries, and palaces were going up everywhere. Then the Eastern and Western churches separated; Venetians, Franks, and soldiers from other countries in Western Europe formed their crusades and pillaged Constantinople. The city eventually fell to the Ottoman Turks, Greece was reduced to an even more insignificant province, and Athens became a small town. The Parthenon was turned into a Turkish mosque.

A Ready Reference for Ancient Greek History

Period	Approx. dates	Key events and people
Minoan	3000 to 1400 B.C.	Knossos (Crete) King Minos The Minotaur Theseus
Mycenaean	1400 to 1150 B.C.	Agamemnon Jason and the Argonauts Achilles Troy
Dark Age	1200 to 1100 B.C.	
Aristocratic Age	800 to 600 B.C.	Athens unites with towns of Attica Draco proclaims severe laws Solon reforms constitution Homer composes the *Iliad* and the *Odyssey*
Persian Wars	520 to 480 B.C.	Themistocles fortifies Piraeus Greeks win at Marathon and Salamis Aeschylus wins Athens drama festival
Classical Age	480 to 430 B.C.	Parthenon built Pericles in power Aeschylus, Sophocles, and Euripides at work
Peloponnesian War	430 to 400 B.C.	Naval battle of Syracuse Erechtheum on Acropolis completed Aristophanes writes comedies Pericles dies Socrates drinks hemlock Sparta triumphs
Macedonian Age	360 B.C. to 300 B.C.	Alexander the Great conquers Aristotle founds school
Roman	200 B.C. to A.D. 300	Rome sacks Corinth
Byzantine	A.D. 300 to 1200	Constantine builds Constantinople Crusaders build forts, sack Constantinople

For the next 400 years Greece remained under Turkish rule. In the early 1600s Venice tried to move in, without success (although you can still see the Venetian influence in places like Corfu). In the early 1800s the Greeks started to muster groups of revolutionaries, and in March 1821 they formally began their struggle for independence when an archbishop raised a new blue-and-white flag at a monastery near Patras. (The date, March 25, is now Greek Independence Day.)

This was the period when Lord Byron and other volunteers rallied to the Greek cause. Byron died at Missolonghi in 1824, but in the end, with the help of Britain, Russia, and France, Greece finally defeated the Turks in a spectacular sea battle off the Bay of Navarino—spectacular and extraordinary because the Turks lost 53 ships with 6000 men on board but the allied fleet didn't lose a single vessel.

INDEPENDENCE, DEFEAT, INDEPENDENCE: In 1829 the "protecting powers" declared Greece an independent nation. Unfortunately, they couldn't agree among themselves on territorial and legal conditions (some of these problems remain undecided to this day). A year later Greece became a kingdom; a 17-year-old Bavarian prince was named to the throne, Prince Otto (or Othon). He lasted until 1862, when he was replaced by the Danish ruling house. Thessaly, Macedonia, and Thrace meantime remained under Ottoman rule, but after the Balkan War of 1912–1913 they became part of Greece, leaving Turkey with only the eastern half of Thrace, including Constantinople (which was then renamed Istanbul). We can leave Greek history there, at least until October 28, 1940, when an emissary from Mussolini demanded that the Greek-Albanian border be opened to Italian troops. The Greek patriot, General Metaxas, replied "Ohi," or no, and thereby brought Greece into World War II. (October 28 is now celebrated as Ohi Day.) Greece was invaded by the Nazis, freed by its own Resistance and the Allies, and settled down once more to the intramural squabbles characterizing the period. Greece is now a republic, with a democratically elected parliament and a president, Constantine Caramanlis, who is held in high esteem both by Greeks and the international community.

Regimes may come and regimes may flounder, but the glory that was Greece remains. Or as Pericles once said, "Future ages will wonder at us, as the present age wonders at us now."

Chapter III

MOUNTAINS, ISLANDS, AND RUINS

An Outline of Modern Greece

ON A MAP, Greece looks almost like an inkblot that landed in one large glob and burst into a score of splotches. The glob is the mainland, the splotches the islands. The total land area of Greece is 51,182 square miles—roughly the size of Louisiana. One-quarter of this area is islands, the remainder is mountains. The island quarter we leave to later chapters in this guide; right now we'll examine the three-quarters that make up the land mass.

It's a complicated land, so let's begin by dividing it, like Gaul, into three parts: the Olympian north, central Greece, and the Peloponnese.

THE OLYMPIAN NORTH: This region includes Epirus, Thessaly, Macedonia, and Thrace. Mount Olympus, the dwelling place of the gods, is up there; so is Mount Athos, with its famous monastery. Thessaly is considered the breadbasket of Greece, supplying most of its wheat, corn, barley, and cotton.

CENTRAL GREECE: This region can be subdivided into six areas —Aetolia, Acarnania, Phthiotis, Phocis, Boeotia, and Attica. The first four names you can forget for the moment, but Attica is the land around Athens (you'll probably be seeing quite a bit of it), and Boeotia is where you'll find Delphi of oracle fame.

GREECE, THE ISLANDS, AND AEGEAN TURKEY

THE PELOPONNESE: To the southwest is a peninsula known as the Peloponnese, which can almost be considered an island since the completion of the Corinth canal which separates it from central Greece. The canal, incidentally, was begun by Nero, way back then, but not completed in its present form until 1893. It's a spectacular tourist sight in its own right.

The Peloponnese is where you find such haunts of the ancient Greeks as Corinth, Mycenae, Epidaurus, Olympia, and Sparta, 4000 years of history, and mountains rising to almost 8000 feet.

THE COUNTRYSIDE: Greece is a land of bleached limestone ridges, brown hills, olive groves, and an incredible collection of bays and coves lapped by green and turquoise seas. In the north, Greece is cut off from Albania, Yugoslavia, and Bulgaria by mountains; in the west, she's isolated by the Ionian Sea; in the south, by the Mediterranean; and in the east, by the Aegean. Because of the mountains and valleys, communities have historically been cut off from each other and have tended to retain their own individual characteristics, and Greeks still tend to identify themselves as Cretans, Athenians, Rhodians, and so forth. This individuality has helped make the country's folk art and folklore so varied and fascinating.

All the groups still retain their rivalries, as you'll find out if you go to a taverna and the singer announces a song from beautiful Thessaloniki (cheers!), then a song from beautiful Rhodes (hurrahs!), and a song from Macedonia (whistles!). The most reliable, charming, tolerant, intelligent of these groups is the one you happen to be talking to at a particular time.

GREEK HOSPITALITY: Over all, however, the Greeks are a lively, friendly, fun-loving, sometimes exuberant, people. And Greek is the only language in the world in which the word for stranger is also the word for guest—*xenos.* They take a great delight in the fact that so many tourists appreciate their country, and a great pride in their country, its heritage, and its ruined symbols of glory.

Hospitality has always been an admirable Greek trait. From the fishing families who open their homes to tourists on the islands (it's more than that they can use the money) to the hotel clerk who acts like he's always known you, the Greek actually seems to like visitors.

Perhaps it's because Herodotus, one of the first world travelers, was so tolerant of other races, and because for centuries Greeks have roamed the world and come back home to settle with a less insular view of things than many other nations. (In almost every small village, there's a local Greek-American—an older man who spent his youth in the U.S., made his "fortune," and came back to settle and be the ultimate arbiter of all arguments about that country and its doings. Sometimes he's living on monthly Social Security checks.)

But perhaps it's nothing more than the innate native sense of drama—the opportunity to take the stage at somebody else's prompting. To any Greek all the world's a stage, just as it always has been—especially the marketplace, the main square, or the cafés along the harbor.

Stop and ask for directions in the street and everybody gathers around and puts in their two-bits' worth. At last, weary of making yourself understood or getting any uniformity out of the replies, you walk away and leave the discussion. When you look back, they're still arguing.

Friendliness, in short, is a characteristic, and you'll often be encountered with the all-purpose greeting *Yiasu!* (good health) by people you don't know. *Kalimera* (good morning) and *kalispera* (good evening) are useful greetings to sprinkle around too.

The Greek government also is trying to be friendly, and has launched an all-out drive to attract tourists. It's done a lot to make them welcome. Overseas, it has opened new offices to tell people about Greece, and has stocked the offices with lavishly enticing brochures. In Greece, it has streamlined arrival and Customs facilities, put up hotels where they were needed, built new highways to get you to the new hotels. The tourists have responded. In 1978, for the first time in history, *5 million* tourists visited Greece—more than double the number who came in 1974. The number is still increasing. That's good news for the hotels and the tour operators, but it causes increasing soul-searching among people who care about Greece's ruins and once unspoiled charm.

THE ACROPOLIS—AND THE CITY AT ITS FEET

Getting to Know Athens

EVERYONE'S IMAGE of Athens is a white, rocky hill with a ruined, but glorious, temple on top. Or maybe a soldier in a skirt with pompoms on his shoes. But your first impression of Athens will be nothing like that.

Your introduction to Athens is a marble parthenon of the 20th century—a gleaming, elegant airport terminal that puts you in the atmosphere of a big, modern, successful city.

On your ride in from the airport you pass through disheveled suburbs of two-story white houses, past women dressed in black, and despite the alien but unmistakable injunction to drink Coca-Cola you're left with no doubt that you're now in a Mediterranean country.

When you get to your hotel in the heart of the city, you're in a sophisticated European city of avenues, jewelry shops, spacious squares, and terrace cafés.

Step a few streets from this chic city and you're treading in the marbled steps of Aristotle, Pericles, and Sophocles.

In other words, there's no point in trying to put Athens into any kind of category. It's unique. It's a city where you brush shoulders with Ancient Greece, Rome, Sparta, Macedonia, Byzantium, the East, the West, Venice, Germany, France, Italy, America. They've all left their imprint, and what you're treated to is a fascinating, intriguing, unbelievably historic but not particularly beautiful city.

Let's pinpoint it. Athens is roughly on the same latitude as Louisville (Kentucky), San Francisco, and Tokyo. Its climate is considered mild, and probably is except when you're trudging around town looking for a hotel at high noon in August. Rainfall is a skimpy 15 inches a year, most of it in short showers in winter (if it rains in summer before the last week of August, it's news). June, July, August, and September are hot, but bearable because the air is so dry. On the other hand, don't try to fit in half a dozen temples between noon and 2 p.m.; try to confine your sightseeing to the early morning or late afternoon. That's the way the Athenians organize things (but we'll come back to that later). In winter, specifically January and February, things can get a little chilly. The cafés and tavernas move indoors, and occasionally you may have to hold on tight for fear of being blown off the Acropolis.

ATHENS: AVERAGE MONTHLY TEMPERATURES					
	Low	High		Low	High
January	45.0	56.3	July	73.6	90.1
February	44.6	57.7	August	73.8	90.1
March	47.7	61.9	September	68.0	83.8
April	53.4	68.7	October	60.6	75.4
May	60.8	75.9	November	52.0	66.6
June	68.5	84.2	December	48.2	59.5

But all the statistics in the weather bureau will never do justice to the Athenian evenings. The air is soft, scented, seductive, scintillating—even alliteration doesn't do it justice, although, to be frank, in recent years it has become less seductive with the increasing hours of *nefos*, or smog, a frequent topic of discussion in the cafés these days.

GETTING THERE

BY AIR: Two airlines can fly you nonstop from New York to Athens with daily wide-body jet service—Olympic Airways, the Greek national carrier, and TWA (which also flies daily via Rome in summer, as well as direct no-change-of-plane flights from New Orleans, San Diego, San Antonio, and St. Louis). From other cities in the U.S. the obvious plan would seem to be to fly to New York and connect with the Athens flights, but check with your travel agent and you may find that this is not necessarily the most efficient, most convenient, or fastest routing. For example, your connecting flight might take you to *La-*

Guardia Airport rather than JFK, leaving you the task of getting from one to the other in time for boarding. Your travel agent may discover from the computers that it's smarter to fly from Atlanta, Chicago, Houston, or Los Angeles with a European carrier like KLM Royal Dutch Airlines or Lufthansa, and make your connection at Amsterdam's Schiphol Airport or Frankfurt Airport. It may sound crazy, but in fact both are one-terminal airports and more efficient than JFK, and your travel time will probably work out about the same—maybe even faster. The fares will be identical. And for a small additional charge you will have the option of stopping off for a few days in, say, Amsterdam, thus adding a whole new dimension to your trip. However, the fare situation is so complicated at the time of writing, I suggest you talk to your travel agent about detailed, up-to-the-minute promotion fares.

BY SEA: Once in Europe, you can get to Greece by boat or train. The usual route is to take the train (or your car) from Rome to Brindisi, where you catch a ferryboat to Corfu or Patras, in the Western Peloponnese. At Patras there are special bus services to take you to Athens, a four-hour trip. However, you may not want to head directly to Athens, since many of the sights you may have come to Greece to visit are along the way or nearby—Olympia, Corinth, Nafplion, Mycenae, Epidaurus. You can rent a car in Patras, or take local buses stage by stage to Athens.

BY TRAIN: It's a long haul, to be sure, but if you're using a Eurailpass you have a real bargain (in 1984, $260 for 15 days of unlimited first-class travel, $290 with a YouthPass for one month of unlimited second-class travel; both passes are also available on some of the ferryboats plying between Brindisi in Italy and Patras in Greece). You have a choice of several trains —four from Paris, the *Hellas Express* and *Acropolis Express* from Germany, the *Venezia Express* from Venice (all via Yugoslavia), and several trains via Rome and Brindisi.

WHAT TO WEAR: Since what you wear in Athens relates to the climate more than anything else, I'll deal with it right now. In summer, wear your lightest clothes. Wear comfortable, *sturdy* shoes for scrambling over all those marble ruins. Men rarely need a jacket, except in the evening for the smarter restaurants or nightclubs. Women should bring along a sweater or stole (you can buy one there inexpensively) for evenings, cruises, or the mountains. But, generally, how you dress is up to you. The Greeks dress casually. Short skirts, slacks, and long hair are now acceptable, although sometimes startling to the peasants in the countryside. You're expected to dress in a respectable manner when you enter a cathedral or church, but there are no hard and fast rules.

WHEN TO COME: As soon as you can get away—now, if you can. From the point of view of things to see and do, any time of the year is fine. For dogged sightseeing, in fact, winter might even be best. On the whole, the best times are April, May, June, September, October, November. Those are the months when the weather is gentlest and the ruins are not swamped (not only by Americans, remember, but also by Germans, British, Dutch, Scandinavians, French, Japanese, and the Greeks themselves). You'll have a better choice of hotels then, also. Avoid the Greek Easter unless you want to stay in Athens: it's a week-long celebration, and everyone heads for the countryside and islands; the airport is a mob scene of people trying to get on overbooked flights. (Remember that I'm talking here only about Athens; some of the islands, particularly Crete and Rhodes, are almost as busy in winter as in summer.) If you're on a tight budget, you'll find at least one advantage in coming in winter: many hotels lower their rates then.

THE LAYOUT OF ATHENS: Let's begin where Athens began— with the **Acropolis.** From the summit of the hill you get the second best view of the city. Around the base of the Acropolis is the **Plaka,** built on the ancient city (you'll be reading more about it later), with some of the most notable archeological finds—the Agora and the Temple of Theseus. To the northeast is the **Hill of Lycabettus;** and beyond that the spreading suburbs and the ring of mountains separating Athens from the rest of Attica. Between Lycabettus and the Acropolis is the heart of the city, distinguished from this height (about 450 feet) mainly by the green patch of the National Gardens and the hint of broad avenues radiating from **Syntagma,** or Constitution Square. To the other side, the west and south, the avenues and suburbs lead off to the coast and the Saronic Gulf, with Piraeus hidden behind a couple of hills.

At street level, the focal point of Athens is Syntagma (which,

ATHENS AND PIRAEUS

Train Station

MARNI

VAS. KONSTANTINOU

PATISSION

Omonia
Sq.

PIREOS

PANEPISTIMIOU

City Hall

EOLOU

STADIOU

ATHINAS

LEOFOROS ERMOU

LEOFOROS ERMOU

MITROPOLEOS

Cathedral

Ancient
Agora

Stoa of Attalos

Roman Agora

PLAKA

APOST PAVLOU

Pnyx

Acropolis

ADRIANOU

Theater of Herod Atticus

AREOPAGITOU

Dionyssos Theater

Hadrian's Arch

Archeological Museum

Grand Harbor

City Hall

Market

Passenger Terminal

KONSTANDINOU

THEOTOKI

SOFIAS

Wall of Moon

SAKHTOURI

Naval Mus.

PIRAEUS

THEMISTUKLEOUS

THEMISTOKLEOUS

IPPOCRATOUS

Lykavitos Hill

Lykavitos

era

ACADIMIAS

University

PANEPISTIMIOU

Kolonaki Sq.

Benaki Museum

VAS. SOFIAS

VAS. SOFIAS

Syntagma Sq.

OTHONOS

Parliament

Byzantine Museum

LEOF. AMALIAS

ATTIKOU

National Gardens

GEORGIOU II

Royal Palace

VAS. KONSTANTINOU

Exhibition Hall (Zappelon)

OLGAS

Temple of Olympian Zeus

as you've just read, is also called Constitution Square, but if you want to ask directions of an Athenian, call it Syntagma). Syntagma is a large square, sloping in the direction of the Acropolis. At the upper end is the neoclassical shuttered facade of the Parliament Building, which used to be the Royal Palace. The other three sides are surrounded by hotels and office buildings (including several airline offices and travel agencies). The great attraction of Syntagma, however, is its cafés. There are cafés on three sides and in the middle. In fact, it has been estimated that there are almost 3000 chairs here (and most of them really are chairs, upholstered and with arm rests).

There are three streets running from the bottom end of Syntagma, all laden with shops and hotels: **Karageorgi tis Servias, Ermou,** and **Mitropoleos.** Mitropoleos leads you to the cathedral, the Agora, the Temple of Theseus, and the Temple of the Winds; and if you make a left turn when you get to the cathedral, you go up into the Plaka, and from there up to the Acropolis.

Back to Syntagma. The broad avenue running off from the top-left corner of the square is variously known as **Venizelou** and **Panepistimou;** it takes you past the magnificent neoclassical facade of the university to the helter-skelter bustle of **Omonia Square,** another swirl of greenery, with a fountain in the middle, but without the elegance of Syntagma. Omonia Square is to Syntagma what Times Square is to, say, Rockefeller Center. From Omonia Square you can follow the avenue known as **October 28** or **Patission** to the National Archeological Museum.

I've just touched on the major landmarks of Athens in this chapter, and will get back to them in detail later on in the sightseeing chapter.

TROLLEYS AND BUSES: The trolley bus and bus routes crisscross the city, and you can get to all the main tourist haunts for no more than 20 drs (20¢). Some of the main routes from Syntagma, for example, are the nos. 3, 5, 9, and 12 trolley buses, which will take you to Omonia Square and the National Archeological Museum; the no. 230 blue bus goes to the Acropolis, the Pnyx, Philopappos Hill; the no. 1 trolley bus to Omonia Square and the Larissis railroad station; no. 161 bus to Faleron; and the no. 40 green bus from Filleninon Street to Piraeus.

If you're in any doubt about which route to take and where to get off, ask your hotel receptionist to write out the number and the stop in Greek and simply show this to the conductor, or one of the passengers (unless you're traveling at the peak hours, when everyone's too busy trying to stay upright to have much time to help a stranger).

TAXIS: Still incredibly cheap. Even the ride from the airport is less than you'd pay in most cities for the fare on the airline bus. The ride to the next town, Piraeus, is around 300 drs ($3), to the nightclubs along the shore about 400 drs ($4). If you're sharing with another couple, taking a taxi in Athens is like taking a bus back home. You don't have to tip the drivers, although they've gotten into the habit of expecting to keep the small change at least; and a few of them seem to have trouble counting out your change in the hope that you may just tell them to forget it. The drivers are, on the whole, honest—but erratic. Shut your eyes and don't look. They also have a tendency to have conversations with other cab drivers as they ride along, since most of them can't converse with their foreign passengers. If you're setting off for a night on the town, it's wise to have the doorman or receptionist at your hotel write down the address in Greek for the benefit of your driver. And, of course, like cab drivers everywhere they disappear at rush hours (in the case of Athens, there are *four* busy periods). The taxis are usually small and relatively new (and yellow), or large and relatively old, and any day now their exhaust fumes are threatening to tumble the Acropolis.

The law allows drivers to pick up additional passengers going in the same direction; conversely, you can now try to flag down a taxi that's already taken. This is a very practical idea intended to save gasoline and space; but the problem is defining "same direction," and you may find yourself making a few unscheduled detours that add minutes (though *not* drachmas) to your trip. If you concur in sharing your taxi, try somehow, stumblingly but politely, to insist that you get to your destination first.

Although taxi fares are still inexpensive, they have gone up yet again. The meter now starts at 20 drs (20¢), but ticks over at the rate of 17 drs (17¢) a kilometer; there's an additional charge between midnight and 6 a.m., 20 drs (20¢), for boarding at an airport or station, each piece of luggage is an additional 10 drs, and there's a *minimum* fare of 70 drs (70¢). Most drivers are honest, but always check that the meter is on Tariff 1 as you set off.

THE SUBWAY: It goes in a straight line—from Omonia Square to Piraeus and from Omonia Square to the hill town of Kifissia (20 drs, or 20¢, in each direction). You probably won't have too many occasions to use it, unless you're staying around Omonia Square and you want to get to Piraeus to catch a ferryboat or cruise ship, in which case it's the fastest and cheapest way to get there.

RENTING A CAR: You could, of course, rent a car, but even a small European runaround won't free you from the frustrations of one-way streets, blue zones, and parking places. While you're sightseeing in the city forget about a car; if you're planning to do some trips out into the country or along the coast, then a car makes more sense. That's a subject I'll come to in the chapter "Touring the Hinterlands."

GREEK MONEY: One **drachma** is currently worth roughly 94 U.S. cents, which means that the dollar is worth 106.94 drs, or thereabouts. For all practical purposes 100 drs equals $1. Check rates and prices in advance. Use the figures in these pages *as a guide only.*

The drachma is made up of 100 **leptas.** There are copper coins for 50 leptas (now almost obsolete), and for 1, 2, 5, 10, and 20 drachmas. Bills are worth 50 drachmas (blue), 100 drachmas (red), 500 drachmas (green), and 1000 drachmas (brown).

Some coins may seem to be worth peanuts, but you'll need them for tipping, telephones, and trolleys.

Note: In the following pages, the dollar equivalents have been rounded off to the nearest half-dollar for the sake of simplicity.

Regardless of the color of the currency, prices have a habit of changing. I've tried to be as accurate about prices as possible. I've checked and double-checked, and to the best of my knowledge, all these prices were accurate at press time (Spring 1984). Rumors are that the authorities will try to hold hotel and restaurant prices to an increase of 10% to 15%, but I can't guarantee it. *So please: Check all prices in advance.*

WHERE TO STAY IN ATHENS

WHAT'S THE HOTEL situation in Athens? Most people visiting Athens for the first time naturally have this question on their minds. After all, Athens is a very, very old city—does it have very old hotels? Do they have private baths? And since summers are hot in Athens, do the hotels have air conditioning?

Well, here's the surprise—most hotels in Athens seem to have been built in the past decade, and those that weren't have been renovated and modernized in the past ten years. Most of them (except in Class D and E) have private bathrooms; most of them have air conditioning.

Nevertheless, the outstanding attraction of hotels in Athens is their relatively low rates. Where else in Europe can you get a room with private bath and air conditioning, smack in the center of a capital city, in peak season, for under $25 a night with breakfast?

If you're seeing Europe on a tight budget, you can probably get a better room, dollar for dollar, in Athens.

If you're traveling on a shoestring, you can survive longer in Athens.

But you'd better hurry: a few years ago the best rooms in the city were going for $54, and you could get simple but comfortable rooms for as little as $8 a night. Now the really deluxe rooms are $100 and up, the budget rooms $12 and up. In addition, the quality of hotel services seems to be declining, and staffs are eager to get their tips despite the fact that a service charge is already included in the bill.

Before going on to individual hotels, here are some general notes on the hotel situation in Athens today.

CATEGORIES: All hotels in Greece are classified by the Greek government. There are six official categories—beginning with L for Deluxe running through Class A and ending with E. In this guide I will confine the reviews to the first four categories, with a quick look at some hotels, guest houses, and hostels in the lowest price ranges. The factors the government uses in judging hotels are the "existence of restaurants, availability of private baths, degree of comfort, and excellence of service."

In reality, the formula for determining the categories must have been devised by the Oracle at Delphi. For example, in Class B hotels every room must have hot and cold running water, at least half of them must have private bathrooms, most of them must have central heating and a telephone, and the staff must speak at least one foreign language (which need not, of course, be English). In Class C hotels, private bathrooms are not compulsory for any of the rooms, and there must be at least one toilet for every six rooms. But in some cases the designations are a holdover from seasons long gone; consequently, some Class C hotels are better than some Class B hotels, and the Class B Athens Gate Hotel, for example, is better value than, say, the Class A Attica Palace. Again, the relatively new Electra Palace Hotel offers more comfortable rooms than most of the accommodations in the traditional Acropole Palace Hotel. In the following pages you'll read about a few hotels that seem to offer outstanding values.

RATES: The government also establishes and enforces the rates for each category. The price and what it includes must be posted in each room—service, taxes, handling of luggage, central heating, air conditioning, meals, and so on. Usually these signs are in English as well as Greek. When you come to pay your bill you should have no problem with overcharging; if you're in a Class B hotel you *know* you'll be paying no more than 2200 drs ($22) (estimated 1985 rate) in a double room, with 15% service charge, in season. However, this does not mean you will not encounter misunderstandings here and there, because hotel keepers are allowed to tack on a few extras: 250 drs ($2.50) for air conditioning ("hot or cold air"); "an increase of 10% may be added to room rates if the stay is two days or less"; "the room rates of hotels located in summer holiday areas, or spas, may be increased by 20% during the period July 1st to September 15th"; "the use of the public bath or shower will be charged at 10 drs for cold water, or 20 drs for hot water." Throw in a slight language problem and there could be a minor international incident. You can avoid any misunderstandings if you reserve your room in advance (preferably through a travel agent) and have a written confirmation *with rates* in your hand.

With all these rules and controls you might think that getting accurate up-to-date hotel rates would be a simple matter. It isn't. When this guidebook was being updated in the spring of 1984, the Greek National Organization for Tourism hadn't established the hotel rates for 1985. Neither had the Hellenic Chamber of Hotels, nor most of the hotel-keepers in Athens; however, the authorities seem to anticipate an increase of 20% to 25% (even more in deluxe hotels).

Therefore, I must report, with regret, that many of the rates included in the following pages are estimates based on information supplied by the appropriate authorities. The figures take into consideration the anticipated 20% to 25% increase, so they should be accurate to within two or three percentage points; however, you should check with your travel agent, or with individual hotels, to determine the precise rate in effect at the time you plan to visit Greece.

TAX AND SERVICE CHARGE: As of this writing, the government tacks on an 8% tax to all hotel rates; there's also a 4.5% *city* tax and a *stamp* tax of 1.2% on the total bill. In addition, hotels are allowed to add a 15% service charge to the bill. Many hotels, however, quote rates that include both service charge and tax. *All the estimated rates quoted in these pages include the government and city taxes and the 15% service charge.*

BREAKFAST: Some hotels also quote a rate that includes service charge, tax, *and* breakfast. That is—continental breakfast, which consists simply of coffee with rolls or toast and butter with marmalade or jam. Recently the government instructed hoteliers to add fresh fruit or fruit juice, but hoteliers seem to have gotten their own back by adding a colored liquid with only the vaguest hint of orange flavor. If breakfast is served in your room, you may have to pay a few extra drachmas. When a hotel quotes "English breakfast" this means eggs and bacon with your coffee and rolls. If you're on a very tight budget, you may prefer a rate that does *not* include breakfast, since you can probably walk around the corner to a neighborhood café and have the same thing for half the price.

HALF BOARD, FULL BOARD: The government also controls the prices of meals served in hotels, and one way a hotel-keeper will try to boost his income is to insist that guests pay a rate that includes meals—*half board,* with breakfast and lunch or dinner (the equivalent of modified American Plan, and sometimes also known as demi-pension), or *full board*, with breakfast, lunch, and dinner (the equivalent of American Plan). This may be an advantage if you're staying in a hotel like the Astor and can dine in the Roof Garden; in most hotels it will probably be a drawback. On the one hand the tourist organization advertises tempting waterfront tavernas; on the other the hotel-keepers force you to dine where *they* want you to dine. Whenever possible, resist half-board and full-board rates and leave yourself the option of dining out.

SEASONS: There are basically two seasons for hotels in Athens: the off-season usually runs from November 1 through March 31, but in some cases it may begin on October 1 and in others end on May 31; some hotels add "shoulder" seasons in spring and fall, while a few hotels no longer distinguish between the seasons, so steady is the stream of visitors, business and vacation, to the city. Get your travel agent to look closely into precise dates, because this may save you several dollars.

CHOOSING A HOTEL IN ATHENS: Once you've determined what price you want to pay, the situation is fairly simple. Most of the hotels are in one of two clusters in the center of town—either around Syntagma (Constitution Square) or around Omonia Square. A few, like the Hilton and the Marriott, are a few blocks farther away, but still convenient to the center of town. Most hotels in Athens are within walking distance of almost everything you want to see, and in any case, taxis are so cheap that getting around the city is not much of an expense—if you can find a taxi in the first place.

COMPARE BEFORE BUYING: If you come in the off-season, when the choice of rooms is greater, it's a perfectly acceptable practice to inspect rooms before taking one. If you give yourself half an hour or an hour, you can walk from hotel to hotel, looking at locations, checking out facilities and the view from the balconies or roofs. Even in the hotel you finally decide on, check out the room, because the standards in some of the older hotels vary considerably from one room to another.

THE VIEW FROM THE TOP: The Acropolis is one of the most stunning sights in the world (even with its present coating of scaffolding). Every corner you turn in Athens brings you another glimpse of this sacred hill. You'll probably want to sit on your balcony at sunset and watch the sunset turn the Parthenon to a glowing honey color. You may even want to sit on your balcony in the morning and watch the Parthenon's columns loom through the morning light. There's nothing like it, so try to get a room with a view, even if you have to give up luxury or space or a private bathroom. And one of the surprising facts about hotels in Athens is that you generally (but not always) pay no more for a room with a view.

RESERVATIONS: During the peak season don't go near Athens without a reservation. You may end up like the Parthenon—without a roof over your head. In the end you'll very likely find a place to stay, but you may spend half your day finding it. Make a reservation in advance. And if you want a room with a view, be sure to specify. In recent years, with more and more visitors flocking to the city, it's wise to make reservations well in advance even during the off-season, if you want to be sure of staying in the hotel of your choice. (This is true not only of Athens but also of places like Delphi and Nafplion.)

LONGER STAYS: Because hotel rates in Athens are so low, you may be tempted to linger a while in that city. If you do, consider renting an apartment rather than staying in a hotel room. Apartments are usually cheaper, well equipped, and they give you a chance to live a more truly Athenian life. It's a particularly economical idea if you have a family. The **Delice Hotel Apartments** and **Riva Hotel Apartments** both offer one-bedroom and two-bedroom suites with fully equipped kitchenettes and air conditioning, 24-hour reception, and telephone service; the Riva also has bar and restaurant service. The Delice is at 3 Vassileos Alexandrou St., the Riva at 114 Michalakopoulou St., both near the Hilton hotel. Double rates are in the region of 3300 drs ($33) to 3900 drs ($39) per night for stays of a month or longer.

SERVICE CHARGE AND TIPPING: A service charge of 15% is included in your hotel bill. The theory behind a service charge was to avoid the confusion resulting from having to tip different members of the hotel staff; the service charge would be added to the bill and that would take care of all tipping. Except that it doesn't. The staff still expects tips. Don't encourage this. Tip only for small *extra* services like shining shoes and fetching cabs.

Here are some tips on tipping in hotels: according to the sign in your room, luggage handling is included in the service charge built into the room rate. So you're not obliged to tip any more, but if you feel like it, offer 50 drs (50¢) a bag (the same rate as porters at airports and stations). In a deluxe hotel you may want to double that. You're also expected to tip the waiter who brings you breakfast in bed. Some people will recommend 50 to 100 drs (50¢ to $1), but this seems unnecessarily high since you're already paying a special charge for room service. Tip what you can get away with.

THE ROOMS: Greeks are traditionally people who like to get out into the open air. And why not, with a climate as balmy as theirs? They'd rather spend a summer evening sitting beneath an olive tree discussing politics or soccer than being cooped up at home watching the telly. Since they spend so much time outdoors, they don't bother about spending a bundle furnishing their homes. By American standards, Greek homes are bare. Ditto Greek hotels, especially the older ones. The lobbies may be like marble palaces, but upstairs the corridors may be spartan, and the rooms furnished only with the essentials. No frills. So don't come to Athens expecting all the trimmings you'd normally find in an American hotel (except in newcomers like the Ledra Marriott or Intercontinental, and the reliable Athens Hilton). The rooms will be spotlessly clean and comfortable, but in many cases they won't have wall-to-wall carpeting, armchairs, radios, and writing desks. You may be discouraged at first, but you'll soon discover that it doesn't matter, because you too will soon prefer to spend your evenings beneath an olive tree.

AIR CONDITIONING: The majority of Athens hotels now have air conditioning, at least in the *L, A,* and *B* categories. Hotels in other categories probably have air conditioning in *some* of the rooms, and you will have to request one of these rooms—and pay an additional charge of around 250 drs ($2.50) a day. Temperatures in Athens in midsummer go up into the 90s by day, and linger in the 70s at night. If you're accustomed to air conditioning back home, you'll probably want it in Athens also, at least in July and August. Moreover, Athens is really a rather noisy city, so you may want to switch on the air conditioning and leave windows and shutters closed to keep out the hubbub.

BATHS AND SHOWERS: There are two types of bathtubs in Athens—the regular kind and the sit-in kind. The sit-in type is about three feet by three feet. It's fine for feet that have trudged all the way up the Acropolis and back, but inadequate for weary shoulders that have carried camera bags and shoulder purses. If you want a real bath, tell the reception clerk when you're checking in. Most hotels have both types. Most baths of either dimension also have hand-held showers, which have one advantage—when you're in your bath you can also switch on the shower *underwater* and use it for a whirlpool bath, or to massage your weary thighs. If you do get an overhead shower, you may not get a shower curtain. The technique is to let the water splash onto the floor, which has been angled to drain off the surplus. It makes sense—but just remember not to leave your slippers or bathrobe on the floor.

RADIO: Many hotels don't have radios in the room. Unless the radio has three channels and one of them picks up the American Armed Forces Network or the BBC, all you will get from your "radio" is a steady stream of taped music.

TELEVISION: Don't expect TV in your room, except at deluxe hotels, which may also have in-house movies. Greece has had television transmission for only 12 years and it's still not the big thing it is in the U.S., and hardly worth paying extra for. (Many new hotels have TV sets in the lobby or the lounge—but that's it.)

SWIMMING POOLS: You'll find few hotels with pools in Athens. Of the ones listed in this guide, only the Athens Hilton, Caravel, Intercontinental's new Athenaeum, Ledra Marriott, Royal Olympic, St. George Lycabettus, Chandris, President, Stanley, Electra Palace, Dorian Inn, and Sirene have pools. Many hotels have sundecks on the roof. But, generally speaking, people come to Athens for sightseeing rather than a tan. If you do want to get in some swimming and sun, stay at one of the nearby resorts—like Glyfada and Vouliagmeni. They're both close enough for jaunts into town for sightseeing and dining.

Deluxe "L" Hotels
(from $110 to $200 double, peak season)

SUPERIOR: The Athens Hilton, Vassilissis Sophias Avenue (tel. 7220-201), is not so much a hotel as a city. On weekends its lobby is filled with wide-eyed Athenians who can't afford a trip to New York but want to see what America is like. There's plenty for them to see—but it's not America. Not with all that marble. There's probably enough marble in the Athens Hilton to have built a second Parthenon—30,000 square meters of it, of 11 types, from Arta, Timos, Pendeli, Yannina, and Salamis. You arrive at the hotel beneath a great curving portico with brown and white marble (a work of art which later centuries may dig up and prize as highly as we prize fragments from Knossos). You walk through hallways with marble floors and marble pillars, down marble steps to a lounge with dozens of plush armchairs, then down a few more marble steps to another wider furnished lounge that looks over the marble pathways leading to the swimming pool. Just inside the hotel entrance are two courtyards (the traditional Greek atrium), 200-year-old olive trees in the middle, and boutiques and shops around the sides—six fashion shops, an antique store, a bank, post office, telegraph office, beauty salon, barbershop, florist, drugstore, travel agencies, airline office, Avis Rent-a-Car office. Without ever leaving the Hilton you can buy designer clothes, records, jewelry, flowers, books, souvenirs, handicrafts, copperware, rugs, bags, cigars.

One of the favorite spots (especially for brunch or weekends) for the Athenian sightseer is the Byzantine Café—an arena of a coffeeshop dominated by a 20-foot-wide copper chandelier. This is where Greeks sample American coffee, American hamburgers, and American apple pie. The Taverna ta Nissia, downstairs, is also full of Athenians, who've come in this case to sample authentic Greek cooking (see the chapter on "Dining Out in Athens"). Next door to the Taverna there's a stylish new, Japanese restaurant, and above both the Pan Bar, a softly lit watering place that's cool in the summer, snug in winter.

On the Hilton roof, 12 floors above the city, you'll find a mini-Las Vegas of entertainment—the Supper Club restaurant/ nightclub (now also open for buffet lunch), and Galaxy Bar with dancing to a live band. But these are no ordinary nightspots. When you step off the elevator you'll see why. Ahead of you, through floor-to-ceiling windows, lies one of the most spellbinding views in Europe—the black, star-speckled mass of the Mediterranean sky, the twinkling lights of the city, and, smack in center stage, the floodlit Acropolis and Parthenon. In summer, of course, you can sit outside on the terrace itself and soak in the view and the soft Athenian air.

All the guest rooms at the Hilton have views of either the Acropolis or Mount Pentelicon, and a few have views of both the Acropolis and Lycabettus Mountain. The Hilton's rooms are spacious and comfortable, as you've come to expect of Hilton hotels everywhere: five-channel radio, color TV with in-house movies, direct-dial telephones, mini-bars, wall-to-wall carpeting, and, of course, sliding glass doors opening onto spacious balconies. The bathrooms (more marble, this time gray) have ice-water taps and American-style shower-baths. The Hilton's maids fix your room twice a day, and turn back the sheets while you're up on the roof dancing. The top two floors are now an Executive Club, with its own exclusive lounge and hostess. Other Hilton facilities include a swimming pool, sauna, massage parlor, photostat service, typewriter rental, garage, and photographer.

The Hilton is located in one of the smart residential districts, among the embassies, beyond the National Park. It's only a 15-minute walk or a $2 cab ride from Constitution Square.

The Athens Hilton is one of the most expensive hotels in town: singles run 9300 to 14,345 drs ($93 to $143), and doubles cost 11,476 to 16,940 drs ($115 to $169), including service charge and tax; these rates (Executive Club, slightly higher), moreover, are in effect *all year,* and if you think the Hilton people are crazy, just try to get a room there.

The **Hotel Grande Bretagne,** Syntagma (tel. 3230-251), is the Dowager Duchess of Athens' hotels. It was built in 1862 as a 30-room annex to the royal family's summer palace across the street (now the Houses of Parliament), and put in the care of Eustace Lampsa, chef to the royal household who knew all the preferences of the royal visitors who'd be staying there. It's still a family-run hotel, with long-serving staff (its two classic concierges recently retired after 50 years of service apiece), but the original three-story building is now seven stories with a total of 450 rooms. Generations of distinguished guests have created a unique atmosphere at the GB (no one refers to it as the Grande Bretagne). Its doors have been whisked open by uniformed attendants for princes, czars, tycoons and millionaires, for composer Richard Strauss, the Grand Duchess Helen, and more recently, Sir Laurence Olivier, Henry Fonda, and Paul Newman. During World War II, the GB was Nazi headquarters; at the end of the war, Sir Winston Churchill stayed here for a few nights and narrowly escaped an assassination attempt which involved using the labyrinthine sewers of the hotel. Today the GB is virtually a "reviewing stand" for state occasions at the Parliament Building and the Tomb of the Unknown Soldier across the street.

The lobby of the GB is one of those monumental Athenian halls of marble—marble floors, green marble walls, marble pillars, Oriental carpets, and plushly upholstered sofas and fauteuils; beyond it is an equally comfortable and spacious lounge with a decorative glass ceiling, and beyond that the dignified, classical dining room. Two contemporary touches are the intime, dimly lit cocktail lounge in one corner, and the new GB Corner café-restaurant in the other. If you simply want to sample the opulence of the GB's public quarters, drop into the lobby for a coffee; it costs a few drachmas more than it would cost in one of the cafés in the square, but it comes to you in a silver pot, on a silver tray, with a silver milk jug and silver sugar bowl—with a wine glass of chilled water, served with great dignity by a waiter in immaculate white uniform.

The GB is one of *the* grand hotels in Europe, and although it may have been overtaken by others in terms of sheer plushness (decor and furniture date from more elegant days), it is constantly being upgraded: latest innovations include direct-dial telephones (with bathroom extensions), mini-bars, air conditioning, and color TV with in-house movies, in a custom cabinet that matches the individual room decor. The prize rooms are those facing the square (especially those on the sixth floor), all now with double french doors and windows to block out traffic noise; but the huge inner courtyard has been restored in its neoclassical style, complete with window boxes and fragrant flowers, and these rooms will be welcomed by people who like to sleep with their windows open—no traffic sounds here. Rates are 8504 to 13,058 drs ($85 to $130) single, 11,172 to 16,896 drs ($112 to $169) double; suites are 20,064 to 97,998 drs ($200 to $980) and up.

At the time this edition was being researched (Spring 1984) the esteemed **King George Hotel** on Syntagma was scheduled for "extensive renovation" and therefore obliged "to limit reservations." More details in the next edition.

FOUR NEW HOTELS: The deluxe hotels listed above now face competition from four newcomers—the Ledra Marriott (1983), the Astir Palace (1983), the NJV-Meridien (1980) and the Athenaeum Intercontinental (1982).

Marriott's 270-room entry in Athens, the **Ledra Marriott,** 113-115 Syngrou (tel. 9525-211), is a near neighbor of the Athenaeum, with a balconied facade of white marble separated from the avenue by a service road and driveway. The hit of the Ledra is, surprisingly, the city's first Polynesian/Japanese restaurant, the lavishly waterfalled and batiked Kona Kai, which has become the smart place for Athenians to be seen and entertained. Other restaurants include a small, stylish Grill Room (serving, among other things, lamb and suckling pig on the spit) and the wicker-and-lattice Zephyros coffeeshop (featuring a Sunday buffet lunch for $13 or thereabouts—including champagne and orange juice on the house).

The Marriott's guest accommodations come in four categories, including sumptuous suites, but even the most "modest" rooms are above average with elegant designer decor (soft tans, ecrus, and browns), individual air conditioning, mini-bar, radio (with extension speaker in the bathroom), color TV, free in-house movies, three direct-dial telephones (bedside, desk, bathroom), armchair and sofa, and extravagant closet space—with drawers and sliding doors that positively glide. Going up the scale you'll have similar accommodations but with a flower-draped balcony and/or view of the Acropolis. Only one-third of the Ledra's rooms have views of the Parthenon, but in nice democratic fashion every guest in the hotel (and only hotel guests, by the way, no "local memberships" allowed) can lounge on the rooftop deck (bar service, barbecues in summer), plunge into a big pool, or soak in a hydrotherapy pool while admiring the Parthenon. For a closer look you can board the free shuttle bus that leaves several times a day for Syntagma.

The Marriott staff is young and a shade less polished, perhaps, than in other hotels, but they make up for that with a politeness and enthusiasm you don't too often find in Athens these days. Rates: singles, 8280 to 13,920 drs ($83 to $139); doubles 9960 to 16,080 drs ($100 to $161); studio suites, from 20,400 drs ($204).

The Astir chain of palace hotels has dominated leading Greek resorts for many years, but the new ten-story, glass-sheathed **Astir Palace Athens Hotel** on Syntagma (tel. 3643-112) is the first time the AH logo has decorated an Athens hotel. The location is ideal, at least in terms of convenience: at the junction of Panepistimiou and Sofias Avenues, facing the Parliament Building on one side, the Hotel Grande Bretagne on the other. Prime real estate indeed, but since the Astir properties are owned by the National Bank of Greece, money seems to be little object. In Athens they've lavished some $100 million on just 79 rooms, two restaurants, and a bar. Even the inner stairwell is lined with white Pendeli marble and decorated with ceramic tile murals.

Extra-large guest rooms feature spacious sitting areas furnished with sofa, armchair, glass-and-marble coffee table, and desk. Other facilities include mini-bar, four-channel radio, color TV with in-house movies (and an extension speaker in the bathroom), direct-dial telephone. Each room sports projecting floor-to-ceiling tinted windows with extra-thick glass (but not extra-thick enough on the lower floors to eliminate completely the round-the-clock rumble of traffic).

The Astir's main dining room, Apokalypsis, hides out on the lower level, an unusual setting of bronze and crystal beneath a reflective ceiling, facing a wall of glass shielding a backdrop that is no less than a section of the 2000-year-old city wall, revealed for the first time when the hotel foundations were being excavated. The Apokalypsis menu is Greek and international on an ambitious scale (budget $50 for two for dinner), but you can dine more simply in the Astir Coffee Shop, one floor above the lobby. The backdrop for this tubular-glass-and-rattan eatery is the passing throng (the tables move outdoors onto the balcony in summer). Here a $12-for-two tab might include Denver omelet and a Reuben sandwich, or a $20 tab could bring scallopine marsala and fishermen's basket—plus, in each case, coffee or dessert.

Rates are 8940 drs ($89) for singles, 10,680 to 15,295 drs ($107 to $153) for doubles; suites run from 18,000 drs ($180).

The striking gray facade of the **Holiday Inn** rises eight stories above Michalakopoulou, a broad avenue just beyond the Hilton, a short walk from the American Embassy. Indoors, it makes most other Holiday Inns look like country cousins, with its lobby in dazzling "disco" decor, a glass-paneled shopping arcade, a contemporary bar/lounge and 12-lane bowling alley. Other attractions are underground parking, hairdresser, coffeeshop (open to 2 a.m.), bistro-restaurant, and disco. Guest rooms, in cool soothing colors, sport radio/TV, air conditioning, direct-dial telephones, two double beds, and efficient bathrooms. Rooms on the top two floors have balconies; of the 190 rooms, only 35 are singles, so solo visitors may be offered a double room at a special rate, one reason, perhaps, why 60% of the hotel's guests are business people. The Holiday Inn, owned and operated by a local company, is located at 50 Michalakopoulou Ave. (tel. 7248-322). Rates are 5610 drs ($56) single, 8760 drs ($88) double.

France's Meridien chain, too, now has a toehold in Athens—and what a toehold! The **NJV-Meridien Hotel** is right on Syntagma (tel. 3255-300), sharing the same block as the GB and King George hotels, and boasting a sleek efficiency the older hotels might envy. Soundproofing has been built in from the beginning, the central air conditioning is unobtrusive, and all rooms come equipped with color TV (including a video channel), radio, automatic alarm clock, mini-bar, direct-dial telephone; bathrooms have thermostatic controls, double vanities, and telephone extensions. The Meridien's 182 rooms include half a dozen singles on each floor, most of them at the rear; upper-floor doubles have balconies overlooking the square, some with views of the Acropolis. On the mezzanine floor, guests can settle into a comfy bar upholstered, paneled, and pillared with leather, and dine off nouvelle cuisine prepared by a French chef in the hotel's spacious restaurant. Meridien rates range from 9800 drs ($98) for singles, from 10,800 to 14,400 drs ($108 to $144) for doubles.

Intercontinental's newcomer is the sumptuous, $60-million, 630-room **Athenaeum Hotel**, at 89–93 Syngrou Ave. (tel. 9023-666), about $2 by taxi from Syntagma. The lobby is a vast multilevel atrium topped by a skylight and surrounded by shops (Zolotas, Dunhill), restaurants (La Rôtisserie for elegant continental dining, the Taverna for Cypriot feasts, Café Pergola for lighter fare), and cocktail and tea lounges. Other attractions include a free-form swimming pool with cascading fountains and sundecks, health club, disco, and a full range of executive services. Extra-large guest rooms feature island decor and local crafts, sitting areas, mini-bars, color television with in-house movies, air conditioning, and direct-dial telephones; about one-third of the rooms have views of the Acropolis, some with plant-draped balconies. This opulence doesn't come cheaply: singles are 8088 to 17,214 drs ($81 to $172); doubles, 11,394 to 20,509 drs ($114 to $205); suites are higher.

More Deluxe "L" Hotels
(from $38 to $100 double, peak season)

The hotels listed above are truly deluxe; the following selection is officially in the category but in terms of facilities and furnish-

ings they are really only a cut above first class. Fortunately, their rates are considerably lower than the group above.

St. George Lycabettus Hotel, 2 Kleomenou St. (tel. 7290-711), is 12 years old with 150 rooms, as many balconies, located on a residential street in the foothills of Lycabettus. Glass doors open to cool, spacious elegance. Gleaming black marble floors are highlighted with upholstered chairs and couches in blends of caramel, pumpkin, and gold, and smoky-glass tables with brass accents. Tony's Bar is down a few steps to the left, and a full floor down there's a cool dining room with gold tablecloths and olive antiqued chairs (prix-fixe lunch or dinner, $5). One floor below that, going down the hill, there's a pâtisserie/coffeeshop. Crowning it all is a rooftop pool and restaurant, eye-to-eye with the pine groves of Lycabettus; and most guests will probably opt for this rooftop restaurant—green chairs among potted oleanders in the summer, indoors in the Grill Room in winter; with dancing to a combo all year round. The 30-foot-long pool is surrounded by "astroturf"-style matting, with comfortable chaises and poolside showers.

The accommodations are trim and contemporary—gold wall-to-wall carpeting, coral upholstery, wood paneling, furniture with brass trim, luxurious bathrooms with tile walls and marble floors, radio, and direct-dial telephones, and now most of them also have TV and mini-bars. The plushest rooms are the corner suites, especially those on the fourth and fifth floors which have balconies on two sides, breathtaking views, two rooms, two bathrooms, and a sense of spaciousness that you might miss in the basic rooms. The St. George Lycabettus (don't get it confused with the plain Lycabettus Class B hotel farther down the hill) is popular with visitors (especially business people) who want modern facilities and comfort in a quieter location with Syntagma, a seven-minute walk downhill and an 80-dr (80¢) cab ride back up. Other facilities include TV, garage, beauty parlor, barbership, and bank. Rates: singles run 4188 to 5124 drs ($42 to $51); doubles, 6219 to 7195 drs ($62 to $72); 20% less during the off-season.

Americans will probably feel at home at the **Amalia Hotel,** 10 Amalias Ave. (tel. 3237-301), even before they step inside because it looks like a modern American resort hotel. The lobby is airy, with tall ceilings, lots of wood paneling, and a marble stairway leading up to the mezzanine. Off the lobby there's a neat little bar (shielded from the outside world by lacy drapes), a tea room, and a restaurant with wooden Grecian-style chairs, chandeliers, and flowers. The lounge in the lobby is as large as you'll find in most hotels, but take the elevator or the marble stairway to the mezzanine floor and you'll find three more lounges—one on a terrace overlooking the palm trees of the National Garden, another with a 23-inch TV, and the third a quiet room that can be shut off for meetings.

The rooms, like the facade, come closer to American ideas than most Athens hotels. You'll find paneled headboards, modern table lamps, armchairs, throw rugs, and those modern one-piece telephones with the dial on the bottom; and the bathrooms have fixed overhead showers. But the furnishings are beginning to show their age (the foam in the lobby chairs is beginning to pop through), and the overall impression is first class rather than deluxe. Of the 100 rooms, 38 have private balconies, and of these 34 face the National Garden. Only six of the rooms are singles, so if you're lucky you'll get a double at the single rate. High-season rates are 4176 drs ($42) double.

The **Royal Olympic Hotel,** 28 Diakou (tel. 9226-411), is slightly off the beaten track, which by the pampered standards of Athens means it's all of ten blocks from Constitution Square. But what a location! If you have a room facing the front, you can throw back the drapes, open the sliding windows, step out onto your balcony, and there in live wide-screen Cinemascope is the entire Temple of Olympian Zeus spread out in front of you. And right behind it, almost growing out of the temple's cluster of columns, is the mountain of Lycabettus, with the greenery of the National Garden filling the gap between. It's a breathtaking sight. And well worth the ten blocks between you and Constitution Square. Into the bargain, this hotel is handsomely furnished —bedrooms as well as the public rooms.

The steps up to the lobby, the floors, and the pillars, are inevitably of marble. The bar separates the lobby from the small swimming pool at the back of the hotel, and on the left of the lobby, there's an elegant dining room decorated with engravings of old Athens. One of the most attractive of the public rooms is the lounge, up a few marble steps, to raise it above the level of the traffic so that you can get an undisturbed view of the temple. (Even if you're not staying at the Royal Olympic, remember this grandstand lounge is a place to drop into for morning coffee or afternoon tea.)

The Royal Olympic's guest rooms are American-style. There are carpets on the floor, computerized direct-dial telephones, radio, air conditioning, balconies, sliding doors of double-glazed glass, amply fitted closets, chairs, coffee tables, well-equipped bathrooms complete down to a second phone, and big towels. The hotel's corner suites can keep an entire family in comfort, with even an icebox attractively disguised as a wood-grained cabinet. There are also a few "businessmen's studios" with sliding screens to separate sleeping area from working area, and equipped with a full-size desk, studio couch, refrigerator, and coffee table. The most luxurious rooms are on the sixth floor. They're a shade more "designed," and they have larger balconies —and of course, the higher you are the more stunning the view and the more muffled the sound of the traffic. But take a room on any floor as long as it's at the front.

With a new wing that opened in 1980, there are now 310 rooms, including eight suites each with different decor, enormous beds, carved inner doors, big oval bathtubs, and large silk prints of recumbent maidens.

If you check into a room without a view you can always head for the glass-enclosed rooftop bar, especially on a summer evening. The dining room of the Royal Olympic is a spruce, chandelier-bright place, and there's also a specialty restaurant called the Templars' Grill, which you'll read about in the next chapter. Rates at the Royal Olympic are 5400 drs ($54) single, 6600 drs ($66) double.

Syngrou, the long straight avenue that links the city with the sea, is currently undergoing a major facelift, and one of the landmarks in this new-style Athens is the glistening 354-room **Athens Chandris Hotel,** 385 Leoforos Syngrou (tel. 9414-824), which opened its automatic doors in August 1977. It's close to the sea, equidistant from downtown Athens, downtown Piraeus, and the airport, and facing the Ippodromo, or race track. The interior is a glistening art deco extravaganza of holiday colors, marble, and contrasting textures. The furniture, imported from Italy, is all Milan Modern—the bedside lamps are like giant ice cubes, the chrome trim of the headboards has a built-in radio, and the ultramodern suites (26 in all) must be among the most luxurious in Athens. On the roof, eight floors up, guests can cool off in a small pool, get a suntan, or enjoy vast views of the city, the mountains, and the Saronic Bay; many guests also have a grandstand view of the races from their balconies. Other Chandris features include a trio of smart restaurants and a late-night coffeeshop. Room-only rates for summer range from 4586 drs ($46) single, from 5227 to 7833 drs ($52 to $78) double—some of the lowest deluxe rates in Athens.

The **Athenée Palace**, 1 Kolokotroni Square (tel. 3230-791), is the elegant building on the corner across from the National Historical and Ethnological Museum—just one block behind Constitution Square. It's one of the grand old hotels of Athens, but a few years ago it was completely refurbished, air-conditioned, and brought into line with modern hotels. The lobby is a cathedral-like place, with marble floors and columns, and a grand stairway leading up to a mezzanine balcony lounge. Over in one corner, down a few steps, there's a snug bar and cocktail lounge; in the opposite corner, a souvenir-and-postcard shop. Above the mezzanine (where you'll find a 23-inch television set), one entire floor is given over to lounges, a beauty parlor, and the dining room. The lounges have big club-like armchairs, Oriental carpets, soft colors on the walls and ceilings to offset the vivid prints on the chairs. The dining room has a red carpet, sparkling table linens, immaculate waiters, and a wall covered with murals of Arcadian scenes.

The Athenée Palace has 150 rooms and 150 full-length, stretch-out-and-wallow-type baths. The rooms are spacious, and the bathrooms are as large as many single rooms in other hotels. (The bathrooms, incidentally, follow a precise hierarchy in marble: in the suites, they have marble floors and marble walls; in the deluxe rooms, marble floors and tiled walls; in the superior rooms, linoleum floors and painted walls.) The rooms are furnished throughout in period style—slightly Victorian, with floral-print covers in an exuberance of reds, yellows, and greens. Some of the rooms have small balconies with a view of Lycabettus popping up over the tops of office buildings, but this is a hotel where the eye-popping attractions are inside.

The Athenée Palace also boasts a quietly efficient front-office staff, and a concierge who seems to be able to handle six problems at once without any trouble whatsoever. Summer rates are 4080 drs ($41) single, 5760 drs ($58) double. Breakfast is included in both cases—good value.

The **Acropole Palace**, 51 Patission (tel. 5223-851), probably has the most elegant facade of any hotel in Athens. It was built at the turn of the century, with some of the embellishments you'd find in a French hotel of that period—bay windows, tiny iron balconies, and a curved corner. Rooms are still furnished as they were originally, and there are antique items in some of the rooms —but several of the rooms are looking dowdy and threadbare, despite continuing efforts to renovate them, including double-glazed windows. The main lobby has a marble and wrought-iron stairway that sweeps gracefully up to the air-conditioned lounges and the circular, domed dining room. Downstairs there's the oddly named Sky Room Bar and the winter nightclub. In summer the dining room and the nightclub are on the Roof Garden, eight high-ceilinged floors up, where you can dine with style and dance to the hotel's two orchestras—one Greek, one British.

The Acropole Palace has many of the facilities you'd expect of a long-established, fine hotel—tea room, beauty parlor, barbershop, American bar, air conditioning. It's a quiet hotel in a convenient location—opposite the National Archeological Museum, about five minutes on foot from Omonia Square and seven minutes by cab from Constitution Square, so if you don't want to be surrounded by tourists (other than groups of Japanese), souvenir shops, and cafés, the Acropole Palace might be the answer. Summer rates are 2102 to 2484 drs ($21 to $25) single, 3156 to 3720 ($32 to $37) double.

The **Park Hotel,** 10 Leoforos Alexandras (tel. 883-2711), is smaller, more intimate, welcoming guests with a club-like lobby of wood paneling and leather decorated in muted colors. It's across the street from one of the city's most spacious parks, and many of the upper rooms have pleasant views overlooking the treetops. Pampering seems to be the philosophy here: bar/refrigerators in all the rooms (plus 24-hour room service), marble bathrooms with extension telephone, fingertip bedside controls for the gadgetry—message light, wake-up alarm, door lock, "Do Not Disturb" sign, heating and air conditioning, radio, and music channels.

In addition to a late-night coffeeshop, the Red House, the Park has, of all things, a pizzeria; but the Latina is like no other pizzeria you've seen—unless you know another one with ovens covered by hand-hammered copper. In summertime, the Blue Peacock bar on the roof garden gives you an even better view of the treetops and a refreshing breeze. The Park's 111 double rooms cost 4800 to 6120 drs ($48 to $61) in summer, 20% less during the off-season.

The modern 520-room **Caravel Hotel,** 2 Vas. Alexandrou Ave. (tel. 7290-721), is a near neighbor of the Hilton. The two hotels seem to be competing on the spaciousness and grandeur of their lobbies; both of them have handsome, contemporary-style tavernas and late-night coffeeshops; both have lobby-level shopping galleries and beauty parlors. The Caravel's rooftop cocktail lounge, the Horizon, has a spectacular view of the Acropolis and Lycabettus Hill; likewise, the sunning terrace around the full-size heated pool, now enclosed in a glass dome for year-round use. Up here you'll also find, in addition to saunas and an indoor gymnasium (with windows to let you admire the view of the Acropolis when you come up for breath), an active Moslem mosque. The Caravel's guest rooms are spacious, colorful, and tasteful, with small balconies, individual room controls for heating and air conditioning, marble bathrooms, and small refrigerator/bars (in addition to 24-hour room service). Summer rates are singles from 3783 drs ($63), doubles from 4875 drs ($81), and suites to almost $200.

Your main interest in Parnes is probably the Casino (discussed farther on), but I'll list a hotel here in case you want a change of pace at some point. The **Mount Parnes Hotel-Casino,** Parnes (tel. 2469-111), is located on the 3000-foot mountain 22 miles from midtown Athens. It's comfortable and clean, the rooms have private baths and showers and central heating, and although it's officially classed as a deluxe hotel there are no frills here. Except that view! All the rooms face Athens, and they all have big terraces (big enough to have a meal on) overlooking the valley and the city, Piraeus and the sea. You get an identical view from the pool terrace. The hotel has a restaurant, snackbar, nightclub, and of course the casino. Also a TV room, tennis, and gardens. What's the point of staying way up there? It's cooler, it's by the casino. Otherwise it's quite dull. The half-board rates in summer are around 6207 drs ($62), single or double.

Class A and B Hotels
(from $25 to $42 double, peak season)

Some of the best buys, and some of the most attractive accommodations, are to be found in these two categories, and for most travelers the following hotels are the ones most likely to match their tastes and budgets. Rates listed include continental breakfast and, of course, taxes, service charge, and air conditioning, unless mentioned otherwise. Remember, please, that the rates are estimates only, and subject to change for the reasons explained elsewhere in this guidebook.

First, details of a half-dozen of the newer hotels in these categories, all of them a slight remove from the clutter of Syntagma and Omonia. The first three are in the part of town known as **Makriyanni,** a predominantly residential area bounded by the

OMONIA SQUARE

LIOSSION

ACHANON

MARNI

STOURNARA

PATISSION

MEZONOS

Vathis Sq.

KAPODI

TRITIS SEPTEMVRIOU

FAVIEROU

MAGER

MARNI

CHALKOKONDYLI

VERANZEROU

KAROLOU

SATOKRIANDOU

National Theater

Karaiskaki Sq.

KONSTANTINOU

Omonia Sq.

STADIOU

KOLONOU

DELIGEORGI

ZINONOS

EOLOU

LEONIDOU

PIREOS

ATHINAS

KERAMIKOU

AGISILAOU

City Hall

SOFOKLEOUS

Acropolis (the side opposite the Plaka), the Temple of Olympian Zeus, and Syngrou Avenue, which is rapidly becoming one of the main business and commercial centers of the city.

The **Hotel Herodion,** 4 Rovertou Galli St. (tel. 9236-832), is located on a quiet side street, but so close to the Theater of Herod Atticus it's especially popular with performers and culture buffs during the Athens Festival; since it's also just five minutes on foot from the Plaka and a five-minute bus ride from Syntagma, the Herodion is a good address at any time of the year. Its spacious marble lobby leads to a lounge and patio garden where you can have drinks and snacks beneath the trees; the dining room is taverna-style, with ceramics and native rugs on white stucco walls. The Herodion's 90 guest rooms are tastefully decorated; many of them have balconies, and in any case there's a solarium/roof terrace with a stunning view of the Acropolis. With the spic-and-span singles going for 4000 drs ($40) and the doubles for 5000 drs ($50), this is one of the better values in Athens. You can get slightly lower rates at the nearby **Hotel Parthenon**, 6 Makri St. (tel. 9234-594), where a cavernous contemporary lobby of shiny marble leads to a lounge, bar, and restaurant; the 79 trim rooms all have private bath or shower and air conditioning. A few blocks away, at the Category B **Hotel Christina,** 15 Petmeza, at the corner of Kallirrois Avenue (tel. 9215-353), the cabin-size guest rooms rent for around 1566 drs ($16) single, 2314 drs ($23) double.

The modern, immaculate **Divani-Zafolia Palace**, 19-25 Parthenonos St. (tel. 9222-945), is popular with tour groups from all over Europe, but the cool, marble lobby is almost spacious enough to accommodate everyone's luggage at one time. There's a pleasant dining room to the right of the lobby (four-course lunch or dinner for $7), a lounge/bar on the left, and down a flight of steps a gift shop shares a foyer with a glass-enclosed expanse of the Wall of Themistocles, dating from 479 B.C. Guest rooms fill six floors, each with marble floors and trim-and-tidy decor in shades of brown, each with individual air conditioning, telephone, radio, and balcony. Parthenonos is a residential street in the shadow of the Acropolis, so street noise is not too much of a problem. Rooms at the front have angled views of the Parthenon, but those at the rear on the upper floors have unobstructed views of Philopappus Hill. The reception staff doesn't project an image of hospitality, but this is an ideal location if you're planning to spend much time at the Athens Festival performances in the Herod Atticus Theater—a five-minute walk away. Rates are 4409 drs ($44) single, 5174 drs ($52) double.

Farther down Syngrou Avenue, the eight-story, Class B **Hotel Ilissos River**, 72 Kallirrois Ave. (tel. 9223-523), opened its doors in the spring of 1980. Its location is perhaps more suited to business travelers than tourists (it's ten minutes by taxi from Syntagma), but anyone would welcome the stylish Class A comfort of its 96 rooms, twin-level dining room, and plush club-like lounge. The rooms (with bath/shower, air conditioning, radio, direct-dial telephone) are good value at 1248 drs ($21) single, 1709 ($28) double.

There's more good value in the opposite direction, four blocks beyond the Hilton and near the Holiday Inn, where $45 gets you a double room with breakfast at the **Golden Age Hotel,** 57 Michalakopoulou Ave. (tel. 7240-861). You're greeted by a multi-marbled lobby with an unusual decorative frieze lining the mezzanine, a streetside café with desultory service, and a comfortable bar/lounge; downstairs, the attractive taverna doubles as a discotheque after dinner in winter. The 122 guest rooms are comfortably furnished (the singles have double beds), and rent for 3912 drs ($39) single, 5038 drs ($50) double.

At 25 Michalakopoulou, the Class B **Hotel Ilisia** (tel. 7244-051), tucks 69 trim and tidy rooms (only seven of them singles) into a corner site just around the corner from the Hilton, next door to the Flame Steak House. The friendly owners don't insist on half board, take in very few groups, and cater primarily to business travelers, many of them connected with the American Embassy. All rooms have air conditioning, bath or shower; most of them have balconies. Singles cost 2172 drs ($22); doubles, 3217 drs ($32).

The high-rise, 530-room **President Hotel,** 43 Kifissias Ave. (tel. 692-4600), is one of Athens's biggest Class A establishments, although its stylishly modern lobby (acres of marble in earthy colors, concealed lighting, pop music) might lead you to believe you'd stepped into a deluxe hotel; bars, lounges, and dining facilities are equally spacious. The guest rooms, on the other hand, are dainty, although pretty to look at and fitted with direct-dial telephone, air conditioning, radio, and balcony. The 22nd floor is given over to a swimming pool, sun terrace, and discotheque, but the President's basement may be the best feature if you plan to do a lot of driving—it has space for 500 cars. Room rates are 2560 drs ($26) single, 3264 drs ($33) double, and the fact that you don't have to take a half-board rate even in summer may compensate for its slightly inconvenient location. The President is located on one of the main avenues leading north from Athens (convenient for touring by car), but a 10- to 15-minute taxi ride from Syntagma.

NEAR SYNTAGMA: The ten-story **Attica Palace Hotel,** 6 Karageorgi tis Servias (tel. 3223-006), is only a few yards down from Syntagma; there's a big sign outside, but many people seem to miss it, and in case you do too, the entrance is in an arcade, among a row of shops, usually clustered with shoppers, office workers, and dispensers of lottery tickets. The lobby is hardly big enough for you and your luggage, the "lounge" is a niche beneath the stairs, and you may begin to wonder if this really is a Class A hotel. Upstairs is a different matter—no scrimping on space up there. The first floor has not one but *three* spacious lounges, one with a bar, and all of them with contemporary furnishings, big modern paintings and sculpture. The dining room is bright and spacious. The upper floors with the guest rooms have hallways of marble—green, red, beige—and each one would be big enough for Socrates and his pupils to sit around in. Guest rooms have contemporary-style desk and dresser units, couches, armchairs, coffee tables, air conditioning, telephone, and private bath and shower. Some rooms have dividers with abstract paintings giving the impression of a small studio apartment; all rooms facing the street have balconies, and from the seventh floor up you get a view of the Acropolis (the top two floors actually have three rooms with big terraces rather than balconies—great place to sunbathe).

About 90% of the Attica Palace's 78 rooms are doubles: 3720 drs ($37) for two, 2388 drs ($24) for singles.

Still another relatively new hotel, still another American-style facade. The **Astor Hotel**, 16 Karageorgi tis Servias (tel. 3255-555), is right in the center of one of the busiest areas of town, with taxis and people constantly passing up and down Karageorgi tis Servias on their way from the Plaka to Constitution Square. Once inside, however, you're not too conscious of noise. The hotel sits back from the street, with its entrance under an arcade that blocks out the traffic noises as well as the harsh sun.

The Astor has 11 air-conditioned floors, with the top floor given over to the Roof Garden. This is one of Athens's few year-round roof gardens, in fact. It sprawls over the terrace in summer, but in winter it's enclosed in glass that doesn't confine the view. And what a view! Look up from your table and there's the Acropolis looking as though it's across the street. Over on the right you can see Lycabettus Hill, and over on the left Mount Pentelicon. You can have lunch or dinner up here for less than $6, even less if you order budget items like spaghetti or omelets.

The Astor has 133 rooms and suites, and most of the rooms above the sixth floor have views (except for the singles, which are all at the rear), and most of them also have balconies. The furniture is nothing to write home about, but again, you'll be too busy looking at the view from your balcony to care much. Down in the basement there's a well-stocked souvenir shop and beauty parlor, and just off the lobby, a small bar. Summer rates are 2760 drs ($28) single, 3600 drs ($36) double.

The **Hotel Electra,** 5 Ermou St. (tel. 3223-223), is another of those modern hotels that look more like office buildings than hotels—especially at street level where the narrow glass door is surrounded by shops and cafés. Once you step through into the lobby, however, you're unmistakably in a grand hotel. The lobby, recently restyled, now has an island reception desk and a stylish bar with decorative tiles, oak counter top, and padded stools with back rests.

The corridors on the guest-room floors have olive carpets, dark-green ceilings, and gray floral wallpaper. The floral paper overflows into some of the rooms, which all have polished parquet floors or spotless linoleum with scatter rugs, marble-floored bathrooms with tiled walls, twin beds, a desk/dresser unit, armchair, phones, and individual air-conditioning controls.

On the eighth floor there are four rooms with 8-foot-square terraces. The hotel is air-conditioned throughout, and all 110 rooms have massage units attached to the beds (10 drs per three-minute massage). The Electra insists on half board all year; in summer, singles are 4430 drs ($44); doubles, 6596 drs ($66).

Turn right into Filellinon Street from the Mitropoleos Street corner of Syntagma, and three blocks later you come to a small square with an old Byzantine church and tower and three palm trees. The **Olympic Palace Hotel,** 16 Filellinon (tel. 3237-611), is the modern building just across the street, with the neat square verandas on three sides. The lobby is the usual palace of glass and marble, leading into a larger lounge with almost enough armchairs to seat every guest in the hotel. There's also a small bar with comfy upholstered chairs, and, one floor up, a big bright dining room with lots of windows and flowers.

All the Olympic Palace's rooms have private baths, music, telephones, air conditioning, modern (but not exactly brand-new) furniture, and the bathrooms have marble floors and floral wallpaper. There are corner suites that sleep three. Despite its location close to Constitution Square, the Olympic Palace is a relatively quiet hotel; and despite the tempting photograph on its brochure, none of the rooms has a proper view of the Acropolis. Rates are 2700 drs ($27) single, 3500 drs ($35) double.

Esperia Palace, 22 Stadiou St. (tel. 3238-001), is on one of the big thoroughfares that link Syntagma with Omonia Square, and 22 is closer to Syntagma than to Omonia. It's a convenient location, but it can get noisy at rush hours so ask for a room high

Imagine staying in a modern hotel five minutes from Syntagma, on the edge of the Plaka, in the shadow of the Acropolis, *and being able to have a swim in a rooftop pool before your siesta.* Then check into the **Electra Palace Hotel,** 18 Nicodimou St. (tel. 3241-401), and have your dreams come true. It is here that you may also find yourself sitting at sundown in a swinging, canvas loveseat, sipping an ouzo and watching the light fade on the Parthenon. This roof garden, with its loungers, bamboo chairs, elevated pool, and bar, is reason enough for staying at the Electra Palace (opened in 1974), but it's by no means the only one. Even without its roof, this would be one of the best values in the city, a Class A hotel with more attractive rooms than many deluxe hotels. For a start, the 106 rooms are "warmer," less institutional than most of the city's hostelries—with brown-gold-red wall-to-wall carpeting, matching headboards, and twin beds, plus a sofa and armchair, occasional tables, desk/dresser, and fitted closets all in warm-hued wood. The tile-and-marble bathrooms have sophisticated fixtures; chambermaids and room waiters are announced by door chimes rather than a rat-ta-tat, and hallways are carpeted for soundproofing. All the rooms have air conditioning, radios (taped music only), telephones; most of them also have balconies with sliding glass doors and sliding screens, and the suites on the upper floors have big terraces rather than balconies. Nikodimou Street is only one car wide, a trifle noisy at times, so ask for a high room. In any case, you have to be above the third floor to get the best view. But even if you can't have one of the upper rooms, stay there anyway—you can always spend your spare hours on the roof. The Electra Palace is owned by the same people who run the highly regarded Electra Hotel a few streets away, so the service is efficient, polite, and friendly. Other facilities include a sunken lounge in a spacious marble-and-mahogany lobby, a cozy bar, mezzanine dining room and lounge/card room, and adjoining garage. Summer rates are 4430 drs ($44) single, 6596 drs ($66) double for half-board (which is obligatory year around).

up or at the rear. (There are balconies of sorts, but only for standing on, so they're not worth making a hassle over.) The Esperia is another of those Athenian palaces with acres of marbled space—a two-story lobby with marble floors and columns, marble hallways on each floor—and the inevitable highly polished floors. The 185 rooms have fresh wallpaper, prints or pictures to brighten them up, colorful bedspreads and curtains, and furniture that's a shade more substantial and comfortable than usual in Greece. High-season rates are 2378 drs ($24) single, 3048 drs ($30) double.

A Class B choice, **Hotel Lycabettus,** 6 Valaoritou St. (tel. 3633-514), is a five-minute walk from Syntagma, on one of the quieter shopping streets, now part of the pedestrians-only mall. The Lycabettus is relatively new and all the rooms on its seven floors have bathrooms, telephones, radio, balconies, and air conditioning. The best of the bunch are on the upper floors (where the balconies are bigger). It's a friendly little place, with a TV bar, coffeeshop, and a breakfast room. Room rates here are 2460 drs ($25) for a single, 3552 drs ($35) for a double, including breakfast. It's not a steal, but it is good value considering the location and the coziness.

Athens Gate Hotel, 10 Syngrou Ave. (tel. 9238-302), is, on the other hand, one of Athens's top values. Location first: a five-minute walk from Syntagma and directly across the avenue from the Temple of Olympian Zeus and its attendant Hadrian's Gate. The entrance to the hotel is flanked by a terrace café sheltered throughout the day by a two-story stoa. There's also a gleaming black-leather, chrome, and marble bar and lounge on the ground floor, but don't linger—head straight for the elevator and press the top button. The roof is eight stories up, a walk-around marble sundeck with a view! All the sights are there—Olympian Zeus and Hadrian's Gate just across the street, the Zappeion and Parliament to the left, Lycabettus in the distance, the Hilton, the Olympic Stadium, and the Royal Palace; then on the other side, the towering Acropolis, and away in the distance the Saronic Gulf.

Most of the 106 rooms come with balconies, and depending on location, you'll probably enjoy some part of this vista without leaving your room. Get your reservation in early, ask for a room on the seventh floor at the rear, and you'll get a terrace rather than a balcony with room for breakfasting or sunning while you look up at the looming Acropolis. The rooms themselves are livelier than the usual in Athens—with fresh razzle-dazzle wallpapers and drapes, carpeted floors, functional mahogany furniture (desk/dresser, armchair), radio, bedside lamps, modern tiled bathrooms, and a couple of features you don't normally find in Class B hotels—air conditioning and direct-dial telephones. Other facilities include room service until midnight, a 100-seat restaurant on the second floor and a new roof garden restaurant with bar, barbecue, and breathtaking views of the Parthenon, Temple of Zeus, Lycabettus Hill and Hadrian's Gate. The manager here is Spiros Zervos, who's been looking after American tourists for years at some of the best hotels in Greece. High-season rates, all half board, are 3816 drs ($38) single, 4792 drs ($50) double. Outstanding value by any yardstick.

Kolonaki is one of the most fashionable neighborhoods in Athens, much sought after by bankers and novelists, and now you can stay there in a quiet residential street, surrounded by high-rent apartments, for less than $25 a night double. The **Athenian Inn**, entered by a flower-decked entrance at 22 Haritos, just two blocks from Kolonaki Square (tel. 723-8097), is owned by a Greek couple who've decorated it tastefully in "Greek village" style (dark beams, white stucco walls, tile floor). The lounge-breakfast-room-bar features an open fire, rustic furniture, and watercolors by local artists; the 28 guest rooms have wall-to-wall carpeting, quaint rustic-style wooden beds, radios, telephones, and bath or shower; 23 of the rooms have balconies, some with a view of Lycabettus Hill. Summer rates: 2355 drs ($24) single, 3435 drs ($34) double, including service charge, taxes, and breakfast in the pretty rustic lounge.

While the outside of the **Hotel Arethusa,** corner of Mitropoleos and Nikis (tel. 3229-431), is gift-wrapped in what looks like Reynolds-Wrap aluminum foil, the interior decor is a lively blend of marble, polished hardwoods, and fabrics in sprightly colors. All 87 rooms in this attractive hostelry are smartly decked out with contemporary furniture, wall-to-wall carpets, air conditioning (with individual controls), radio, telephone, big bathroom. Up top there's an indoor-outdoor roof garden (superb view, drinks, dinner for around $6), and you can have an after-dinner drink in the modern bar (with TV), one hushed floor above busy Mitropoleos. This is an unusually handsome Class B hotel, and the rates are reasonable—1973 drs ($20) single, 3008 drs ($30) double.

One of the newer Class B hotels in Athens, the **Sirene Hotel** at 15 Lagoumtzi St. (tel. 922-9311), features a pool and view of the Acropolis from its seventh-floor roof. It's only a medium-size pool of course, but then you're not here for the Olympics. You can also stretch out on the sundeck, and there's a bar within hailing distance. The remainder of the hotel is no letdown either: rooms are trimly furnished, with carpets, bath or shower, radio, telephone, big closets, and individual air conditioning controls. The comfy lounge includes a writing room, TV, and bar; lunch or dinner in the cool, modern restaurant is less than $6. The Sirene doesn't have the most convenient location in town (you can't have everything), but it's still only a ten-minute bus ride to Syntagma, or a five-minute ride plus a ten-minute walk to the Acropolis. The Sirene's summer rates, with breakfast, are 2805 drs ($28) single, 4208 drs ($42) double.

You can't get a much more central location than the **Minerva Athens Hotel,** 3 Stadiou St. (tel. 3230-915)—the upper floors of the business center above the arcade that runs from Syntagma to Stadiou Street. The Minerva was transformed into a Class B hotel in 1960, 50 rooms on three floors (6, 7, 8), all with private tub or shower, room phones, and most of them with air conditioning. No restaurant. A spiral staircase leads from the arcade-level lobby to a small lounge where you can sit down to the continental breakfast that's included in the room rate—2500 drs ($25) single, 3600 drs ($36) double, with air conditioning.

Appollonos Street is hotel row. It runs for half a dozen blocks from the Plaka to Constitution Square, and it's full of good budget hotels. The **Omiros Hotel,** 15 Apollonos St. (tel. 3235-486), is one of the newer and smaller ones. It has 37 rooms, all with pink or green tiled bathrooms, telephones, radios, and air conditioning. It's a dapper little hotel. The lobby has handsome wood paneling with Ancient Greek ceramic decorations on the walls, and a coffee corner at the back. There's also a small but uncongested bar-and-restaurant one floor up. The rooms are equally compact, some with head-to-head beds along one wall, a small couch along the other. The rooms facing the street have balconies overlooking the narrow, typically Athenian street, with balustrades, arcades, shutters, and pots of flowers. Most of the rooms have scatter rugs on linoleum floors, and the furnishings are standard. There's taped pop music everywhere at the Omiros—in the lobby, in the elevator, in the rooms, on the roof. The pride and joy of the Omiros is its Roof Garden, which has one of the most unobstructed views of the Acropolis in the entire city (it's amazing how a modest little hotel can take on a new dimension of majesty with a superb Roof Garden vista of that omnipresent sacred hill). You can have dinner up there for around $6 or $7, or you can just sit on the swing chairs with your date/wife/husband/boyfriend and a Coke and while away the hours gazing at the great white flank of the Acropolis rock.

The Omiros's rates are 1944 drs ($19) for a single, 2778 drs ($28) for doubles.

NEAR OMONIA SQUARE: King Minos Hotel, 1 Piraeus St. (tel. 5231-111), is a Class A hotel, close to Omonia Square. It's only a few steps from the square, but its glass-and-grillwork facade is more reminiscent of the Caribbean. The hotel has a spacious lobby, with a marble frieze of King Minos's Palace in Knossos dominating one wall. Up on the mezzanine floor are acres of lounges, two desks with typewriters, an American bar, fountains, birds in a gilded cage, and a restaurant. There are seven floors of rooms, and since this 16-year-old was recently refurbished, the furnishings are fresh and modern, with roomy closets, chairs and desks, and marble balconies. Bathrooms have full-size bathtubs, marble floors and walls, and piles of towels; studios have twin beds arranged at right angles, around a brace of chairs and a coffee table. If you feel cramped, you can always sit out on the balcony and watch the action in Omonia Square. Or go up to the roof to sunbathe. The King Minos is air-conditioned throughout. Peak-season rates are 2592 drs ($26) single, 3600 drs ($36) double.

Hotel Stanley, 1 Odysseos St. at Karaiskaki Square (tel. 524-611), is another hotel with a pool on the roof—this time a moderately priced Class B. It's a slight distance from the center of town, but its roof is one of the coolest, breeziest places in town at high noon, with a great view as a bonus. The 400-room Stanley dominates the big square at the end of Aghiou Konstantinou Avenue, between Omonia Square and the Larissis railroad station. It's a modern air-conditioned hotel, where every room has a bath or shower, balcony, and telephone. The rooftop pool and garden are open from May through October; in winter, the roof becomes a disco. An attractive first-floor restaurant with Scandinavian decor and mottled marble floor is open year round (with three-course meals for less than $8) and there's also an inexpensive cafeteria. Despite its size, the Stanley is usually full, so if you don't have a reservation call ahead first. It's an exceptional value, with singles for 2360 drs ($24) and doubles for 3368 drs ($34).

Two of the best values in and around Omonia Square are

relatively new Class B Superior hotels—the Titania and the Dorian Inn, both opened in 1976.

A stylish tinted-glass facade rising eight floors above a street-level shopping arcade identifies the **Hotel Titania** at 52 Panepistimiou Ave. (tel. 3609-611). Up on the roof, the terrace and bar (sometimes with music) have impressive views of Lycabettus Hill and the Acropolis. The Titania's 400 rooms and a score of suites fill six floors with bright colors and trim design; all the rooms have telephones, individual heating/cooling controls, fitted wall cabinets, and tiled bathrooms with tubs and hand-showers. Public facilities include a colorful coffeeshop (there's also room service from 7 a.m. to 11 p.m.), spacious restaurant (lunch or dinner for $7), and lounge/writing room on the mezzanine. Summer rates are 2694 drs ($27) single, 3978 drs ($40) double. Good value in a convenient location (the traffic hurtling along Panepistimiou is not too intrusive with the windows closed, but if you want complete quiet, ask for a room at the rear).

The **Dorian Inn Hotel** is located on the far side of Omonia Square at 15-17 Piraeus St. (tel. 523-9782). Its 117 comfortable, carpeted rooms and 29 junior suites have direct-dial telephones, individual controls for heating and air cooling, and half of them have balconies; there's room service from 7 a.m. to midnight, a restaurant, a bar-lounge with TV, and another bar on the roof, 12 floors above the city, with an excellent view of the Acropolis. But the Dorian's main attraction for many people will be the rooftop pools—one for adults, one for children. Peak-season rates are also 2916 drs ($29) single, 4056 drs ($41) double.

The Class B **Grand Hotel,** 19 Patission St. (tel. 5222-011), doesn't quite live up to its name—but then neither do its rates. The wallpaper may be peeling here and there (not so much from age as from sloppy hanging) and the decor is not very inspired, but the tiled bathrooms are shiny clean (some have bath and shower, some shower only). The mezzanine floor is given over to spacious lounges, bar, and dining room, and the high-ceilinged lobby has three elevators to speed you to your room. The 100 guest rooms come with air conditioning, telephone, two channels of music, and balcony. The Grand is located in a bustling part of town, just off Omonia Square, a few blocks from the National Archeological Museum; if you want complete silence check into one of the viewless rooms at the rear, but with windows and shutters closed, the rooms overlooking the traffic are tolerable. Doubles cost 3190 drs ($32).

Acadimias Street runs parallel to Venizelou, and about halfway along, just behind the university and National Library, the nine-story **Hotel Acadimos,** 58 Akadimias (tel. 3629-220), rises at the corner of Hippocrates Street. You can't ask for a more cultured spot than that. The hotel's 130 rooms have balconies, telephones, baths or showers, and many of them have fine views of the Acropolis or Lycabettus Mountain, but there's no air conditioning here. There's a cocktail bar and lounge on the first floor, and a restaurant where for 500 drs ($5) you can have a good lunch or dinner and watch the latter-day Aristotles ambling from library to class to shaded bench. Peak-season rates at the Acadimos are 1296 drs ($13) for a single, 1872 drs ($19) for doubles; only 10% less in winter.

At first glance, the **Hotel Ionis,** 41 Halkokondyli (tel. 5232-311), looks like yet another modern office building on a street of undistinguished office buildings, but once you step through the smoked glass doors you enter an oasis of style. Gleaming gray marble, polished wood, and brightly colored ceramics create a welcoming lobby; a marble stairway winds up to a mezzanine restaurant, spacious lounge with TV, and a bar with ceramic friezes depicting willowy nymphs. Corridors are carpeted, windows are double-glazed, cheerful curtains and bedspreads are color coordinated, and each room has air conditioning and two-channel radio. Rooms on the street side have balconies (on the upper floors, terrraces rather than balconies). Although Halkokondyli is not the "smartest" street in town it has some advantages: it's quiet in the evening when all the office workers have gone home; it's only five minutes on foot from Omonia Square and 15 to 20 minutes to the National Archeological Museum; and rooms cost less than they would on more fashionable thoroughfares. For 2493 drs ($25) single and 3281 drs ($33) double (both with breakfast), you probably won't find smarter rooms in Athens.

If you enjoy browsing around markets, the **Athens Center Hotel,** 26 Sofokleouus St. at Klisthenous (tel. 5248-511), puts you within walking distance of the central meat, fish, vegetable, and fruit markets, and close enough to the flea markets at Monastiriki. This may not be the most congenial corner of the city for ladies traveling alone, but the hotel itself is bustling with small tour groups and there's an amiable atmosphere around the lounge/bar and rooftop terrace. All 136 rooms have private bath or shower and air conditioning; a few have balconies, and other amenities include a snackbar, restaurant, and parking garage for

25 cars. But at 1808 drs ($18) single and 2664 ($27) double it hardly measures up in value with, say, the Ionis.

Class C Hotels
(from $12 to $25 double, peak season)

Good news for budget travelers: the official hotel guide to Athens includes more names in categories C and D than in all the others put together. In all, there are well over 100 hotels in Athens offering rooms between $12 and $25 a night for doubles in peak season. This guide can't possibly review all of them, but in the following pages you'll find a selection of some of the best budget hotels in the city.

NEAR SYNTAGMA: The ten-year-old **Hermes Hotel**, 19 Appollonos St. (tel. 3235-514), has an entrance like an airline terminal, but its severe facade is softened somewhat by hints of shrubbery draping over the balconies. It's a small hotel—only 45 rooms—all with balcony, phone, bath or shower. The rooms at the rear look on a school playground; the upper floors have views of the city, and in some cases the Acropolis. Dinner costs around $7, but there's also an à la carte menu with snacks and sandwiches. Room rates are 1490 drs ($15) for a single, 1870 drs ($19) for a double—all the rooms are actually double-size.

One major advantage of the **Royal Hotel**, 44 Mitropoleos (tel. 3234-220), is you don't have to take a coach tour to visit the cathedral. You just cross the street. The hotel's entrance faces a tiny square with a circular garden in the center and trees all around, a few shops, a café or two, and the curved back of the cathedral; and it's right next door to the bronze-faced headquarters of the Greek Shipowners' Association. The location is the best part of it. The hotel has a peculiarly Athenian facade, with marble on the street level, and tall narrow windows, very classically proportioned, going up four floors. There's a bright indoor café facing the street, and a mirrored lobby one floor up. The doubles with bath are spacious and liberally furnished—couch, chairs, dressing tables, large windows and good-size bathrooms; the singles are quite a bit smaller. There are telephones in every room. Doubles with bath are 1900 drs ($19); doubles without bath are 1700 drs ($17).

The Royal Hotel's neighbor, the **Imperial Hotel**, 46 Mitropoleos (tel. 3227-617), has a slightly Germanic facade—square cut with small windows. It doesn't have a lobby at the entrance, but when you go up one flight you'll find a pleasant sitting room, and the manager, G. Klissouris, who speaks English, is anxious to please, and enjoys meeting all the Americans who stay in his hotel. The Imperial's rooms are simple, clean, and large, and all but two have shower or bath. All have a telephone, balcony, and central heating (but no air conditioning). The singles have double beds and tend to be roomier than most singles in this price range. There's free parking in the square across the street. Most of its balconies look toward the cathedral and Acropolis. There are 21 rooms on five floors; rates are from 1500 drs ($15) single, from 1940 drs ($19) double. Pricey.

Kolokotroni is the street that begins at the National Historical Museum and runs more or less parallel to Ermou and Mitropoleos. The **Hotel Carolina,** is about halfway down at 55 Kolokotroni (tel. 3220-837), easily identified by its freshly painted facade. It's one of those places you walk into and instantly feel at home. It was run until 1984 by two Greek-American brothers who came over from Carolina several years ago and converted what was once an apartment building into a 35-room hotel. Now the Carolina is being run by a longtime associate of the owners, Athanasios Papayiannoulas, and his brother George. Every room faces the front or side, most have balconies, and they share eight bathrooms. The best rooms are on the top floor, but since this is the kind of hotel where you'll be constantly meeting new friends and dashing off to a favorite taverna in the Plaka, the view probably doesn't matter much. There's a small snackbar on the first floor, a few steps up from the lobby. The single rates are 1100 drs ($11) without bath, 1250 drs ($13) with bath; doubles are 1350 drs ($14) without, 1500 drs ($15) with. Breakfast is 150 drs ($1.50). The fun is free.

For people who want to be in the heart of things you can't be much closer to the heart of old Athens than the intersection of Iperidou and Asteriou Streets in the Plaka. Here the ten-year-old **Hotel Nefeli** at 16a Iperidou St. (tel. 3228-044), squeezes 18 spic-and-span rooms into a three-story wedge, each of its chambers equipped with modern bathrooms, room phone, trim furniture. Nothing fancy, but comfortable and functional. The spacious, cool lobby is dominated by an orange plastic phone bubble, and there's a pleasant breakfast room-lounge right on the corner. Obviously not the quietest spot in the city, and when the Plaka wakes up so will you, but here are modern rooms in a central location for only 1440 drs double, or just under $15 for room, breakfast, and taxes. First choice in this category.

Here's a real little find, opened in 1983—the **Hotel Hera,** 9 Falirou St. (tel. 9236-682), facing a small square in a residential section between the Acropolis and Syngrou Avenue, a five-minute walk from the Plaka. The stylish facade, like a miniature Ledra Marriott,, fronts a spic-and-span split-level lobby that opens onto a lounge with TV and a coffeeshop with marble-topped tables, which in turns leads to a quiet patio café. The 49 guest rooms, on five floors, are compact to be sure, but sensibly designed (plenty of storage space for suitcases or backpacks), each with direct-dial telephone, radio, twin cot-size beds covered with brightly colored spreads, skimpy drapes covering sliding windows that shut out most neighborhood noise. The tiled bathrooms (showers only) are spotless. For Acropolis views you have to head for the rooftop terrace. It's a good value at 2362 drs single ($24) and 3038 drs double ($30).

The **Philippos Hotel,** 3 Mitseon (tel. 9223-611), is something of an oddity—it's on the *other* side of the Acropolis, the side with the classic picture-postcard view. This is a residential district, except during the Athens Festival when it becomes a funnel for the crowds heading up the road to the Pnyx for the Son-et-Lumière show. If you're staying at the Philippos, you don't have to join the crowd, you simply step out onto your balcony and there's the whole show, right there.

The Philippos is a simple little hotel, only a few years old, and completely redecorated in recent years. You go up a few stairs to the tiny lobby and TV-fitted bar, where there always seems to be American college girls sitting around reading Aeschylus. The Philippos is another of those cozy, communal, everybody's-a-buddy places. In the rooms on the upper floors you'd better be—because each one can sleep five. The other rooms are slightly cramped, even when they're supposed to sleep two, but if you're in the first flush of Aeschylus you probably won't notice. The bathrooms are clean, tiled, and fitted with hand-showers. There are balconies in all the rooms, and on the upper floor they're as large as terraces. The Philippos's restaurant, incidentally, is a cheerful pseudo-taverna with stucco arches, chandeliers, and air conditioning. However (and a surprise for a small budget hotel), you can phone down for sandwiches, snacks, or omelets any time from 7 a.m. to midnight. You can sunbathe on the hotel's roof, and if you want to go sightseeing, you can catch the bus two blocks away and take it to Constitution Square and Omonia Square. Rates are 924 drs ($9) single, 1159 drs ($12) double in summer.

NEAR OMONIA SQUARE: The **Omonia Hotel,** right on Omonia Square (tel. 523-7211), has ten floors and 275 rooms, each of which has an iron balcony and picture windows which give the building an airy appearance. The lobby, one floor up above the entrance to the sunway, is surrounded by a bar-café facing the square, with a restaurant at the rear. There's always plenty of activity around this friendly, spotless hotel; all rooms have private baths and showers, phones, and comfortable furniture, and they're particularly spacious, especially the singles. Good value at half-board rates of 2195 drs ($22) single, 3299 drs ($33) double (but the hotel will try to help you, if you want to pay for room and breakfast only).

The **Asty Hotel,** 2 Pireos (tel. 5230-424) is a slightly younger hotel than its competitor on the next block—the Omonia. It has 128 rooms, most with balconies, half of them facing the square with its fountains and greenery, clean and comfortable but rather "institutional." The Asty's restaurant, on the mezzanine overlooking the square is, incidentally, one of the more popular eating places in the neighborhood. Rates: doubles without bath cost 2120 drs ($21), and with bath, 2348 drs ($23).

The **Hotel Pythagorian,** 28 Aghiou Konstantinou (tel. 5242-811/4), is another of those good-guy Class C hotels in the region of Omonia Square. The attractive entrance with square marble columns and vinyl "wood" paneling leads to a lobby and dining room with a white spiral stairway that goes up to a mezzanine lounge with green marble floor and overstuffed chairs. The 56 rooms, spread over seven floors and topped with a roof garden, all have tiled bathroom with baths and bidets, rooms with typical lino-floor-plain-modern-furniture decor. Rooms at the front have balconies. In-season rates are 1800 drs ($18) single, 2000 drs ($20) double, with breakfast.

The street that runs from Omonia to Ermou is called Athinas, and halfway down it crosses Evripidou. Aghiou Demetriou is where the two streets meet. Okay? The **Hotel Kronos,** 18 Aghiou Demetriou (tel. 3211-601), is actually in a convenient location for either the hustle and bustle of Omonia or the hustle and bustle of the Plaka. It's a small modern hotel, in a small square with a church, trees, and grass. Most of the rooms (comfortable and spotless) have private baths. Rooms with bath are 900 to 1300 drs ($9 to $13) in a single and 1200 to 1700 drs ($12 to $17) in a double. (*Note:* A sister hotel, Neon Kronos, a few blocks away at 12 Assomaton St., is also good value.)

Theater Square, unfortunately, no longer has a theater—it's now backstage Athens, a beehive of importers and exporters by day, and quiet as a church by night (but probably not for single ladies). The 16-year old Hotel Alkistis, 18 Plateia Theatrou (tel. 3219-811), has a sleek ten-story facade of glass, steel, and marble, and 112 rooms and eight suites with motel-modern decor, private baths and showers, and telephones. Ninety-six of the rooms have balconies, and if you pick the right one, you'll have a fine view of the Acropolis. All the rooms and hallways are spotless and freshly painted; the comfortable, spacious lounge has TV and a bar and the roof garden boasts a panoramic view (there are tables and chairs, but no bar service so you have to bring up your own drinks). Manager "Papou" (or Grandfather) Georgiou claims to be an honorary citizen of New Mexico, Minnesota, and Oklahoma, although he has never set foot in the U.S., but he does host lots of young Americans each year—students who come to earn credits in Greece under the auspices of the American Institute of Foreign Studies. When you step into the Alkistis's two-story, marble lobby you may have trouble believing you're in a Class C hotel, but one look at the rates and you will be persuaded that this is another of the city's remarkable bargains. Summer rates are about 1250 drs ($13) in a single with bathroom, 1750 drs ($18) in a double with same. These low rates are reduced by 10% in the off-season. *But get your reservations in early—the Alkistis is one of the most popular Class C hotels in Athens.*

The Hotel Nestor, 58 Aghiou Konstantinou (tel. 5235-576), has a rather olive-drab exterior but the 50 rooms themselves are bigger than usually found in this category, bright, with handsome furniture, pastel-colored walls and balconies, and all have bath or shower. There's an outdoor café, and a dining room enlivened with fresh flowers on every table. The friendly, 50-room, seven-story Nestor has been popular for years with Scandinavians: now it's the turn of the Americans. Singles are 1716 drs ($17) and doubles are 2106 drs ($21) in peak season.

Another gleaming, marble-facaded hotel with its front steps in the market is the Omega Hotel, 15 Aristoghitonos (tel. 3212-421). This one has a roomy, wood-paneled lobby, a pleasant lounge and coffee bar. Its 54 rooms have private bathrooms, but the furnishings are fairly basic. Hardly a steal at 720 drs to 900 drs ($7 single, $9 double) for stays of three nights or longer.

Plateia Exarcheia is a charming triangular plaza lined with trees and cafés, with its apex at the **Hotel Exarcheion.** This Class C hotel, built in 1973, has 68 rooms (all with private bath or shower, most with balconies), and there's a splendid view across the city from the rooftop bar, six floors up. Double rooms are 1538 drs ($15); breakfast is an additional 110 drs per person. If your first stop in Athens is the National Archeological Museum, and you want to be in an area that's Athenian rather than touristy, then this is a good address to head for—55 Themistokleous (tel. 3601-256).

The **Hotel Museum** is a friendly, pleasant, spotless C-class hostelry located right behind the National Archeological Museum, 16 Bouboulinas St. (tel. 3605-611). Of its 59 rooms, 52 are doubles with balconies, all at the front, and the remaining seven are singles, all at the rear; all 59 come with private shower, telephone, and taped music. The mezzanine floors are given over to a cafeteria and bar/lounge. Singles cost 1500 drs ($15), doubles 2000 drs ($20)—which makes the Museum popular with visiting professors and students.

Rock-Bottom Accommodations for Adventurers and Students

In a city like Athens, where $10 will set you up in a single room in a first-class hotel in the off-season, you hardly need to bother with the local rock-bottom prices. However, thousands of young (and some not so young) people arrive in Greece each year with minimal dollars in their pockets and backpacks on their shoulders, and Athenians seem to go out of their way to cater to them, although in 1983 the government started to clamp down on many of the pensions and hotels offering dormitory-type accommodations.

The **YWCA,** or **X.E.N.** as it's known in Greece, hardly deserves the title rock-bottom, because it's in a big, modern building that at first glance seems more like a first class hotel, in a convenient location—at 11 Amerikis St. (tel. 3624-291), just a couple of blocks from Syntagma and the American Express office. X.E.N. has a hairdressing salon and library, as well as kitchen and laundry facilities on every floor. Membership costs less than 500 drs ($5) a year for girls under 16, more for adults, but you don't have to be a member to stay there. Each room has beds, tables, chairs, marble floors; there's no air conditioning, but the sunless rooms at the rear are cool even at midday in midsummer. June through October, rates for stays of one to three nights are from 700 drs ($7) for a single without bath, double that for a double room with bath.

The **Athens Youth Hostel** at 57 Kypselis St. (tel. 8225-860) charges about 300 drs ($3), with facilities for breakfast and light meals. It's open all year, but you need an International Youth Hostel Card (you can buy one on the spot for 720 drs or $7, and it's valid all over the world). *Note:* The hostel now organizes group tours at appropriate rates. Ask for details.

Since the government decided to eliminate most dormitory-style accommodations for backpackers and students, Cleo's Guest House has gone and now there's only **Cleo's Hotel** (or Cleopatra, in the official listing), consisting of a dozen rooms at 3 Patrou St. (tel. 3229-053). It's located more or less in the Plaka, across the street from the Hotel Hermes, and a few blocks from the cafés of Constitution Square. Doubles are 1730 drs ($17); triples 1956 ($20). The **Phaedre Hotel** is a Class D establishment, but its rates are so modest it can reasonably be included in this category. Its location, at 16 Cherefontos St. (tel. 3238-461), belies the ominous overtones of its legendary namesake—on a quiet little square facing the palm-filled courtyard of St. Katherine's Church, surrounded by neighborhood tavernas and narrow streets, one block from Filellinon Street, near the Monument to Lysicrates. The rooms are relatively big, but none of them has a private bathroom, just washbasins, with three toilets to every floor—but then consider this bargain rate: 1300 drs, or just $13, double. Hot showers are free.

Kaisariani Church (ancient church near Athens)

DINING OUT IN ATHENS

YOU MAY HAVE heard some people say Greek food is dull. Dull? Try this for starters: *caravides*—fried crayfish with Russian dressing; *koheli*—lobster, mussel, crab, shrimp, or red snapper baked in a shell with cognac; *moussaka*—chopped meat with eggplant, cheese, and béchamel sauce; *teropita*—those delicious little cheese puffs filled with feta; *yigantes*—white lima beans in tomato sauce; *dolmadakia*—vine leaves stuffed with meat, onions, and spices, and served with lemon sauce.

That's not a random selection from many menus. It's not even a random selection from one menu. It's only the start of one recent meal, what the Greeks call *mezedes,* or hors d'oeuvres—which was concluded with mixed grill of lamb chop, veal, and kidney, tomato and spring onions, followed by a deep-fried fritter served in a hot sugar sauce, followed by apple spiced in honey.

So let's straighten out some of the facts about dining in Athens. Greek food is *not* dull. Maybe if you're staying there for a week or longer, your palate may lose its enthusiasm for more Greek food because so much of it is cooked in oil and flavored with lemon, or because so often it's lukewarm when served (on the theory that hot food is not good for you). But for the average visit of two or three days, you won't have time to sample all the dishes you're going to want to sample. If you do stay longer and you do want a change of pace, you can always go to one of the restaurants serving American food in its infinite variety—hamburger, club sandwich, and steak.

Most Greek restaurants also serve a few dishes that are popular in Greece but that are not Greek dishes. Most of the inexpensive restaurants feature spaghetti, cannelloni, wienerschnitzels, omelets, and steaks. Remember, Greeks have been entertaining tourists from other European countries for a long time now, and try to cater to them. There always has been a choice of French and Turkish eating places, but now Athens has acquired Chinese and Japanese restaurants, even an English pub or two.

The other rumor you hear about Greek food is that it contains some unsavory ingredients. This is sometimes true in the country, and in the lambing season partially true in Athens. If anyone ever asks you if you'd like to try *ameletita,* just smile and say no thank you. Even in Greek it means unmentionables. Plural. Or if someone suggests *kokoretsi,* decline. It's second cousin to a Scottish haggis and we all know what a yummy that is. And don't be surprised if you take your Greek date to a seafood restaurant over by Piraeus and she gobbles up the entire fish—head, eyes, and all. It's not that she's starving. It's simply the Greek custom. You don't have to follow suit.

If you're tentative about what you eat (and when you're traveling, changing time zones, and generally rushing around, you have every right to be), stick to basic dishes like roast lamb and veal. They're cooked on the spit, with only a whisper of spices.

Unfortunately, as you will see a few pages from now, inflation has been catching up with kitchens in Athens, and some of the basic Greek dishes are getting close to the point where they're not worth the price. Nevertheless, if you're on a tight budget your dollars will buy you more sustenance in Athens than in most European capitals. If you're really counting your leptas rather than drachmas, stick to restaurants *(estiatorion)* rather than tavernas, to *ouzeri* rather than cafés.

Types of Eating Places and Dining Tips

The one thing that Greece has that most countries don't have is **tavernas.** There probably was a time when a taverna was something quite distinct from a restaurant—and even more distinct from a nightclub. But that's no longer the case. A taverna can be a pub, a restaurant, a café, a nightclub, or a combination of all of them. Since many of them provide music, and are really for an evening on the town, you'll read about them later on in the chapter on nightlife.

The other unusual feature about Athenian eating places is the **roof garden.** Apparently the roofs of Greek houses used to be flat in order to collect rainwater, which was then drained off and fed into a tank under the soil; when proper plumbing and water systems came along, people didn't need their roofs as dams, but they then discovered that they were refreshingly cool places to spend an evening. So they started turning them into gardens, or at least terraces. The idea spread to restaurants. Now many of the new hotels in Athens include a roof garden, and you should certainly plan to spend at least one evening up there. The basic, authentic roof gardens are on tavernas in the Plaka, and the ultimate roof garden is probably the King George Hotel's, which is baronial Tudor, half indoors, half outdoors (but which may be closed for renovation while you're in town).

Athens at midday in midsummer is often too hot for sitting down to a meal, and this has probably given rise to the city's varied types of **snackbars**—the Western-style snackbar, the tea and pastry shops, the fig-and-nut store, the pastry vendor, and the souvlaki shop. Keep these snackbars in mind if you're on a budget, or if you're having problems adjusting to the curious meal hours in Athens (a subject I'll come to in a minute).

The Pastry Vendor

He's the local equivalent of the pretzel man. He sells two, sometimes three, items. First, there are rolls and hero-style breads, plus a bread known as *koulouri*—a large, thin bagel with sesame seed on top. It costs only a few drachmas—the perfect inexpensive snack. The pastries include plain *bourekia*, a sort of doughnut with sugar sprinkled on top. You can buy bourekia either in a "long-john" shape, or in a rounded shape with a small smidgen of jelly in the middle. *Bougatsa* is a pastry pie with cream inside, and sprinkled with powdered sugar. When filled with apples rather than cheese, it's known as *milopitta*. Some pastry vendors also have ham sandwiches, or *piroski* (bread with sausage inside).

Fig-and-Nut Shops

They sell figs, dates, prunes, walnuts, pistachios, almonds, honey, raisins, syrup, and so on. You buy by the drachma, and these goodies hit the spot if you're on a budget, or if it's a long time until your nine o'clock date.

Picnics

What with all that sunshine and all those scented lemon trees, you may want to find a corner of some centuries-old agora and have a picnic. To stock up, visit a grocery store or the Pris-Unic-Marinopoulos supermarket. Start with some cheese. The main types are *graviera* (Greek-Swiss), *feta* (Greek goat cheese), *kefalotiri* (a yellow, salted cheese), *kasseri* (a hard, yellow cheese), and *roquefort* (which in these parts is any kind of bleu cheese). The olives are stored in large wooden barrels and aged for months (order them by the drachma). Yogurt is ladled from large vats and spread onto wax paper. Six drachmas' worth is probably your limit. You'll never taste fresher yogurt than in Greece (try it served with honey for breakfast). You may also want to check with the restaurant the **Stage Door,** at 14a Von Kourestion, which lists picnic boxes on its menu—mostly salads and sandwiches—for $5 or thereabouts.

Pastry Shops

The Greeks have sweet tooths. Shamelessly so. *Baklava* is a gooey goody made of layers of paper-thin pastry called *filo*, honey, nuts, pastry, honey, nuts, etc. *Kataifa* is equally gooey but filled with sweetened nuts and shredded wheat, and in its most glorious state, served with a mound of chantilly cream. *Galaktoboureko* is much simpler—a hollow pastry filled to overflowing with custard cream. Greek chocolate, like Greek olives, is bitter, and you can sample it in the form of layer cakes, tub cakes, or flaky mounds. Many pastry shops (or *zacharoplasteions*) in Athens also sell coffee, so you can sit down and enjoy yourself right there and then—simply pointing to what you fancy.

Cafés

As in most Mediterranean countries, people pop into a café or *caferion,* at the slightest opportunity. In winter, they'll have a quick espresso as a pick-me-up; in summer, something cooler. The café is an institution. Almost an epidemic—Constitution, or Syntagma, Square can seat 3000 imbibers at one time. The café waiter is no less immaculately attired or competent than his counterpart in a real restaurant. Even the simplest order is attended to with style. Ask for a lemon juice and he'll bring you a tall glass with freshly pressed lemon juice, a carafe of water, and sugar on a silver tray—all for something like 120 drs ($1.20). And having paid your dues, you're free to sit in this informal "club" all afternoon watching the world go by, flirting, dozing, writing postcards. In Athens, as in other parts of Europe, it's perfectly proper to sit at an empty chair even when there are other people at the table.

Refreshments

Coffee. Ordering a cup of coffee for the first time in Athens is almost as bewildering as trying to order a sandwich in New York if you're a stranger (white, wholewheat, rye, pumpernickel, toast, etc.) The list of coffees on café menus in Athens goes roughly as follows—espresso, cappuccino, French, Viennese, Nescafé, Greek (which had been known as Turkish coffee until the troubles flared up in Cyprus in 1974). If you just say coffee, you get either Greek (if the waiter thinks you look Greek) or Nescafé (if he thinks you look American). What you probably want is, in fact, French. Nescafé is instant coffee brought to you with a cup and some hot water and you mix your own. Cappuccino comes from those hissing Italian coffee machines, and is a combination of coffee and cocoa with a white froth on top, sometimes served with a pinch of nutmeg or cinnamon. Coffee for the Greeks comes in three degrees of sweetness: *metrio*— medium strong, medium sweet; *vari-glyko*—strong and sweet; *sketo*—no sugar. Most Greeks seem to drink it *metrios,* and that's the way you'll probably prefer it. Besides, it's the easiest to say.

Wines and other liquid refreshments. You can't *not* drink wine in the land of Bacchus. Most people think of *retsina* when they think of Greek wines, but there's more to it than that. Retsina is resinated wine. Originally the resin was added to preserve the wine, then everyone liked it so much that way the resin stayed there. However, it's an acquired taste. Most visitors prefer the regular Greek wines, from the bottle rather than the barrel. There are hundreds of them, some good, some okay, some yugggh. Order the following and you won't go far wrong:

Reds: Demestica or robust Castel Danielis, both from the Peloponnese; Caviros or Cellar from Attica (the closest thing to a local Athenian wine); Naoussa from Macedonia; or Chevalier de Rhodes from Rhodes. Of these, Demestica is the least expensive, Caviros the most expensive. Porto Carras is a sturdy wine from new vineyards associated with a new resort in the north.

Whites: Again, Demestica, Santa Helena, or the muscadet-like but light Santa Laura, all from the Peloponnese; Robola from Cephalonia; Pallini, or the pricey Cava Cambas and Elissar from Attica; and Domaine Carras blanc de blanc from Porto Carras.

Rosés: Roditis, Cimarosa, King, Cellar.

Be adventurous and ask for half a kilo (yes, wine is measured by the kilo) of the open wine if they have it. This will be the local wine—the white will probably be resinated, the red probably not.

Although retsina is an acquired taste it's surprising how fast many foreigners do acquire the taste and at prices around 60 drs (60¢) a kilo, who can blame them? Obviously you take pot-luck, but the wine from Attica, the region behind Athens, is usually good.

The main Greek aperitif is *ouzo*, a clear anise drink that turns misty gray when you add water. *Mastic* is a thick white gum from a tree that grows only on the island of Ios—it's dropped into a glass of water still clinging to the spoon and it's stickier and sweeter than anything in the world.

There seem to be no Greek beers these days, so the most popular brews are the Dutch Amstel and Heineken, and the German Henninger, all of which are brewed in Greece. Beer is sold in two sizes—550 grams and 330 grams; remember to ask for a small beer (330 grams), about the size you're accustomed to back home.

Water

It's one of the most refreshing drinks in Athens, and comes automatically to the table—even when you order coffee—but without ice. If you prefer bottled water, carbonated water is more reliable than the still variety. In the country, never drink water that has come straight from a well. A popular Greek refresher is the lemonade—fresh lemon juice, the real kind, squeezed into a glass, and usually served with a separate glass of water so that you can mix to your own taste. You can spend an entire afternoon in a café nursing one lemon juice. Two other popular Greek refreshers, on sale almost everywhere: Coke and Pepsi.

Dining Hours

To understand Athenian meal times, you have to understand traditional Athenian office hours. Most people trudge into their offices at 8 or 8:15 a.m., work nonstop until 1 or 2 p.m. (unless, they're executives, in which case they nip out for a quick ouzo at noon), stop for lunch and a siesta until 5 p.m., then go back to the office until 8 or 8:30 p.m. Shops follow the same basic schedule. Thus lunch is closer to 2 p.m. than to noon, and nobody thinks of starting dinner before 9 in the evening (even later in summer). If you have a date, arrange to meet for drinks at 9 p.m., then go on from there. If you're accustomed to eating earlier, you'll have problems. Most restaurants don't start serving dinner until 9 p.m., but a few (mostly in the budget category), which are probably accustomed to serving tourists from northern Europe, will serve you a meal from 6 or 7 p.m. on. Now you know why there are so many snackbars in Athens! (Memo to business travelers: In Athens you're more likely to be invited to a business *dinner* than a business lunch.)

Prices

This is probably the most tempting part of the subject, despite inflation—but thanks to a record-high dollar, you can go to the finest restaurant in Athens, pick out the most expensive dish, and still end up spending less than you would on an average meal back home. If you want to shoot the works, Athens is the place to shoot. If you have to survive on pennies a day, you needn't get skinny in Athens. There are plenty of restaurants in this guide where you can eat, and eat *well,* for under 500 drs ($5).

Restaurant prices, like hotel prices, are controlled by the government, specifically by an organization referred to on the menus as the Marketing Police. Each type of restaurant is fitted into a category and must supply meals within those limits. Individual items will vary on the à la carte menus of different restaurants, but all restaurants within a given category, except deluxe, must supply fixed meals at a fixed price.

Column A and Column B

Most menus in Athens have two columns of prices. The first column is the price of the dish. The second is the price of the dish plus service and taxes. You'll be charged the price in the second column, and I've no idea what will happen if you try to pay the price in the first column. Theoretically, it's probably a good idea to show customers how much they're tipping—except, as in the case of hotel service charges, people may still feel obliged to tip more. See below.

Tipping

Despite the service charge, most people round out the figure on the bill and leave the change as a bonus tip. You don't have to, but some Greek restaurants, even the humblest, are swarming with busboys and assistant waiters who rely heavily on tips. If your busboy, or *miero*, is particularly attentive about getting rid of empty plates and so forth, tip him separately by placing a few 20-drachma coins *on the table,* not the saucer.

Taxes

The government imposes something called a luxury tax on restaurants—anything from 3% to 17%, and some restaurants unsportingly add this tax to their clients' bills, which they're allowed to do. Usually 3%. In fancier places with music you may also find something called an entertainment tax listed on the menu; if you don't feel like paying it, don't go in. At Easter or Christmas you may also find a "bonus," 2% or 3%, added to your bill—government authorized.

Restaurant Dining

Now for the restaurants themselves. What you will find in the following pages is a listing of Athens dining spots arranged by type (Greek, steak houses, international) in the case of the moderately priced and expensive restaurants, followed by a roster of recommendations (restaurants, snackbars, and cafés) where you can dine for 600 drs ($6) or less. Since you've come to Greece for local color, I'll begin with restaurants and tavernas that have a distinctive Greek flavor and ambience.

THE TAVERNAS: Nothing could be more Greek than the taverna. The simplest tavernas (and for many people, these are the most enjoyable) are plain rooms in nondescript buildings, or in patios and gardens under arbors and olive trees; furnishings usually consist of plain-jane wooden tables and chairs, the tables covered with white paper on which your waiter sets glasses of water. The kitchen is usually open to view, and the selection of food is either still in the pots or spread out in glass-enclosed showcases—diners simply walk over to the pots or display, size up the various dishes, then indicate to the waiter what they want. Simple—especially for foreigners who don't speak Greek. Menus follow the same basic pattern—that is, moussaka, dolmadakia, arni souvla, barbounia skara, and some regional variations of these basic dishes. In some tavernas, on the other hand, you have no choice, and it matters not whether you speak Greek or Swahili because waiters simply arrive at your table with platters of food, beginning perhaps with the selection of *mezedes*, or appetizers, mentioned at the start of this chapter.

In Athens, the most famous of these fixed-menu tavernas is **Taverna Myrtia** at 35 Markou Moussourou-Mets, somewhere behind the Olympic Stadium (say, a $3 taxi ride from Syntagma); it's fairly typical of its kind, with rush-matting walls, beamed

Greek Menu Terms

Hors d'oeuvres

Taramosalata	Fish roe with mayonnaise
Tiropita	Cheese pie
Spanakopita	Spinach pie
Melitzanosalata	Eggplant salad
Tomates yemistes me risi	Tomatoes stuffed with rice
Midia Fassolia salata	Dandelion salad
Piperies yemistes	Stuffed green peppers
Tzatziki	Cucumber with yogurt

Fish

Astakos (Ladolemono)	Lobster (with oil and lemon sauce)
Bakaliaro (Skordalia)	Cod (with garlic)
Barbounia (Skara)	Red mullet (grilled)
Caravides	Crayfish
Garides	Shrimp
Glossa (Tiganiti)	Sole (fried)
Kalamarakia (Tiganita)	Squid (fried)
Kalamarakia (Yemista)	Squid (stuffed)
Oktapodi	Octopus
Soupies yemistes	Stuffed cuttlefish
Tsipoura	Dorado

Meats

Arni souvla	Spit-roasted lamb
Arni yiouvetsi	Lamb in tomato sauce
Arni avgolemono	Lamb with lemon sauce
Brizola moscharisi	Beef or veal steak
Brizola hirini	Pork steak or chop
Dolmadakia	Stuffed vine leaves
Keftedes	Fried meatballs
Kotopoulo souvla	Spit-roasted chicken
Kotopoulo yemisto	Stuffed chicken
Loukanika	Spiced sausages
Moussaka	Meat and eggplant (or potato)
Paidakia	Lamb chops
Pilafi, risi	Rice pilaf
Souvlaki	Lamb (sometimes veal) on the skewer
Youvarlakia	Boiled meat balls with rice
Yuvetsi	Lamb with noodles

ceiling, a collection of island pottery and copper lamps, a few paintings. Myrtia also regales you with a strolling trio. It's the most expensive of the tavernas listed here, about 4000 drs ($40) per person for a meal of innumerable courses (probably more food than you can manage) but it lends itself to convivial evenings: the tables are covered with jolly red cloths, and waiters squeeze and maneuver through the crammed tables with platefuls of tiripitae, beans plalci, artichokes, octopus, followed by shrimps, swordfish, quail, followed by liver, beef pie, lamb and pork in a wine sauce. Since it's an indoor taverna, Myrtia is closed June to September, and you must always call ahead for a reservation (tel. 7012-276).

Steki Tou Yianni at 1 Trias St. (about five minutes from the National Archeological Museum by taxi) sounds like a steak house but in fact the name translates as "Yianni's Lair." Like Myrtia, it's an excellent introduction to Greek food for those who feel they ought to try some traditional fare but may be nervous about doing so. Decor is basic Greek rustic: walls paneled to the waist with wood, the remainder with that basket-weave that's almost *de rigueur* in tavernas, and as you enter, you walk past a row of aging barrels filled with the house wines. Typical dishes are squid in batter with a cocktail sauce, seafood pie served from an oyster shell, moussaka, tiropitakia with spiced sausage and beans, dolmades, and finally, stifado (or Greek stew). Followed by (if you can still cope) Greek desserts. Yianni's fine house wine comes from Attica, and is served in attractive earthenware jugs. Reckon on spending about 2000 drs (about $20) for two with the house wine (more, if you order à la carte). Steki Tou Yianni's is closed on Sunday and for a month or two in summer.

Many Athenians will tell you that one of the best unspoiled, untouristy tavernas is **Xynou**, at 4 Angelou Geronta St., a back street in the Plaka. It's basically a cluster of leafy courtyards with soft lights, murals of life in ancient Athens, and a trio of balladeers singing gentle songs. Xynou is where well-to-do Athenians dine (you'll see more jackets here than in most tavernas), but prices are still moderate: a good meal with house wine should cost less than 750 drs ($7.50) a head. Reservations: 3221-065. Open 8 p.m. to 2 a.m., closed Sunday.

One block behind the National Archeological Museum and popular with students and well-to-do Athenians as well as with visitors, **Taverna Costoyannis** serves consistently top-rank meals in a big, rambling, busy taverna at 37 Zaimi St. Unlike other restaurants that remove only the roof in summer, Costoyannis discards its walls too, so you can dine virtually in a garden surrounded by whitewashed walls and luxuriant creepers. Costoyannis has a stunning selection of appetizers, with a special recommendation for shrimps with bacon, tzatziki, eggplant Imam, and swordfish souvlaki. Visit Costoyannis with a few friends, order half a dozen dishes and dip in. Call for a kilo of the house wine, called "brusco," or "kokkinelli," and you'll still be amazed when your bill comes—about 400 drs ($4) a head! If you want to splash out, or if you can squeeze in yet another dish, the grills, both meat and fish, are excellent. Costoyannis fills up from 9 p.m. on, so go early or reserve (tel. 8220-624) unless you don't mind waiting for a table. A taxi from Syntagma will cost another 70 to 80 drs (70¢ to 80¢) each way. Costoyannis is closed for lunch and all day Sunday.

The Hilton Hotel's award-winning **Taverna Ta Nissia**, big, beautiful and airy, is said to represent an island taverna, but surely a very classy taverna on a very classy island. The ceiling, 40 feet high, is redwood, the floor is marble, ditto the trout tank; decoration consists of lots of copperware, the table linen is persimmon, the china, deep turquoise with brown and orange stripes, and the menus come in hand-woven binders—that sort of place. The food doesn't let you down either, beginning with the ten-dish *mezedes* for just over 700 drs ($7). For the main dish you might want to sample the spit-roasted Olympia lamb with fresh mint and rice pilaf or *gourounaki souvlas*, which is roast suckling pig basted in its own juices, and served with crackling skin. Budget roughly $15 to $18 per person for a full meal. Reservations: 7220-201. Open daily, dinner only, from 7 to 11 p.m. Except similar prices, but with cuisine in the Cypriot manner, at the equally stylish **Taverna** of the new Athenaeum Intercontinental Hotel. Reservations: 9225-950.

Other tavernas worth bearing in mind (in most cases, less expensive than those above) are **Rodia**, in a whitewashed courtyard at 44 Aristipou St. (tel. 7229-883), and **Rouga**, at 7 Kapsali St. (tel. 7227-934), both in the fashionable Kolonaki district.

OTHER TYPICALLY GREEK RESTAURANTS: The following selection is similar in style and cuisine, but these are considered restaurants rather than tavernas.

Gerofinikas, at 10 Pindarou St. (between Syntagma and Kolonaki), is considered by many to be the finest of the Greek/

Levantine restaurants, and it certainly is not the sort of place where you can expect to be seated without a half-hour wait if you forget to make a reservation. You enter it through a long, unprepossessing passageway that leads you into a surprisingly leafy indoor "courtyard," which is air-conditioned in summer; displays of Oriental desserts and great bowls of fresh fruit greet you at the door, and off to the left there's a big open kitchen with the day's dishes set out for your inspection—lamb fricassee, eggplant Beyendi, *doner kehap* (grilled veal) and *mouskari*, or veal with vegetables cooked in a paper bag. The succulent desserts include the syrupy sweet *ekmek kataif,* topped with chantilly in summer, with thick cream in winter. With prices of main dishes in the 400- to 650-dr ($4 to $6.50) range Gerofinikas is one of the best buys in town, but if you want to dine there you'd better call ahead for a reservation: 3636-710 or 3622-719. Open 12:30 to 11:30 p.m.

Vladimiros, at 12 Aristidemou St. (tel. 7217-407) is a delightful restaurant on the way up to the Lycabettus funicular. It's an ideal spot for American visitors—a neighborhood restaurant catering to a local clientele who may want a change from their native moussaka, so without acting like a tourist you can enjoy beef, pork, lamb, and veal dishes cooked over charcoal and garnished in continental style. Vladimiros is equally popular in summer for its garden beneath the pine trees of Lycabettus, in winter for its piano bar and cozy rooms filled with paintings. Budget $8 or $9 for main courses. Daily, from 8 p.m.

A few streets closer to Syntagma at 36 Loukianou St., **Jimmy's Cooking** is located at the point where a steep street becomes steep steps. There's a cozy, comfortable interior, but the main attraction is the small warm-weather terrace shaded by a canopy and screened by greenery. Jimmy's cooking consists of a variety of Greek and continental dishes in the 450- to 650-dr ($4.50 to $6.50) range.

One of the brightest little restaurants in Athens is **Fatsio's,** 5 Efroniou, a few blocks from the Hilton and fewer still from the Caravel, where walls and ceilings are hand-painted in the style of Thessaly, with cornucopias and flowers in sunny blues, yellows, and reds. Even the linen napkins are sealed in clear plastic. The display of dishes includes baked veal with eggplant, baked swordfish, veal with tomato sauce—none of them over 450 drs ($4.50). Reservations: 717-421. Open for lunch only, noon to 5 p.m.

The air-conditioned **Corfu** at 6 Kriezotou, just around the corner from Panepestimiou, is classed as a "luxury" restaurant although the decor suggests something more modest. Likewise the food. As its name might lead you to expect, it features several Corfiote specialties, like beef "Pastitsada," which is boiled beef and spaghetti, at 430 drs ($4.30), and sirloin of beef "Sofrito," which is sliced beef in a wine sauce with noticeable amounts of garlic, at 470 drs ($4.70); the rest of the Corfu's menu ranges from moussaka at 350 drs ($3.50) to lobster at 900 drs ($9). A place to drop into in a thunderstorm if you can't make it to one of the better spots near here; but if you want to call ahead for a reservation, the number is 3603-411. Open daily from noon to midnight.

DINING AT THE TOP: By any standard, the King George Hotel's **Tudor Hall** is one of the most striking restaurants anywhere, filling the top floor of the luxurious King George Hotel. The name gives you a clue to the decor—like a baronial hall in an old English stately home, the walls and ceiling covered with dark, carved wood and hung with immense tapestries, sconces, and chandeliers. But there's another distraction to keep you from enjoying it throughout the meal—the view of the Acropolis (although only half the tables are in the right position). The fixed-price dinner up here will cost you about $25 to $30, service included, but the view far outshines the cuisine. Be sure to call ahead in case the restaurant and/or hotel is closed for renovations (tel. 3230-651).

Another popular spot for sky-high dining (highest in the city, in fact) is the **Dionysos Restaurant** on top of Mount Lycabettus (tel. 7226-374 for reservations), with a menu similar to its namesake near the Acropolis—in other words, you can choose from a wide-ranging menu and enjoy a dinner for anywhere from 500 to 1200 drs ($5 to $12) per person.

Farther down Mount Lycabettus, you can dine at **Le Grand Balcon,** the rooftop restaurant of the St. George Lycabettus Hotel, 2 Klemenou St. (tel. 790-711). In summer you get a magnificent 360-degree view from the outdoor terrace; in winter you're tucked away snugly in the elegant Grill Room. In both cases, you're entertained by a combo for dancing. À la carte dinners here will average somewhere between 1200 and 2000 drs ($12 to $20).

You can get an even closer view of the Acropolis from the Roof Garden of the **Astor Hotel,** 16 Karageorgi tis Servias (tel. 3255-555), one of the city's few year-round eyries (in winter it's enclosed in glass that doesn't block the view). This is another place for lingering. Once you get up there, order a bottle of Santa Elena or Cimarosa, and slowly scan the menu; you'll be reluctant to rush through your meal and get back down to earth, literally and otherwise. Enjoy roast lamb, shish kebab, or the complete 920-dr ($9) dinner with moussaka or soup as a first course, roast lamb or chicken with rice, dessert, and/or feta cheese. If it's still too early to drag yourself away, order some Greek coffee. Then follow it up with a Metaxa. Two people can still leave with change from $30—having enjoyed a better view (and better value) than diners in the pricey Tudor Hall. Open to 10:30 p.m. only.

FRENCH AND CONTINENTAL RESTAURANTS: The Balthazar, 27 Tsocha St. at Vournazou Street, near the American Embassy, a $1.50 to $2 cab ride from Syntagma (tel. 6461-215), is an imposing corner town house with a curving driveway, steps at the front, and a secluded garden for summer dining in the rear. The first things that greet you as you come in through the main door are crystal chandeliers, beautiful walnut paneling, lofty ceilings, and marble fireplaces. The three-story mansion was built at the turn of the century for a well-to-do Athenian family (not shipping—textiles), but in recent years it was rescued from decay by a young consultant economist, Nikos Paleologos, who had his passport removed by the regime of 1967, so he had plenty of time on his hands to put the place in order. He imported a special craftsman from London to restore the elaborate ceilings, decorated the walls with his private collection of contemporary Greek art, and decked the windows with his private collection of antique glass bottles (some of them are real curios). The setting may be elegant, but the Balthazar is, in fact, fairly casual about its elegance: the waiters are in shirt sleeves, and Paleologos commutes from the kitchen to the tables in blue denims. The name, by the way, comes from a reference in *Cyrano de Bergerac* —"faire un Balthazar," meaning have a feast or big meal—and that seems to be the clear intent of Nikos Paleologos and his wife. Their meals are hearty. Some suggestions from their varied menu: minute steaks with brandy and mushrooms, the daily

Eastern curries served with homemade chutney; for openers, try the spiced cheese log which is a blend of island cheeses and herbs. Menus vary from season to season, but you can expect main dishes to be in the $6 to $9 price range. A large open-air bar has now been added to the restaurant's summer garden—so you can always drop by just for a cocktail. Dinner only, from 7 p.m. to 2 a.m.

The next restaurant is over on the far side of the Acropolis, near the Herod Atticus Theater and Philopappos Hill, with one of the best views of the Acropolis in the entire city. The **Dionysus** is difficult to fit into one category, since it's several restaurants in one: it serves Greek food and continental food (escalope Holstein, chicken Negresco, crêpes suzettes) in its glass-walled restaurant and terraced garden; and snacks in its vine-covered courtyard café, which is almost right opposite the main entrance to the Acropolis. Dinner in the restaurant will cost about 1130 to 1550 drs ($11 to $15) a head; in the courtyard, there are tourist menus for under 825 drs ($8), and simple dishes like omelets, spaghetti, and sandwiches cost well under 1030 drs ($10). With these prices, and this setting, Dionysus is a very popular place. For reservations call 9233-182.

One of the most highly regarded French restaurants in town is the award-winning **Prunier,** a pretty little three-room bistro at 63 Ipsilantou, two blocks from the Hilton. Interesting menu, attentive service. Reservations: 7227-379. The newest French restaurant in town is the **Brasserie des Arts,** the dazzling glass-and-copper dining room on the second floor of the Hotel NJV Meridien. A French chef oversees the *nouvelle cuisine* brochette d'espadon and carré d'agneau; the pastry chef has his farm-fresh butter flown in from Normandy; and it's the only eating place in the city with tableside telephone service. Expensive, and marred by an amplified combo that's more obtrusive than it should be in a space like this (although they're actually playing in the lounge). Reservations: 3255-301. Open daily from 1 to 4 p.m.

Most of the continental restaurants I've been talking about here serve only indoors, but up in Kolonaki, at the corner of Xenokratous and Aristidimou, **Je Reviens** has a stylish indoor salon (with piano music and chanteuse in the evenings) *and* a pleasant terrace with checked tablecloths and lanterns strung from the mulberry trees. For a dinner featuring coq au vin or cotelettes de veau, expect to pay around 1000 to 1200 drs ($10 to $12), but for a light lunch of omelet and salad you can get by on 400 drs ($4). Reservations: 7223-605. **L'Abreuvoir,** next door at 51 Xenokratous (reservations: 7229-061), is the oldest French restaurant in town and for many Athenians still the best, but many visitors find it too stuffy and expensive.

Welcome Additions

One of Athens's oldtime favorite restaurants, Vassilis, has given way to what may well prove to be another favorite, the **Stage Door,** 14 Voukourestiou (tel. 3635-145). The new co-owner, Greek-American Nikos Sokaris of the Stagecoach (below), has restored the lovely old turn-of-the-century building and installed a long bar with padded stools on street level, and upstairs, a wicker-and-shrubbery restaurant with circular booths, print fabrics, and, alas, piped music. Bar lunches (or suppers) range from BLTs to omelets to chef's salad—200 to 350 drs ($2 to $3.50). The restaurant menu features seafoods—filet of sole six ways plus daily specials, at 750 to 900 drs ($7.50 to $9) depending on the catch—as well as moussaka at 650 drs ($6.50), fish souvlaki at 680 drs ($6.80), and seven cuts of steak, ranging from 650 to 900 drs ($6.50 to $9). In other words, a three-course meal up here will cost anywhere from $12 to $20 a head, without wine. Closed Sunday; open for lunch from 1 to 4 p.m., for dinner from 8 p.m. to 1 a.m., and the clubby bar stays open to 2 a.m.

One of the most interesting restaurants to open in Athens in recent years is the new **G. B. Corner** in the prestigious Hotel Grande Bretagne, with one entrance in the glittering, elegant lobby, the other on Panepistimiou Avenue. The G. B. Corner has an Edwardian, masculine air, all dark wood and cut glass, brightened by clusters of globe lamps. The most surprising feature of this newcomer is its moderately priced menu and its innovative dishes—including hamburger chasseur. A welcome addition to the Syntagma scene, it's a pleasant place to visit any time of the day or half the night (it's open until 2 a.m.) for a drink, a coffee, or a full meal, which could be as little as 600 drs ($6) or as much as 1100 drs ($11). **Le Bistrot Athenian,** on the next corner of the same Syntagma block, adjoins the lavish Brasserie one floor up in the new Meridien but serves less expensive fare—say, omelettes aux choix for 320 drs ($3.20), hamburgers for 450 drs ($4.50), or brochette de filet de veau for 900 drs ($9). Open 7 a.m. to 2 a.m.

ITALIAN, ORIENTAL, ET AL.: Each year Athens is becoming more and more cosmopolitan, and although you're probably not coming to the land of olives and feta cheese to eat pizza and tempura, you may like to know that they are available—together with the cuisines of Lebanon, Turkey, Spain, Korea, China, Cyprus, and now, with the arrival of the Ledra Marriott's Kona Kai, Polynesian. Here's a sampling of international restaurants.

The smartest Italian restaurant in town is **Da Walter** (tel. 7248-726), located in a modern apartment building at 7 Evzonon St. at the corner of Anapiron Polemon in Kolonaki, somewhere between the American and British Embassies. The decor, in tones of mocha and coffee, is chic and modern (although the thickly upholstered modular sofa/chairs would probably be more appropriate in the lobby next door), and the fresh flowers and lemon-colored napery tell you that the dapper staff takes a pride in the place. Prices are moderate to hefty—peti di pollo al marsala or filetto Voronof (veal in a cognac and mustard sauce) will cost $5 to $8; but if you avoid pricey appetizers like prosciutto crudo and salame de Milano, you can dine well for under $12. Dinner only, from 8 p.m. to 1:30 a.m. For reservations, call 7239-163; taxi fare from Syntagma is about $1. If even these prices are too lofty, the **Al Convento Pizzeria** is just around the corner, open every evening from 8 p.m. to 1 a.m.

At the **Kona Kai** in the new Ledra Marriott, 113-115 Syngrou (tel. 9525-211), the lower-level location is deftly disguised with waterfalls, pools, hanging batiks, and a striking backdrop photograph of a South Sea isle matched in extravagance only by the exotic cocktails. In addition to Polynesian fare there are also several Japanese tepanyaki tables. Expect to pay $20 to $25 a head, depending on your resistance to the fancy drinks. Dinner only, 7 p.m. to 12:30 a.m.; closed Sunday.

Tucked away in a narrow street (near Farmaki Square) in the Plaka is a Japanese restaurant, **Michiko,** 27 Kidathineou St. (tel. 3220-980), in a Japanese courtyard, complete with fish pond, fountains, butterfly bridge, and kimono-clad waitresses. The 20-odd tables are distributed along flagstone paths on two raised terraces beneath frilly red awnings, and the whole place is sheltered by a venerable tree and decorated with colored lanterns. Sukyaki and tempura may not be what you've come to the Plaka to savor—they're not exactly bargains here ($8 to $12)—but they're there if you feel like a change of pace from moussaka and eggplant some evening. Open to midnight; closed Sunday.

If you have an uncontrollable longing for the flavors of Canton and bamboo furniture, the hot new Chinese place is **China** at 72 Efroniou, near the Caravel. Expensive. Reservations: 7233-200.

STEAK HOUSES: The **Steak Room,** at 6 Aiginitou between the Hilton and the American Embassy (tel. 7217-445), is one of those restaurants you might want to try if you weary of moussakas and veal. Some people will tell you it serves the best steaks in Athens, prepared in the American manner and served with baked potato and sour cream or butter. The Steak Room's owner, Michael Papapanou, a Greek who spent ten years in Canada, gets his beef loins from the north of Greece, ages them, then cuts them right at the charcoal fire. For any cut (from porterhouse to filet steak), the price ranges from 650 to 950 drs ($6.50 to $9.50). His stint in Canada also taught Mr. Papapanou the mysteries of extra-dry Beefeater martinis and Irish coffee.

The air-conditioned Steak Room is open from noon to 3:30 p.m. for lunch Monday to Friday (with a special lunch menu), and from 7 p.m. to 1 a.m. for dinner; closed Sunday. The Steak Room claims to have been the first steak house in Athens, and if so, it started quite a trend. They're now all over the place.

Templars' Grill, the steak house in the Royal Olympic Hotel (tel. 9226-411 for reservations), is the most spectacular. It flies its Aberdeen Angus steaks in from Scotland and they're reputed to be the tenderest in town, prepared and grilled by a chef who spent several years in the States. Daily, from 8 p.m. to midnight. Prices for main courses are 600 to 1000 drs ($6 to $10).

Flame Steak House is only a few blocks from its rival the Steak House, at 9 Hadjiyanni Mexi, on the corner of Michalakopoulou, near the Hilton. Restaurateur Elias Dialektakos picked up the tricks of his trade in Chicago, then packed up some American-style light fixtures, amber glassware, and ashtrays, and returned to his homeland. His 12-year-old eatery has knotty-pine paneling and bar, and comes equipped with air conditioning and taped stereo, and hand-hammered copper plaques depicting Michelangelo paintings, all set off by burgundy rugs and peach tablecloths. Most dishes on the menu are charcoal-broiled—like filet mignon at 750 drs ($7.50)—but there are also items like golden french-fried shrimps for under 600 drs ($6). One of the restaurant's nicest features is a roomy terrace for sidewalk dining, with an orange awning and trellised greenery to shut out the traffic. Every evening from 6 p.m. to 2 a.m. Reservations: 7238-540.

The **Stagecoach,** 6 Loukianou St. in Kolonaki, is located across the street from the residence of the British ambassador, but when you push aside the swinging doors it's an informal setting complete with long brass-railed bar, wooden booths, and wooden gallery. You'll find six cuts of steak on the menu here, at 700 to 1800 drs ($7 to $18) for that old ranch favorite, chateaubriand, but over the years the Stagecoach has acquired a reputation for fine prime ribs. The Stagecoach is airconditioned, open for lunch from noon to 4 p.m., dinner from 7 p.m. to 1 a.m., and the number for reservations is 7237-902.

Meals for Under $6
Restaurants, Cafés, and Snackbars

Despite the steady rise of prices in Athens in the past few years, and helped by the strength of the dollar, there are still many entries in this category. Some of those restaurants and tavernas mentioned above have a few items on their menus that could, with judicious selection, bring you a meal for under 600 drs ($6); conversely, some restaurants in this section list a few expensive dishes which *could* put your meal over the $6 figure. On the whole, however, you should have no problem keeping within your budget at any of the restaurants, cafés, and snackbars listed below. There's no need to detail the menus in each of these places: they all follow a basic pattern—moussakas, dolmadakia, keftedes and various lamb, veal, and pork dishes in assorted Greek styles (such as those listed earlier in this chapter). Many of them also have a sprinkling of international dishes like omelets, spaghetti, schnitzels, escalopes, and, of course, fish. In most cases, the waiter will offer you a menu in English. You can expect a cover charge of 20 or 30 drs (20¢ or 30¢), and a small charge for bread and butter.

RESTAURANTS AROUND SYNTAGMA: The two-story, air-conditioned, wood-paneled **Delphi,** just off Syntagma at 13 Nikis (tel. 3234-869), has a wide-ranging menu with budget-priced roast chicken with rice at 270 drs ($2.70) and shrimp with rice for around 700 drs ($7), as well as a selection of dishes within that price range—rice with minced meat, veal with okra, moussaka, and a choice of unusual salads featuring squash, dandelion, beetroot, and cabbage. Don't come looking for a leisurely, relaxed meal—those waiters *move.* The Delphi is open daily from 11:30 a.m. to 1 a.m.

Just around the corner at 10 Exnofondos St., the tables of the new **Diros** spill out on to the sidewalk beneath the stoa. A refrigerated glass case displays some of the attractions within—roast veal at 350 drs ($3.50), moussaka at 240 drs ($2.40), omelets from 80 to 130 drs (80¢ to $1.30), grilled grouper or grilled shrimp at 450 to 650 drs ($4.50 to $6.50). Side dishes cost around a dollar; a half bottle of Demetrios is 140 drs ($1.40). In other words, you can easily put together a meal with wine at Diros for under $5. Air-conditioned.

In a city where misspelled menus are two a drachma, **Sintrivani** at 5 Filellinon takes some kind of prize, for where else in Athens have you been offered "duddelions"? Nobody, to our knowledge, has actually partaken of this intriguing vegetable dish but if you're prepared to settle for lamb or swordfish kebabs, at about 300 drs ($3), then you won't be disappointed by Sintrivani tou Syntagmatos—"the fountain of Syntagma." Go through the main room in summer and you can dine in a very pleasant garden; service is friendly, and it's only a two-minute walk from the square.

Another restaurant in this down-to-earth Greek style, with moussakas, dolmadakia, omelets, and spaghetti in the 300- to 400-dr ($3 to $4) range, is the recently remodeled **Kentrikon**, which overflows into the arcade just off Kolokotroni Square, next to the National Historical Museum.

There's almost a generation gap at the new **Drugstore**—students and hippies to the left and upstairs in the ouzeri and café, oldsters to the right in the restaurant decorated with lively reds and overhead spotlights. It's located at 4 Korai St. (tel. 3226-464), near Klathmonou Square and Stadiou, and although its features include a newsstand and video store, it doesn't quite have the personality of its Parisian namesake. The music is as assertive as the service is tentative. But if you're in no hurry, you can linger over items from an eclectic menu, like omelets at 160 to 190 drs ($1.60 to $1.90), canelloni at 290 drs ($2.90), hamburgers at 330 to 350 drs ($3.30 to $3.50), or côte de porc at 380 drs ($3.80), and something identified as "sandwitches." Open seven days a week from 8 a.m. to 2 a.m.

SNACKBARS AROUND SYNTAGMA: First, two with similar names: the **American Coffee Shop**, on the corner of Nikis and Karageorgi tis Servias Streets, offers southern fried chicken for around 150 drs ($1.50), but you can pamper yourself with other nostalgic dishes for just less than a couple of dollars—fish and chips, charbroiled hamburgers, or two eggs any style. Open from 7 a.m. to midnight. The **American Snackbar** is located directly across from the post office at 3 Mitropoleos, and greets you with signs announcing the day's special—which is liable to be hamburger with french fries followed by apple pie, for around 300 drs ($3); inside, there are cozy booths where you can try the nondaily specials—breaded fish fry with french fries and salad, fried chicken, pancakes with syrup, or complete lunches and dinners for around 350 drs ($3.50).

The **Elysee**, at 1 Mitropoleos St., in an L-shaped corner arcade that has a row of tables and chairs, is a cool, shaded place to have a snack and still not shut yourself off from the excitement of the square. The Elysee's prices and menu are similar to the American's. Now cross to the other side of Syntagma and walk a few doors down Stadiou Street to no. 7, where you'll find another arcade and the **Elite**; this is an attractive snackbar with trim modern decor, dark walnut booths, and a welcoming burgundy-colored carpet. The usual menu, the usual prices, but open only during shopping and office hours.

Another pleasant stop for refreshment in this general area is **Hermion,** in the arcade at 15 Pandrossou, on your way to the Flea Market. In warm weather it spills into the colorful canopy-topped courtyard; otherwise it's a clean and shiny 20-table restaurant attended by white-jacketed waiters. Even the most expensive items, like veal Hermion, cost less than 400 drs ($4). Open for breakfast, lunch, and dinner. Just inside the Plaka, at 91 Adrianou, **McMilton's** offers sandwiches for 200 drs ($2), schnitzels for 400 drs ($4), plus other Greek and continental dishes. Air-conditioned indoors, it has a small terrace surveying one of the liveliest corners of the Plaka. Open noon to 2 p.m.

In the Plaka, the people-meeting place is **Café-Restaurant Posidon** (or Possithonos), in tiny Kapnikareas Square opposite the Roman Agora. The menu is extensive, but if you prefer, and if there are tables to spare, you can spend the evening nursing a beer as you watch busking hippies, old ladies selling fluffy shawls, and Greek Adonises sizing up the latest influx of Swedish maidens.

Two small snackbars that have opened in the streets to the west of Kolonaki Square: **Mövenpick** (no connection with the Swiss chain of the same name), at the corner of Akadimias and Pindaroiu Streets, serves a variety of light meals from donuts and pastries on up; and **Jimmy's Coffee Shop,** on Valaoritoun Street, next to the Hotel Lycabettus.

DINING AROUND OMONIA SQUARE: Over in the Omonia Square area prices tend to be a few drachmas cheaper than around Syntagma. One of the busiest eating spots (at least at lunchtime) in this neighborhood is **Ellinikon** at 3 Satovriandou, just off the square, with seating for 100 diners. Prices are modest —100 to 200 drs ($1 to $2) for items like moussaka, pastitsio, spaghetti, or meat pie. Closed Sunday. Directly across the street, prices are a few drachmas higher at a newer establishment called **Taygetos,** the place on the corner with the yellow walls and smart wooden trim. Here main dishes are in the 200- to 400-dr ($2 to $4) range.

While you're in the square, you might also take a look at two hotel restaurants—those of the **Omonia** and **Asty;** both serve a three-course lunch or dinner for 500 drs ($5).

The best of the snackbars in this neighborhood is probably the **Floca Self-Service,** two blocks from the square at 16 Emanuel Benaki St. Since it's a member of the Floca chain, it's reliable, spotless, and good value: stuffed vine leaves, moussaka, roast chicken—in other words, a tasty Greek meal for 210 to 290 drs ($2.10 to $2.90). The Floca is air-conditioned.

Also on Benaki, this time at no. 3, between Panepistimiou and Stadiou Streets, you'll find one of the most attractive and spacious restaurants in this area—**Nea Olympia.** Its extensive menu includes moussaka and omelets for less than 210 drs ($2.10), veal dishes for around 360 drs ($3.60).

Still near Omonia Square but a block or two toward Syntagma, at 46 Panepistimiou, the **Ideal** serves omelets at 90 to 190 drs (90¢ to $1.90) and various meat dishes from 280 to 480 drs ($2.80 to $4.80) in an attractive pseudo-rustic setting, and a brick-and-wood entrance flanked by displays of seafood and fruit.

THE CONVIVIAL CAFÉS OF ATHENS: The third type of eating place in this price group is the café. In some cases the cafés are also snackbars; in some cases they also have restaurants. They're listed here because their *main* role is as a café—a place where you can idle away hours over a coffee, lemon juice, Coke, or ice cream, or enjoy a light lunch of pan pie, cheese puffy, or sandwiches.

There are three main centers for cafés in Athens—Constitution Square (Syntagma), Kolonak Square, and Fokionos Negri Street.

Syntagma is the largest, with 3000 chairs (armchairs at that) deployed around its sidewalks and around the fountain in the center of the square, shaded by cypress, laburnam, and three palm trees. One of the cafés is operated by the deluxe **King George Hotel**; it's waiters have to cross from the square to the hotel to collect your order and it can be disconcerting to see your baklava floating on a tray through the traffic (they rarely lose either a baklava or a waiter). If you're gasping for a drink, go to a *red* chair in the square, and you will be served by the excellent Dionysus kitchen (notable for especially good pastries from its associated restaurants, Zonar's and Dionysus, two favorites in town). These cafés serve sandwiches—veal, ham, cheese at 100 to 210 drs ($1 to $2.10)—pastries at 110 to 220 drs ($1.10 to $2.20), orange or lemon juice and tea or coffee for less than $1.

For Americans, the most popular café is **Papaspyrou,** the one surrounding the American Express Office, on the west side of the square. Papaspyrou is at its busiest around 5 in the afternoon, when the mail arrives at American Express and the tables fill up with beaming or crestfallen faces, depending on the mailman.

Phivos, 2 Othonos, is the café with the blue awnings and green chairs at the corner of Syntagma and Filellinon. It bills itself as a pâtisserie/cafeteria/snackbar, so you can satisfy any degree of hunger here. But take a peek inside at the pies, pastries, baklavas, and chocolates, and you'll probably decide to settle for something light. And sweet. Hot dishes—like hamburgers, dolmadakia, cannelloni, and moussaka—are around 250 drs ($2.50).

A café where you can get an exceptionally good cup of coffee is the **Café Do Brasil** in the arcade that cuts the corner between Constitution Square and Stadiou. The Brazilian is part of a chain, with a stand-up counter downstairs and tables upstairs where executives look down on the tourists scurrying among the stores in the arcade. Coffee costs from 55 to 70 drs (50¢ to 70¢); pastries, 55 drs (55¢); and ice creams 55 to 65 drs (55¢ to 65¢).

One spot where you can dine nostalgically or Greekly, in some style, is the **Byzantine Coffeeshop** in the Athens Hilton. This is a big circular arena beneath a dome with a corona of copper lamps; one wall is decorated with unusual mosaic panels of women in the costumes of Ancient Greece; the floors are marble and the tables are marble. Some coffeeshop. If you're nostalgic for home you can try hamburgers, frankfurters on a bun, apple pie, one egg any style, or even a BLT. Greek specialties include moussaka and dolmadakia avgolemono at 380 drs ($3.80). For a simple snack try the bourekakia—flaky pastry filled with cheese, three pieces for 450 drs ($4.50). Prices are, of course, a drachma or two higher than in most other coffeeshops, but you can still have a light lunch for around 300 to 400 drs ($3 to $4).

Another attractive coffeeshop in the Syntagma area is the **Brazilian Coffee Stores**, at 1 Voukourestiou, the sort of stand-up place where you pop in for a quick espresso or cappuccino and enjoy a pastry and the aromas of a dozen types of coffee. A few doors down, on the corner of Voukourestiou and Stadiou, the new **Everyday** is a cavernous, split-level mecca for coffee imbibers, this time with chairs and tables and a menu of snacks and light meals. For sweet tooths there are two new tearoom/confiseries in town: the dainty **Désiré** at 8 Dimokritou in Kolonaki, and **De Profundis**, at 1 Angel Hatzimihalis St. (near the Center for Folk Art), with French decor, English teas, and taped classical music (but closed for most of August).

Kolonaki Square

Syntagma is where the tourists go, but **Kolonaki Square** is where the Athenians sip their coffee, and talk business or gossip. Kolonaki Square is only a few blocks from the National Gardens and Syntagma, just off Vassilissis Sofias. It's something of an oasis (although at times it looks more like a parking lot), with a grove of trees and a fountain in the center and a café on almost every corner. Pick almost any café on Kolonaki Square. By day your choice is determined by the position of the sun; at night, by wherever you can find a seat.

Fokionos Negri, our third café haunt, is over in Patission, the residential district beyond the National Archeological Museum and slightly off the beaten track. But if you're spending more than a few days in Athens, and you want to get beneath the surface of Athenian life, hop into a taxi, or take either the no. 3 or 12 trolley bus, and ask the conductor to let you off at the stop nearest to Fokionos Negri. This street is sometimes called (but never by Athenians) the Via Veneto of Athens, and you'll soon see why. It's a broad, plaza-like street with trees, fountains, café tables, and umbrellas in the center, and cafés on the corners. Some of these cafés are so popular they have two or three corners each. The remainder of the street is taken up by flower shops, beauty parlors, cosmetic shops, and other services pampering to the needs of Athenian society. Again, you can choose almost any café, but if you plan to sit indoors, try the **Oriental,** at no. 25 and 27, which is one of the most luxurious cafés ever. You don't sit at tables—you plop into armchairs and sofas, with your coffee, pastry, or ice cream laid out on coffee tables. Fokionos Negri also has some fine restaurants, among them **Taverna I Thraka,** where a Greek feast for two, with wine, will cost approximately 1500 drs ($15); and **Paesano,** with the burning Olympic torch above the awning, for pizza.

Two of the most famous *zacharoplasteions* in Athens are, in fact, on none of these squares, but on Panepistimion Avenue, two blocks from Constitution Square. **Zonar's** is the huge café on the corner with a row of red tables and chairs beneath a bright-red awning. The interior of Zonar's is an Expo for sweet tooths—with display cases piled high with candies, chocolates, pastries, baklavas, galaktoboureko, and bougatsas, as well as the classical pastries you'd find in Vienna or Munich. Even the decor carries through the theme—chocolate-brown walls, cream-colored ceilings, icy chandeliers, and marble-topped tables (although the management is whispering about redoing it). At the rear, a few steps lead up to the restaurant, and a few more lead down to the cozy American bar. You can have snacks here (sandwiches are 200 to 280 drs—$2 to $2.80), but most people come to savor the pastries (130 to 220 drs—$1.30 to $2.20); and sip the espresso, cappucino, Viennese coffee, Nescafé, French coffee, and Greek coffees. Zonar's is half a block of self-indulgence. Don't miss it.

The 100-year-old **Floca's,** next door, also tempts with heaps of pastries, snacks, and coffees. Its menu also features a few spectacular ice cream dishes ($1.50 to $2.50)—Bé-Bé (parfait of vanilla and strawberry ice cream, fruit salad, meringues, whipped cream, and biscuits), and Hippy (chocolate, pistachio, and mocha ice cream, meringue, chocolate sauce, whipped cream, cherries, and Hippy biscuits). Floca's confectionery counter looks like Christmas; if you're on a diet, stay outside on the terrace.

THE OUZERI OF ATHENS: Here's an opportunity for some authentic local color: the ouzeri are traditional "pubs," neighborhood bars, where Athenians stop in at any time of the day for a quick refreshment of ouzo (the local apéritif with an anise base), whisky, or coffee. The decor is usually quite basic, the clientele is mostly male (although women are "welcome" to use them too), and most of them serve local snacks or sandwiches (meatballs, sausages, shrimps, etc.). There are two close to Syntagma Square. If you walk to 10 Panepistimiou, then through to the end of the arcade with the Nikis & Takis shop, you find yourself in a high-ceilinged but rather shabby bar called **Apotsos,** which may well be the oldest ouzeri in town; you sit at a small wobbly marble table, surrounded by walls plastered with antique metal signs advertising Huntley & Palmers Biscuits, Taylor Brothers Mustard, and Johnnie Walker Whisky, and order a beer or ouzo and any of the following: saganaki (delicious fried cheese), dolmades, their own sausage or meatballs. You'll be refreshing yourself here in the company of politicians and journalists; another favorite haunt of journalists is the ouzeri across the street, at 7 Panepistimiou—**Orfanides,** just around the corner from the GB Hotel, with a few tables on the sidewalk at the corner of Voukourestiou. **Athinaikon** at 8 Santaroza (near Omonia Square) is the gathering place for lawyers and judges (the law courts are nearby), and there's another ouzeri halfway up the hill to **Lykavittos,** which is a godsend for thirsty, camera-toting pilgrims. With the exception of the latter, these ouzeri tend to be less expensive than the regular cafés (lawyers and judges are no fools).

RESTAURANTS OUTSIDE OF ATHENS: In summer, most Athenians don't come into the center of town for dinner: they drive out to their favorite hideaways on the outskirts of town—in the countryside or by the sea. You might want to follow suit, in which case here are some tips on where to go.

Kifissia

Kifissia is a village some ten miles from the city center, once primarily a resort, now both a resort and residential suburb, which in recent years has become a home away from home for many Americans who have come to live and work in Greece. It's not the sort of place you'd come to if you're in Athens for only a few days, but you may want to spend an hour or two here to cool off in summer, or stop off for a meal on your way to Delphi or other points in the hinterlands. You can get to Kifissia for 20 drs (about 20¢) on the subway from Omonia Square, or for about $4 by taxi; once there, take a 20-minute, 100-dr ($1) ride around the town center in a horse-drawn carriage before or after your meal, or pay a brief visit to the **Goulandris Natural History Museum** and its displays on flowers and zoology.

Some of the most popular restaurants in Kifissia are the **Edelweiss, Blue Pine Farm, La Belle Hélène, Alt Berlin,** and the small but stylish **Lotophagus.** At the restaurant of the **Grand Chalet Hotel,** you can sit in the garden as you sip or dine and look across at the marble quarries on Mount Pentelicon. (You may have gathered from reading the chapter on hotels that the Greeks use marble the way Americans use Formica, much of it from Pentelicon; and in case you were thinking that by now the mountain must be a molehill, take a look across the valley— Pentelicon still stands.) These are all pleasant spots for a meal, but they are "international" rather than Greek in flavor; for more typically Greek settings go to Varsos or Taverna Moustakis.

Varsos, just off the main square, is a cavernous pastry shop that's been pleasuring sweet tooths for over 100 years, where diners linger over kataifa, baklava, and that unique ice cream with a texture like Turkish delight known as kaimaki, 24 hours a day, 365 days a year.

Taverna Moustakis serves its Greek delicacies indoors in winter (in a cluster of wood-and-wicker rooms around an open kitchen where you can order your meal by pointing), in a tree-shaded courtyard in summer, serenaded by strolling bouzouki players. The Moustache is a popular spot with Kifissians, so call ahead for a reservation (and directions, if you're driving); the number is 8014-584. Open also for lunch on Sunday.

Mikrolimano

The other popular dining spot on Athens's outskirts is in the opposite direction, by the sea, but less than $5 away by taxi. Until a few years ago it was known as Turkolimano ("Harbor of the Turks"), but in post-Cyprus Greece the signposts now direct you to Mikrolimano, "Little Harbor." Little *and* circular. It's a marina filled with sailboats from the seven seas, and crowned on the far hill by the ultra-chic Royal Hellenic Yacht Club. The entire waterfront is ringed with seafood restaurants, each with its terrace set up beneath brightly colored awnings across the street by the edge of the quay. Some of these restaurants have no-nonsense, unadorned interiors; others (the newer ones) are interior-decorated. A few of them have their own fishing boats, or their own sources of supply, and theoretically they should sell less expensive fish, but it doesn't always work out that way as you'll discover on a stroll along the waterfront checking out prices. *Note:* All fish prices are quoted automatically "per kilo," but are invariably sold *whole;* therefore the price you pay is the price per kilo times the weight of the fish.

When you visit Mikrolimano, here's the procedure: check out the restaurants and menus to see what the day's catch has been, and how much you'll have to pay. Next, find yourself a table across the street by the quayside, order an ouzo or a bottle of Demestica. Then go back to the restaurant, ask the waiter to open the icebox with the fish, and make your selection—*barbounia* (red mullet), *garides* (shrimp), *glossa* (sole), and so on. Have your waiter weigh the fish right there and then and tell you how much your choice will cost. Finally, tell him how you would like to have it cooked—*skara* (grilled) or *tiganiti* (fried). Before returning to your waterfront table, select as an appetizer one of the Mikrolimano specialties—baked shrimp with tomatoes and feta cheese, or pikilea, a sort of seafood hors d'oeuvre (one portion is usually enough to appease two appetites until the main course is ready). Then you can settle back and spend the rest of the afternoon or evening sipping your wine, listening to the water lapping the hulls of the schooners and yawls. Afterward, get one of the weathered boatmen to row you around the harbor for less than half an hour (about 600 drs, or $6, for the boat, which will hold up to six passengers). You could almost be in Hydra or Mykonos or one of the other romantic Greek islands—yet you're only a $5 to $6 cab ride from your hotel.

Every Athenian has his favorite restaurant in Mikrolimano, although there is really only a marginal difference in prices, usually in the region of 650 drs ($6.50) a kilo for sole, 800 drs ($8) a kilo for red mullet—which should work out at 1500 to 1800 drs ($15 to $18) a head per meal, without wine (prices used to be much lower, but fish are getting scarce and no one wants to go fishing anymore, even in Greece). In summer, you may have little choice between one restaurant or another—you simply grab whatever table is available; if not, you should check out **Semiramis, Zefiros, Ta Prasina Trehantiria, Kokkini Varka,** the newish, three-story **Aglamer,** or, perhaps most famous of them all, **Canaris.**

Zea Marina

If you go one bay beyond Mikrolimano you come to a larger but equally circular harbor known as Zea Marina, which is the part of Piraeus given over to pleasure boats rather than cruise ships; and if you're joining one of the Greek shipping tycoons for a cruise, chances are this is where you'll come to board his floating palace. Zea Marina is a pleasant spot to keep in mind on a stifling Athens day when you want to get a breath of fresh air. Take the subway or bus to Piraeus and join the folks on a stroll around the promenade, stopping off now and again to admire a particularly handsome yacht, or taking a break in one of the cafés in the main square (there's usually music and dancing on weekends in summer). If you want to mingle with the owners of the yachts, have a drink or meal in the **Landfall 3 Makriyianni** at the far end, on the side farthest from Mikrolimano (tel. 4525-074). If you're hungry, drop into one of the local tavernas for a meal (try **Vasilena**, at 72 Etikon [tel. 4612-457] and you won't go far off course). Better still, check out one of the marina cafés and sit by the edge of the marina dreaming of a Mediterranean cruise on the three-masted schooner *Creole*.

Country street vendor

NIGHTLIFE IN ATHENS

Breaking Plates in the Greek Tradition

ATHENIANS DON'T paint the town red—they say "Let's go and break a few plates together!" It's an old Greek custom. When the audience is enjoying itself, it's expected to show its appreciation exuberantly. Greeks used to do this by smashing plates or glasses, or throwing flowers on the stage. The plate- and glass-smashing is now banned by the police, and the audiences started throwing flowers or plastic baubles instead; but you'll still find occasions when the music, the stars onstage, the stars above, and Dionysus combine to rouse the audience to smashing pitch. Just in case it happens some night when you're around, don't insist on a ringside table. Sit well back. (And don't break any plates because the taverna will charge a hefty premium for them.)

Athens itself is, of course, the greatest show of them all. The way to enjoy it is simply to go to the nearest café, find a table, and watch the performers—the lottery sellers, the sponge sellers, the souvlaki vendors, the taxi drivers, the stately old ladies all dressed up for a gala at the Grande Bretagne.

If you insist on paying for your entertainment, there are plenty of options open to you. Athens has a few ideas on nightlife you'll find nowhere else in Europe. Take your pick. You can watch ancient Greek drama in a theater dating from the time the plays were written. You can relive the history of the Acropolis in the awesome Son-et-Lumière, or Sound-and-Light, spectacle. You can sit on a roof garden beneath the floodlit Acropolis and watch a folklore show—or you can get up and dance a Zorba-like *syrtaki.* You can listen to a world-famous orchestra playing Beethoven in a 2000-year-old amphitheater. And so the possibilities go on and on.

Whatever you decide to do, you'll soon discover one of the most appealing features of nightlife in Athens. Not only is it varied, not only is it unique, but it's priced so low you can enjoy almost everything it has to offer—even if you're on a tight budget. The only restraint on living it up right through the night is the thought that tomorrow you still have so many ancient wonders to see.

The entertainment pages of *Athens News, 30 Days,* and *The Athenian* are the best guides to local events in Athens, what's playing in theaters, concerts, operas, cinemas, nightclubs, tavernas, and restaurants.

Sta Bouzoukia— (To the Bouzouki Clubs)

Long before the movies *Never on Sunday* and *Zorba the Greek* there was bouzouki. This six-stringed lute-like instrument was popular with *rebetes,* men who scratched out a living on the fringes of society in places like Piraeus, persecuted by the police for their crimes and drugs. Unsavory characters, indeed, but their music had an appeal that reached out and touched Greeks everywhere. No one knows exactly when *rebetika*—the songs of the *rebetes*—began to be sung, but it was probably in the 1820s, around the time of Greek independence; they were played by the poor and the social outcasts, in bitter but stoical protest against the injustices of their lives—much like the early blues songs. With the songs came the dances: the *zebekiko,* an intensely individualistic dance which the *rebetis* performs for himself and not for the people around him; the *hasapiko,* another traditional *rebetic* dance for two or three men, no more, and again a private introverted dance. What you may recall from *Zorba the Greek* was *syrtaki,* which is a modified and faster version of the *hasapiko.*

Over the years bouzouki became fashionable with all strata of society, reaching its peak in the early 1950s. Then it declined, due mainly to commercialization; to make the instrument more versatile another pair of strings was added, then the instrument itself was electrified. Instead of just the traditional guitar for accompaniment, the sophisticated Athenians who went out for a night *sta bouzoukia* (to the bouzouki clubs) came to expect guitars and drums and piano, and possibly double bass and electric organ, besides a couple of bouzoukia. This is basically what you'll hear today when you go *sta bouzoukia;* the unamplified bouzouki has all but disappeared, and the districts where the *rebetes* themselves used to hang out have all been pulled down. However, you can still hear good modern bouzouki music in several taverns in Plaka, in downtown clubs in the winter months, and in the seaside clubs in summer.

At some point during your visit, you should try to listen to this authentic Greek music. Even their pop tunes have retained that haunting, bittersweet quality. Their love songs are not so much about falling in love as being clobbered by love (some samples, roughly translated, from the current repertoire: "I hate my eyes since I've looked at you/ you've made my eyes a little toy" . . . "Talk to me, talk to me/ I've never kissed you/ and I can only kiss you in my dreams." . . . "Believe that you met me some night in a dream/ but for me it wasn't a dream"). Even when the songs are not about love, they're not exactly joyful jingles—"The worry beads broke/ and fell on the ground/ and all the men started to cry/ the lamp has blown out/ and the last ship has sunk. . . ." If you have active tear ducts, better take along plenty of Kleenex when you set off for a night on the town in Athens.

IN THE PLAKA: Until recently, to take a few steps inside the Plaka was to realize that pandemonium is indeed a Greek word. Before World War II there was only one taverna in the Plaka (it's still there) and the other buildings were private homes. Now every home seems to be a taverna and every other sidewalk and rooftop an extension of a taverna. Tavernas set up their tables in patios, on rooftops, even on the stepped streets climbing up the base of the rock. Most of the tavernas have music, which would be fine if they didn't also have amplifiers to blast out their sounds, reverberating through the alleyways and across the rooftops. Into the bargain, the Plaka had acquired a form of entertainment known as the open-air light show, a rooftop discotheque pounding kilowatt upon kilowatt of *noise* into the air.

Fortunately for all of us (and especially homeowners and hotel guests, within earshot), the new minister concerned with the environment has banished rooftop discos, cut down on other noise, and encouraged authorities and people to gut and restore all those wonderful old buildings. A few years from now the Plaka will once more be a unique experience. Meantime, if you're not in the mood for curling up with Aristotle it can be a lot of fun. Tremendous fun. If you don't want to get yourself involved in the raucousness, you can still find an occasional taverna without music in a quiet (well, relatively quiet) terrace or courtyard, with the music arriving distantly across the rooftops.

Finding Your Way Around in the Plaka

Finding a particular club is not easy since most of the streets are identified in Greek only. However, you'll get there if you follow these basic directions. First, go to Cathedral Square. From the steps of the cathedral (facing out to the square), turn left and follow Palieloghou Venizelou Street until you come to a modern white marble building on the corner; bear right, past the Greek arts shops, Stathis and Zorba's, until you come to Adrianou Street, at right angles. Now go left on Adrianou, past a few gift shops until you come to McMilton's bar-restaurant on the left, a streetful of boutiques dead ahead. The street on your right is **Flessa Street,** and you'll know you're in Flessa because on the right there's a building that looks something like a misfit from Kyoto, which is the Taverna Palia Athena. Continue up this street to the fork in the road and bear right. This puts you on **Lissiou Street,** which is where most of the action is—here and on **Mnisikleos Street,** which runs at right angles to it.

Coming *from* the Acropolis, follow the path past Areopagus, past the **Café-Bar Acropolis** (which has a magnificent view from its pathside terrace); there's an intersection on the left, but keep going along the path at the base of the hill, past an old church, then follow a curve to the left and down to a white wall; now go right. From that point follow the bustle, and from there you'll have to negotiate steps cluttered with tourists just listening to the music, tables filling up every inch of flat surface, waiters trying to get to the tables, people trying to get to the tables, people trying to get to the Acropolis, and occasionally someone trying to pinch a bottom.

Once you're in the Plaka, how do you go about selecting a taverna?

Picking a Place in the Plaka

On a busy weekend, the only valid piece of advice is: grab the first table you come to. There's really not so much difference in food or decor or service between one restaurant and another; if you can, get to the Plaka about half an hour before you're likely to feel ravenous, wander around and look the places over until you see something you fancy—in a patio, on the sidewalk, on

steps, or on a rooftop (assuming you're visiting in summer).
Within each category you have also a choice of noisy, *noisier*,
NOISIEST.

Check out the prices too as you go along. Tavernas with music
cost more than tavernas without music; tavernas with shows cost
more than tavernas with only music. To give you some idea of
what you can expect to pay, here is a sample of prices from
Taverna Kalokerinou at 10 Kekropos St. (tel. 3232-054): main
dishes (lamb chops, shrimps) from 400 to 750 drs ($4 to $7.50);
appetizers cost anywhere from 100 to 140 drs ($1 to $1.40);
desserts, 100 drs ($1); a bottle of local wine will be 120 to 240
drs ($1.20 to $2.40); and there's a cover charge of 50 drs (50¢).
Work all that out and you'll find that an evening here, or in a
similar taverna, will cost about 1500 to 1800 drs ($15 to $18) a
head, with wine. This figure may be higher in other tavernas,
depending on such variables as music tax, entertainment tax,
show tax, and who is performing. *Prices in tavernas without
shows are a few dollars less.*

Taverna Kalokerinou (above) is one of the most reliable of the
tavernas with shows (folk dancing and belly dancing from 10 to
11:45 p.m., and nonstop music from 9:30 for singing, dancing,
or just plain finger-snapping and foot-tapping). The management
here bans tour groups, so that couples and foursomes can get
well-placed tables rather than being shoved into a corner. Like
most other tavernas in these parts, the show is indoors in winter,
on the roof in summer.

The corner of Lissiou Street and Mnisikleos Street is where
you'll find one of the liveliest concentrations of tavernas, one on
each corner.

I'll start with the **Mostrou**, because it's the only one around
that has its name in large English characters on a sign above the
door. It's your landmark, as well as a potential destination, if you
don't mind spending an evening surrounded by other tourists.
It's a big place with a roof garden for warm weather (the remainder of the year, you're in a semi-rustic room with a ceiling that
looks like a TV studio with its complex of lights and spots for
the floor show). The Mostrou show, indoors or outdoors, features a noisy modern band and vocalists for dancing, six dancers
(in folk costume, but backed by an electric-organ/electric-gui-
tar/electric-drums type of music), and the inevitable singer with
hand-held microphone who always manages to sound like Bar-
bra Streisand doing an imitation of Judy Garland. The show is
at its best when the dancers and band cut out the jazz and get

down to some serious Greek dancing. Then you can't even catch the waiters' attention. The Mostrou menu is probably one of the biggest in the Plaka, and there's a cover/bread/roll charge of 100 drs ($1), and an "entertainment tax" of 7%. It's more expensive than most—grilled swordfish at 620 drs ($6.20), chicken dishes at 520 drs ($5.20)—but then it has a bigger floor show than most. The music begins at 9:30 p.m., the show runs from 11 p.m. to 12:30 a.m., followed by more music. Closed on Sunday.

Directly across the street is another multifloored taverna with a roof garden—**Dionysus.** It's more relaxed than Mostrou, prices are a few drachmas less, and here you have a chance to inspect what you're going to eat when you walk past the display case and kitchen at the entrance. Under its new management, it's been spiffed up, the waiters are courteous, the atmosphere much more welcoming than at Mostrou, but the breaking of plates is banned. For reservations, call 322-7589.

Across the street are two tavernas in the simple, peasant style, popular with Greek families (no tour groups), and consequently much cheaper. The one on the right as you face the steps that take you up the hill is the **Taverna Kritikou,** and you'll probably hear it before you see it. Its tables spread over the steps and through the doors to the dance floor, and if the only free table is at the rear, allow yourself three or four minutes to squeeze through. This was the first taverna in the Plaka, by the way. There's a minumum of decor here—a few murals in Plaka-primitive style and a less-than-classical arch of corrugated plastic above the band. It's a four-piece combo—with electric organ, guitar, drums, and bouzouki—but it gets the place going, encouraging a steady stream of men getting up to dance, egged on by the audience to perform wilder, more contorted leaps than their predecessors. Its attractive menu is decorated with paintings of the beast, fowl, or fruit you're about to order—and the attractive prices include moussaka for 195 drs ($1.95), chicken or squid for 400 to 520 drs ($4 to $5.20), Cretan wine from 260 drs ($2.60).

Again across the street—**Plakokiti Taverna O Fandis,** which translates as Jack's. This is another boisterous place that caters mainly to Athenians but welcomes out-of-towners. If anything, it's even more basic, more congested, and noisier than Kritikou, but it's spread out through three small rooms separated by arches and decorated on every inch of wall and pillar with the traditional Plaka-primitive murals. The band is raised to shoulder height, and the stamp-size dance floor is half in one room, half in another. It's an infectious place, and most visitors probably wish they could do Greek dances. Some visitors actually try. To enjoy the fun you have to eat, but that's no strain on the budget. The Fandis has an inexpensive and varied menu: shrimp or octopus for less than 600 drs ($6), veal and potatoes or veal and onions for less than 500 drs ($5). Retsina costs about 250 drs ($2.50) a kilo, and domestic white or red wine is 280 to 500 drs ($2.80 to $5) a bottle. Open seven evenings a week.

Now, follow the steps up the hill and continue up and up until you come to 4 Stratonos St., where you'll find **Taverna Vlachou.** You'll recognize it by the plaster drunk leaning on the lamppost at the door. The Vlachou has what appears to be a vacant floor on street level, so take the stairs up to the next floor, then another flight of iron stairs which you climb to get to the topmost floor, where you'll find an unrestricted view of the entire city. Movie companies have filmed panning shots of Athens from up here, and it's the view that makes the Vlachou worth the hike up the hill. It's a good thing you have such a spectacular view to keep you entertained while you're waiting for your waiter. Service isn't exactly coffeeshop sharp, partly because there are so many tables, but mainly because the kitchen is three floors down and the waiters have to walk up those narrow little stairways with every order. Try not to forget to order the salad—if the waiter has to make a special trip you won't be terribly popular. Veal in wine sauce with rice (called "Veal for Drinkers") or grilled shrimps in oil and lemon sauce cost less than 500 drs ($5); wines average 180 to 260 drs ($1.80 to $2.60) a bottle.

Some Other Plaka Tavernas

Taverna Klimatiria is located in a quiet corner on the outskirts of the Plaka, just under the Acropolis, at the corner of Thrassyvoulou and Klepsydras Streets. Climb the steps into the taverna and you are in what appears to be a very noisy, roughly decorated cellar with brick arches in the walls, the whole area crammed with tables, apart from the end where the musicians stand in a niche beneath one of the brick arches. Klimatiria has all the usual *mezedes* and a large selection of wines from all over Greece, from retsina to Robola; main courses are principally grills—shish kebab, veal chops, and beef steak. In summer the roof comes off and the music (a couple of guitars, piano, and bouzouki) fills the air until about 2 a.m. A nice, friendly place, this one, where dinner for two should cost 1500 drs ($15) or less.

When you decide you've had enough of music while you eat, try a meal at **Café Restaurant Aerides** at 3 Markou Avriliou. This is on the edge of Plaka and in summer you eat on the pavement opposite the Tower of the Winds; from here you also have a glimpse of the Erechtheon up on the Acropolis, and hills away in the distance. They also have a raffia-and-greenery covered patio and a couple of rooms upstairs in an old Plaka house. You can get a three-course meal for 420 to 540 drs ($4.20 to $5.40). Or, if you're really only here for the view, there's moussaka, dolmades, and stuffed tomatoes at 195 drs ($1.95) each. Good selection of wines and several varieties come in half bottles. Service is courteous. Unlike most tavernas, Aerides is also open for breakfast and lunch.

Head down Diogenou away from the Tower of the Winds and in 30 seconds you'll find yourself in a quiet, shady little square with tables and chairs under the trees, and **Taverna O Platanos** and a little *cafenion* facing each other. Another taverna without music for your battered eardrums, this is one of the oldest in Plaka and specializes in grills. Try a brizola moscharisi for 280 to 300 drs ($2.80 to $3) and a Greek salad at 120 to 140 drs ($1.20 to $1.40); a perfectly acceptable kilo of open wine from the barrel is a mere 60 drs (60¢). Lots of Greeks go there—perhaps they too like to get away from meat and music sometimes. When you've finished, slip over the square to the *cafenion,* have a cup of Greek coffee and ask for a backgammon set as you digest your brizola moscharisi. The official address for O Platanos is 4 Diogenou. Open for lunch from noon to 3:45 p.m., for dinner from 8 p.m. to midnight (sharp!); closed on Sunday.

Tavernas, like everything else these days, have their ups and downs, and it might be wise to check with your hotel receptionist to see which are the brightest, liveliest places when you are in town. A current favorite—the tree-shaded terrace of **Taverna Nefeli** at the top of Panos Street (at no. 24), opposite the Kanellopoulos Museum, is an attractive, quieter spot for "outdoors" weather, but the interior is dull and dreary. However, the prices are reasonable—roast chicken for less than 200 drs ($2), veal with rice for less than 400 drs ($4).

When you walk around the Plaka looking for these places, you'll pass dozens of others, and if you see one that looks interesting, just drop in; the list above doesn't claim to be *the* top ten or whatever, but simply a sampling to let you know what to expect.

Nightclubs by the Sea
(and in Athens)

At midnight, when coaches turn into pumpkins, Athenians turn into swingers. Drop into any Athens nightclub just after dinner and you can almost certainly have a choice of ringside tables, overwhelming service, and a dance floor all to yourselves. At worst you may have to dodge a few tangoing tourists (until midnight, all the bands sound like Guy Lombardo). Come midnight, the whole atmosphere changes. The local swingers start filing in, the bouzoukis are plugged into their amplifiers, and the air fills with bittersweet Greek melodies. Everything keeps blasting away until three or four in the morning, or until the last plate has been thrown.

Before listing a few of the more popular clubs in Athens, here are some ground rules about nightclubbing in the city. You don't have to dress to the nines, but you'll find that most men wear jackets and ties. Most nightclubs don't have a separate minimum or cover charge. They usually incorporate it in the price of the first drink—somewhere in the region of 900 to 1200 drs ($9 to $12), regardless of what you drink. Subsequent drinks are usually a bit costly as well. If you have dinner to while away the evening until midnight, your drinks will cost less, but, of course, you'll still end up paying at least 1500 drs ($15) if you have Greek dishes, up to 2500 drs ($25) if you order steaks. That's not unreasonable when you consider what you're getting in return—three, four, five, or six hours of entertainment, frequently with one of Greece's top singing stars, plus dancing.

Athens nightclubs set such a hot pace that the air conditioning can't keep up with them; so when the weather warms up the nightclubs pack up for the shore, and set up their music stands and stages all the way from Piraeus to Vouliagmeni. The night owls of Athens then scan the newspapers to find out where their favorite stars are singing and follow them. The actual club is relatively unimportant—it's the performers that count. If you plan to follow suit, here are some of the names to watch for—Marinella, Dalaras, Bithikotsis, Zambetas, Voskopoulos, Dionyssiou, Tsitsanis, and Kokotas. They're the ones who get the plates flying.

One of the newest and swankest of the shoreside nightclubs is **Delina**, in a dazzling year-round anchorage out near the airport. You enter it through a tunnel of aggressive multihued spotlights, which lead into a softly lit big circular bar; a concealed door then guides you into a vast area like a circus big top, so vast it could almost house the entire menagerie of Barnum & Bailey. The seaside end of this area is taken up by a large stage normally filled with a 22-piece (*twenty-two*) orchestra. The international floor shows are at 11 p.m. and 1 a.m. Minimum charge is around 1000 drs ($10), which is the cost of your first scotch and soda, but that will, if you wish, keep you going until the club closes at 2 a.m. Dinner will set you back about 5000 drs ($50), with wine. A stunner of a nightspot. Reservations: 8940-205.

Heading south along the coastal highway, there's the **Neraida** in Kalamaki (tel. 981-2004), possibly the loveliest setting, by the sea, beside a new marina. Minimum charge is around 1000 drs ($10). **Fantasia** (tel. 9810-503), by the beach, opposite the old airport, is the least sophisticated of the group, but currently one of the most popular. And the **Asteria,** at Glyfada Beach (tel. 8945-675), which is part of the hotel-bungalow complex, an attractive, modern, red-and-white taverna opening to the bay, the beach, and the sky, and worth the cab ride; this is a sophisticated taverna with music rather than a cabaret, and most of the music is international pop. Dinner is around 5000 drs ($50), with wine, per head.

Note: None of these clubs is more than $10 by taxi from downtown Athens, and you can always get a taxi to bring you home in the wee hours.

Back to Athens, the new **Copacabana** (behind the Royal Olympia at 4 Kallirrois Ave.) bills itself as a nightclub/music hall, featuring a six-piece orchestra, a juggler, exotic dancers, belly dancing (sort of), striptease (sort of), assorted singers, and a Greek folk troupe—all adding up to a show that lasts three hours somewhere between 10:30 p.m. and 2 a.m. A meal at the Copa (no relation to its New York namesake, by the way) will cost you from $30 a head, domestic wines about the same price per bottle (without dinner), and a full bottle of champagne or scotch (probably the best bet in the long run) costs 1200 to 1600 drs ($12 to $16). For reservations call 9232-648.

Another strong recommendation is the **Supper Club** of the Hilton Hotel. It's something special—a nightclub 12 floors above Athens, plush, spacious, and stylish. The price of the floor show, band, and dancing is included in the meal, say, 1400 drs ($14) a head, without wine (slightly higher on Friday). If you want to enjoy the show without dinner, come up after ten for a drink (open 8:30 p.m. to 1 a.m.; closed Sunday and Monday). The Supper Club is on the left of the Hilton roof when you step off the elevator; if you walk along the terrace to the *other* end of the roof, you come to the Galaxy Bar's dance floor—indoor in winter, outdoor in summer (open to 2 a.m.). Just think, if you've come to Athens to see the Acropolis, all you have to do is come here to the Hilton rooftop, dance yourself skinny, and see the Acropolis without missing a beat. But the drinks are expensive.

Discotheques

With all that lively Greek dancing going on around you there's not much need for discos. However, if your feet start to itch for the big beat, here are a few suggestions.

Since discos tend to boom in and out of fashion in Athens as elsewhere, your best bet is to pick up a copy of *Athens News, 30 Days,* or *The Athenian* and study the latest listings; alternatively, ask someone at your hotel to recommend something that fits your tastes. Generally speaking, discos have no entrance fee, but drinks will cost around $5. That said, some of the current "in" spots are **Nine Plus Nine**, at 5 Aghras St. near the Olympic Stadium (tel. 7222-258), and **Papagayo**, at 37 Patriarchou Ioakim St. in Kolonaki (tel. 7230-135).

Three other well-established favorites with Athenians are **Nine Muses** at 43 Akadimias St. (in summer at the Astir Palace Hotel in Vouliagmeni), **Athinea** at 6 Venizelou (in winter), and **Annabella,** on a promontory at Aghios Kosmos in Glyfada, with dancing on a breeze-cooled patio beside a pool in summer (in winter, everything moves indoors; first drinks cost about 350 drs ($5.83). Hotel discos much frequented by well-to-do locals and visitors are the **Galaxy Bar** of the Hilton (on the roof, from 10 p.m., with a great view of nighttime Athens, first drinks 250 drs or $4.16), and the **Horizon Dancing Bar** of the Caravel Hotel, again on the roof with a dazzling view.

Other Nightspots in Athens

THE BOÎTE: If you think the decor in a taverna is fairly basic, wait until you see a *boîte.* The typical Athenian boîte is small, crowded, smoky, and the seating may be "kindergarten" stools rather than chairs—but it can be a lot of fun. The boîte is strictly for music—*rebetika,* folk songs, pop hits and, occasionally, resistance songs (although you may have trouble in determining what they're in resistance to). Performers are usually unknowns, but occasionally you may have an opportunity to hear one of

Greece's more famous singers or composers. There are usually two shows nightly (the first one is never before 9 p.m.), and the admission charge of 250 to 300 drs ($2.50 to $3) usually includes the first drink. Since the evenings can be long (you may have to sit through supporting acts until the star arrives) your best bet usually is to order a bottle of wine, and make it last the evening.

Some notable boîtes: **Zygos** at 22 Kidhathineon and **Skorpios** at 15 Kidhathineou in the Plaka, where you can sometimes hear the famous singer Hadziz (a great favorite with the ladies, as he has been for generations); **Skolion** at 10 Mnisikleos, also in the Plaka, which is run by a debonair young Greek Dino Constantinidos, patronized by his countrymen rather than by tourists, and offers piano, amplified bouzoukia, and dancing on a cramped patch of floor.

LATE-NIGHT BARS: No shortage of these in Athens, and you may have found your favorite nook on your first night in town. If not, here are some suggestions: **George's Bar** at 17 Voukourestiou, identified only by a large 17 on a door leading to a dimly lit basement which nevertheless has shelves crammed with paperbacks for its clientele of writers and other literati; **Larry's Bar,** near the top of Likavitou Street (at no. 20), is another favorite with the inveterate late-nighters in the Kolonaki district; and **Dewar's Club,** 7 Glykonon St., also in Kolonaki; **Montparnasse** at 30 Haritos is yet another of Kolonaki's lounges, popular with writers and artists, and decorated with 1920s posters, glass-topped tables, and overstuffed cushions in the shape of fruit. Plus there are the **G. B. Corner** in the Grande Bretagne, the **Galaxy** in the Hilton, the **Stage Door** at 14 Voukourestiou, and the **Balthazar** at 27 Tsoha.

Other Nighttime Activities

MOVIES: You probably hadn't planned on taking in a movie on your trip to Athens, but if you're going to be in town for several days you may feel like one some evening as a change of pace from Aristophanes and Euripides. In any case, movie-going in Greece is an experience in itself. Around the end of May the indoor cinemas close up for the summer and take to the open air—wherever there's a space that's not currently a construction site or car park. The movies are usually reruns, but no matter, since you have a chance to catch up on something you've missed. If you go to the first performance, around 8:45 or 9 p.m., the sound is audible but the picture is faint; if you wait for the second show, after the sun has properly set, the picture may be clear but the sound may be almost inaudible so as not to antagonize the people living in nearby apartments (who have been known to show their resentment by turning their own radios and TVs up loud and switching on every available light). The films themselves are shown in their original language with Greek subtitles. Grab a Coke or beer and a bag of potato chips as you go in (everyone does). It may not be for the serious movie buff, but on a warm evening a visit to a movie can be fun, and inexpensive—rarely more than 60 to 70 drs (60¢ to 70¢).

In case you want to call ahead for starting times, here are the telephone numbers of some of the leading *indoor* movie houses in Athens, open in winter only:

Appollon, 19 Stadiou St. (tel. 3236-811).

Asty, 4 Korai St. (tel. 3221-925).

Attikon, 19A Stadiou St. (tel. 3228-821).

Embassy, 5 Patriarchou Ioakim (tel. 7220-903).

Pallas, 1 Voukourestiou St. (tel. 3224-434).

Radio-City, 240 Patission and Lissiatrion (tel. 8674-832).

DORA STRATOU DANCE THEATER: The south side of the Acropolis can be a congested spot in summer. The crowd that's not heading for the Pnyx and the Son-et-Lumière show is probably on its way up the Hill of Philopappos following the sign for the Dora Stratou Dance Theater. The Dora Stratou Company is a group of folk dancers that was founded about 20 years ago and has earned a lot of bravos since then, both in Greece and on tours around the world, including the U.S.A. The show consists of a warm-up overture by the Zygia, a small orchestra made up of clarinet, violin, lute, santouri, and drums. The players are dressed in typical Greek native costumes—black waistcoats, mini-skirts, blouses, white stockings, and snub-nosed shoes. Like evzones in mufti. The dances and songs are dances and songs that Greeks have been dancing and singing for 2500 years, and there's no finer place to watch them than under the feathery trees, on an Athenian hillside, a stone's throw from the Acropolis. You can almost see Pan and the nymphs dancing here. A typical program might include the Florina-Kratero from Macedonia, the Dodoni from Epirus, and the Ierissos from Chalkidiki.

You can get to the Dora Stratou Dance Theater by bus 16

from Constitution Square. The dances are performed every evening at 10:15 p.m., from May through October. On Wednesday and Sunday there are "matinees" at 8:15 p.m. Admission prices range from 145 to 250 drs ($1.45 to $2.50), and your ticket reserves a specific seat in the amphitheater (real seats, not bleachers).

CONCERTS AND OPERA: Throughout the winter months, there are performances of opera by the **National Opera** in the Olympia Theater, 59 Akadimias (tel. 3612-461); concerts by the **Athens State Orchestra** (as of this, its regular house, the Kotopouli Theater at 48 Venizelou, has burned down and it's concerts are being rescheduled in other venues); and there are often recitals and chamber concerts at the **Gloria Theater, 7** Ippokratous (tel. 3626-702). Ticket prices range from 100 to 400 drs ($1 to $4), depending on the performers.

Nearby Piraeus has recently developed into a miniature cultural center, and you can sometimes take in concerts, operas, and recitals in that rejuvenated seaport.

The best place to find out about all these events is in the pages of *The Athenian, 30 Days,* or *Athens News,* or from the concierge at your hotel. He'll also tell you how to go about getting tickets, and in the better hotels he'll probably get them for you.

SON-ET-LUMIÈRE: If you arrive in Athens anytime between the beginning of April and the end of October, make a point of spending at least one evening watching the Sound-and-Light spectacle at the Acropolis. Son-et-Lumière involves batteries of lights—1500 in all—that are flooded onto the Acropolis hill and the Parthenon in various combinations, to tie in with a commentary relating the history of the city. It's a stupendous show (with a pretentious commentary). It takes place every evening at 9 and 9:45 p.m. in English, except on Good Friday.

To see the Sound-and-Light show, you go to the small hill called Pnyx, which is on the south side of the Acropolis—the *far* side, if you're near Omonia or Constitution Squares. If you don't want to walk, take bus 230 that goes along Dionysus Areopagitou, past the Acropolis, and get off one stop past the Herod Atticus Theater, where you'll find a sign that says Son-et-Lumière. (Or take a taxi—it should cost no more than 80 drs, less than $1, from either square.) From there, just follow the crowds. The 45-minute show costs 80 drs (half price if you show a student card). If you don't want to spend even 80 drs (80¢), go to the Areopagus Hill; from that vantage point you can see the show, but you won't hear the commentary or the music.

The Son-et-Lumière show is part of a much more broad-ranging show—the Athens Festival.

THE ATHENS FESTIVAL: The Athens Festival takes place from mid-July to mid-September at the 1800-year-old **Herod Atticus Theater,** on the slopes of the Acropolis. There you can sit on marble bleachers (now with free plastic cushions), beneath the stars, and watch some of the world's finest orchestras, musicians, singers, dancers, and actors in a setting unsurpassed anywhere in the world. The theater (sometimes known as the Odeon) was built by Herod Atticus as a memorial to his wife, Appia Annia Regilla, so the architecture is Roman, not Greek. It hold 5000, every seat has a perfect line of vision, and the acoustics are extraordinary, even for a Chopin nocturne.

At the time of this writing the final program for 1985 had not been announced, but to give you an idea of the caliber of per-formers, recent visitors have included the Royal Philharmonic Orchestra with Vladimir Ashkenazy; the Netherlands Dance Theater; Natalia Makarova; Rudolph Nureyev; the Vienna State Opera and Philharmonic; the Utah Symphony Orchestra with Maurice Abravanel; Béjart's 20th Century Ballet; the Royal Swedish Ballet; the Washington National Symphony; the Am-sterdam Concertgebouw with Bernhard Haitink conducting. When you add to that the splendor of the setting, the balmy night air, and the stroll back to the hotel or the Plaka, you have the ingredients for the evening of a lifetime. Here's your chance, for example, to see local companies such as the National Theater, the Amphi-Theater, and the Art Theater perform plays by Eu-ripides, Sophocles, Aristophanes, in an almost authentic setting. They will be in Greek (you can buy a synopsis) but there's plenty to enjoy even if you don't understand the words. (However, if you don't want to wait for the last act, at least wait for an intermission before you get up and leave.)

Ticket prices for the Athens Festival range from 100 to 1500 drs ($1 to $15). You can get details and tickets from the **Athens Festival Office** in the Spyrou Miliou Arcade at 4 Stadiou St., which is one block from Constitution Square (tel. 3221-459 and 3223-111, ext. 240). You can also get tickets from the box office at the Herod Atticus Theater (tel. 3232-771 and 3223-111, ext.

137). English summaries of the Greek plays, at either location, are 50 drs (50¢). (*Note:* Additional performances take place at a second outdoor theater on Lycabettus Hill.)

A NIGHT AT THE TABLES: If nightclubbing is too tame, take a taxi to **Mount Parnes** and try your hand at blackjack or roulette. The casino on top of Mount Parnes is one of the largest in Europe (17,000 square feet of glitter and plush) with girl croupiers (some from England, most from Greece). About 1500 gamblers a day make the trek up the hill to have their fling at blackjack, roulette, punto banco, baccarat, chemin de fer, boule, and craps. And it is a trek. Mount Parnes is an hour's drive from Athens; when you get there you can either drive all the way up the mountain, or you can take the *téléferique* from the base at 55 drs (55¢) each way, a five-minute ride (but it runs only every half hour or so).

The casino is open every day, except Wednesday, from 8 p.m. until 2 a.m. All you need to get in is a jacket and tie, and a passport; be prepared to fill out at least one form. The casino is out of bounds to civil servants and bankers. If you discover that the goddess Tichi, the Greek's Lady Luck, isn't running with you, go to the grotto-like two-tiered circular nightclub and watch jugglers, equilibrists, and dancers. Admission to the nightclub is free, but the first drink is around 600 drs ($6) and dinner costs 1500 to 2000 drs ($15 to $20) per person. For information call 3229-412.

NIGHTTIME TOURS: The simplest way to sample the nightlife of Athens is to take one of the special "Athens by Night" sightseeing tours. This kind of tour is more fun in Athens than in most cities because it usually includes a drive past the floodlit Acropolis, then along the edge of the sea to Castella in Piraeus, with refreshments in a typical taverna and dinner at a Greek nightclub, complete with floor show and folk dancing. **American Express, CHAT, Key Tours,** and **Viking** operate these "Athens by Night" tours and "Theater Night" tours that take you to performances of the Sound-and-Light Spectacle *and* the Greek dances at the Dora Stratou Theater. The "Theater Night" tour costs 950 drs ($9.50), including tickets but without dinner, and the "Athens by Night" tour costs 1500 drs ($15) with dinner. A special "Casino by Night" tour, from 7 p.m. to 2 a.m., costs 1700 drs ($17), with dinner.

SIGHTSEEING IN ATHENS

IF YOU HAVE ONLY one day in Athens, your best bet is to take a guided sightseeing tour. But even if you're staying a few days and plan to do a lot of sightseeing, it's still a good idea to take the tour to get an idea of the lay of the land, and find out what really interests you. Then you can go back yourself and take in the spots you want to cover in depth.

Let's assume, however, that you plan to see the city on your own, and you've decided to begin with breakfast in **Syntagma,** or Constitution Square. The square itself is a sightseeing attraction (you've already read about its cafés). On the bottom side you have one of the highlights of the square as far as Americans are concerned—the office of **American Express,** usually surrounded by swarms of visitors, young and old, rich and poor, student and professor, booking trips to the islands, waiting for mail and/or money from home. The mail is delivered at 5 p.m., by the way, and this is the time to be there to meet old friends, catch up on gossip, make new friends, and sympathize with those who didn't get that check. The café on the corner, Papaspyrou, gets the brunt of the sorrow and elation. You have to move nimbly to get a table here.

However, the main sight of Syntagma is the former Royal Palace, now the **Parliament Building.** This is a large, squarish yellow building with a marble forecourt facing the square. Apparently, this site was chosen personally by young King Otto (the Bavarian who was put on the throne after the war with Turkey), and his site-selection technique was to hang pieces of meat in various parts of town and select the location where the maggots were slowest to develop. The main attraction here, apart from the constant arrival or departure of dark limousines, is the **Changing of the Guard.** This ceremony, complete with evzones and their pompoms, takes place every hour, 20 minutes before the hour, and on Sunday at 11 a.m., accompanied by its regimental band. If you get there late, you can always photograph the new evzone on duty at the **Tomb of the Unknown Soldier,** in front of the building.

You can spend whole days sitting in the cafés of Syntagma, enjoying the daily routine of the city—the crowds cramming into the offices in the morning; the lottery ticket sellers promising riches; the sponge sellers, more interested in sitting in the shade than selling a record number of sponges; the jet-setters dashing in and out of the NJV Meridien and Grande Bretagne; the tourists checking into the airline offices, the limousines heading for Parliament, the Americans clustering around American Express; the shoppers disappearing into the arcades of Ermou and Karageorgi tis Servias Streets; the crowds cramming out of their offices and cramming into the buses; young hippies; young blondes; young Greeks trying to pick up the blondes; young Greeks trying to pick up the hippies; the elderly gentlemen who've been congregating here through several reigns and regimes, as timeless as the Acropolis.

But sooner or later you'll want to leave the comfy café chairs and the shade of the awnings and go see the other sights of Athens, mainly the Acropolis. *Note:* In the following paragraphs, where mentioned, the winter period is from November 1 to March 31, and summer is from April 1 to October 31—but there's a lot of leeway, depending on the whim of individual hoteliers.

Archeological Sites

THE ACROPOLIS: "Future ages wonder . . . " and they admire, and huff and puff up the hill for a closer look. The Acropolis (meaning "upper city") is built on a rock 515 feet above sea level. The rock has been there, presumably, since the Creation; the walled fortress on top of it has been there for many millennia; but the Acropolis you see today, with its temples and its Parthenon, is a creation of the fifth century B.C. Let's simplify the upper city. The "Acropolis" is the entire plateau; it contains four ancient buildings and one very discreet modern building, which is the **Acropolis Museum.**

The first of these ancient structures is the **Propylaea,** an imposing entrance consisting of a central gateway with two wings (one of which was originally a picture gallery, the Pinacotheca). Just to the right of the Propylaea is a small temple known as **Athena Nike,** or Nike Apteros ("Unwinged Victory"). It was built in the fifth century B.C. to commemorate the victories of the Greeks over the Persians, and its beautiful friezes portray scenes from that war.

The **Erechtheum** (pronounce it er-ek-the-*um*), was begun in 421 B.C. and completed in 407 B.C., on the site of a temple to Erechtheus, a legendary king of Athens. In some ways this is the most hallowed spot up on the hill, because it is the spot where, so the legend says, Athena herself, the guardian of Athens, created the first olive tree. Legend also has it that the invading Persians destroyed this tree, but when they were driven off the tree miraculously grew again. It's a curious temple by Athenian standards: it's built on two levels, it's asymmetrical, and its two porches have no relationship to each other. The smaller porch of the two is the famous one supported by the six **caryatids**, or stone maidens. During the Turkish occupation, the military governor housed his 40 wives here.

But the crowning glory of the Acropolis is the great temple dedicated to the virgin goddess herself, the **Parthenon**. At one time the temple sheltered a gigantic statue of Athena, finished in ivory and gold, and its anterooms were stacked high with the treasures of the city. The Parthenon was built during the time of Pericles, between 447 and 432 B.C., and designed by what may have been the most successful architectural team of all time—Phidias, Ictinus, and Callicrates. They started out with a very uneven foundation, so that one end of the building rests on 35 feet of marble to bring it level with the rest of the structure; the temple lies east to west, with 17 columns on the north and south walls and eight columns on the other two sides.

But the numbers mean little compared to the grace and grandeur of the temple's lines. The Parthenon has no straight lines. Horizontal lines curve in the middle and the 50 columns bulge in the center then taper off toward the top. Traces of iron in the marble (from the hill of Pentelicon, on the edge of the city) give it a golden glow. In its youth the Parthenon had statues and friezes and other decorations, but over the years they've been removed by various conquerors or explorers (the British Museum's famed Elgin Marbles come from the Parthenon). But long before Lord Elgin scrambled up the hill, the Parthenon had undergone various humiliations—for 1000 years it was a Christian church, then it became a Moslem mosque complete with minaret, and then a Turkish arsenal. It was hit by a Venetian shell during a siege in 1687, and that one hapless shell destroyed the interior and the roof of the temple. All the bits and pieces that were left lying around were put back into place during a restoration project that began in the 19th century and didn't end until 1930.

Take a breather now. What you see from up here (with the exception of the museum)—the Stoa, the Plaka, the Areopagus, and Pnyx—was the extent of the city of Athens in its Golden Age. This was where it was all at. Pericles, the orator, aristocrat, general, and statesman, was the grand panjandrum. The plays of Euripides, Aeschylus, Aristophanes, and Sophocles were being premiered at the Theater of Dionysus. Philosophers and men of learning were gathering there and exchanging their wild ideas: Anaxagoras with his absurd theory that the universe was an organized system; Democritus mumbling about all matter being made up of atoms; Herodotus, the so-called father of history, researching his book on the Persian Wars. It must have been an extraordinary, exciting place.

Now for the rest of the Acropolis. The Acropolis Museum is a low structure tucked into the northern end of the plateau, hidden from the outside world. It was built in the last century to store the various statues and fragments of stone reliefs found on the surrounding hills—pediments, friezes, the *Moschophoros* (man with calf), *Athena Meditating,* and a collection of statues of women, known as "Korai" famous for their smiles (which certainly make a change from *Mona Lisa* and her mystic smile). The museum helps you visualize how the buildings must have looked centuries ago.

The Acropolis is usually open Monday through Saturday from 7:30 a.m. to 5:45 p.m. (on Sunday and holidays from 8 a.m. to 4:45 p.m.). The Acropolis Museum's hours are the same as those of the Acropolis, except that the museum is closed on Tuesday (all year). Admission to the Acropolis is 65 drs (65¢), and another 65 drs gets you into the Acropolis Museum. Please check these facts and figures when you get to Athens, before hiking up that hill, because they may change, due to preservation work to counteract the effects of air pollution—and too many admirers. The sad reality is that much of the Parthenon and Erectheum are encased in scaffolding, the caryatids have been carted off to the museum and replaced by plastic replicas, and the actual temple itself has been roped off to prevent more wear and tear on the marble. As of this writing, the Parthenon is a sorry sight, and the preservation work will continue for several years, but there's a good chance that these priceless treasures will survive for a few more centuries.

THE AGORA: We can still stay within the orbit of the Acropolis and feel its presence over our shoulders. The second most important corner of antiquity is the region around the Agora, at the base of the Acropolis on the northwest side. In Ancient Athens the Parthenon was the center of religious life, but the Agora was where the business was done and the fun was found. Pericles's Aspasia probably headed right for this spot. One of the former arcades, the **Stoa of Attalos** has been rebuilt (by the efforts of the American School of Classical Studies), and now houses a museum filled with the bits and pieces found around the Agora, including models of the Acropolis and the Agora, which will help you understand both sites better—so go there first. Originally, the Stoa was the market, and housed some of the first government offices of a democracy. The dominant feature here, however, is the majestic **Temple of Hephaistos,** usually referred to as the "Theseion," or "Theseum." It may be even older than the Parthenon, and unquestionably it's the best preserved of all Greek temples. The Ancient Agora Museum in the Stoa of Attalos, to use its full title, is open from 8 a.m. to 6 p.m. Monday through Saturday, to 5 p.m. on Sunday and holidays, and closed on Tuesday. Admission is 100 drs ($1) each for the site and the museum.

Other sites in this neighborhood include the old **Dipylon Gate,** which used to be the first landmark on the road from Athens to Piraeus; the **Keramicos,** the cemetery of Ancient Athens where you can still see some old sculptured memorials and stelae in the graveyard itself, and funerary tablets and ceramics dating from the 11th century B.C. in the adjoining museum. The Keramicos Archeological Museum (to give it its formal title) is open from 9 a.m. to 3:30 p.m.; Sunday and holidays, from 10 a.m. to 3 p.m.; closed Tuesday. Entrance fee is 50 drs (50¢) for site only, another 25 drs (25¢) for the museum.

Still in this general region, but not in the Agora itself, you can visit the so-called **Tower of the Winds,** a clock built in the Roman period in the shape of an octagonal tower, with figures of the winds, a weather vane, and a unique hydraulic mechanism.

Farther to the east, between the Acropolis and the National Garden, is the **Temple of Olympian Zeus** (what a resounding name!), at the junction of two avenues—Amalias and Olgas—facing the southern entrance to the National Gardens. Begun in the sixth century B.C., the temple was built on a terrace 225 yards long, but today it's very much a ruin, and most impressive when it's floodlit in the evening. The best place to admire it from is not the site itself but from the lounge of the Royal Olympic Hotel, or the roof of the new Athens Gate Hotel. The temple site is open in winter from 9 a.m. to 1:30 p.m. and 4 to 6 p.m. (10 a.m. to 4:30 p.m. on Sunday and holidays); in summer from 8:30 a.m. to 12:30 p.m. and 4 to 6 p.m. (9 a.m. to 3 p.m. on Sunday and holidays). Nearby **Hadrian's Arch,** built by the Emperor Hadrian in the second century B.C., marked the boundary between the ancient quarter of the city and the new Athens, or Adrianople as it was then called.

The Museums

NATIONAL ARCHEOLOGICAL MUSEUM: At 1 Tositsa St. (but the public entrance faces Patission Avenue).

Don't rush in. Enjoy the setting first. From Patission you walk through a spacious garden with cafés beneath palm trees, up to a long, classical facade above a sweep of marble steps—usually crowded with footloose young travelers in search of a heritage, or a companion, and crowds of tourists pouring from sightseeing buses. It's not unusual for 8000 people to visit this museum in one day.

Once in the exhibition rooms proper you're left with no doubt that here is the world's grandest collection of antiquities. Years after you've visited the National Archeological Museum, its treasures will be imprinted on your mind. You need several hours, if not several days, to see everything here. Go on your own rather than on a tour, when you'll be whisked through so quickly you won't remember a thing; on the other hand, if you have time for several visits, it might be an idea to take a tour first time round, make a mental note of exhibits you want to see in a more leisurely manner, then return again on your own.

All the treasures from Mycenae are here in Athens, and the distant site really comes alive before your eyes when you see the fantastic collection of objects discovered at the dig by the famous German archeologist Schliemann. Note the magnificent beaten gold mask of a man with beard and moustache taken from the fifth Shaft Grave: Schliemann claimed, having removed the mask, to "have gazed upon the face of Agamemnon." The Mycenaean Hall contains a staggering variety of finds: intricate gold and silver dagger blades, gold-leaf portrait masks, breastplates, swords, libation cups, and many representations of animals and birds—all dating from around 1550 B.C.

Contrast these objects of exquisite craftsmanship with the

comparatively crude statues of the seventh and sixth centuries B.C.—the stiff, upright *Kouros* or youth is represented naked with one foot forward and the *Kore* or maiden is draped. Examples of this sculptural style have been found all over mainland Greece and the islands. Another remarkable category of exhibits (not grouped together) consists of bronzes, some of which have lain beneath the sea for the past 2000 years.

You should also visit the exhibition of the finds from Santorini (or Thira, as it has now been officially named), the frescoes alive with colorful representations of swallows, monkeys, dolphins, and elegant figures of youth and maidens. Thira/Santorini was an island civilization that flourished at the same time as the Minoan, back there in the second millenium B.C. The islanders built luxurious homes and decorated them with gorgeous murals and pottery. But one day, as legend has it, "Enkeladus in the bowels of the Earth was roused with undescribable fury," and the ensuing earthquake wiped out Thira (you'll read more about this in the chapter on the Greek Islands).

These paragraphs describe maybe one-millionth of this museum's treasures; unless you have time to pay several visits, confine your tour to a couple of halls, and within each focus on a couple of showcases—such as the displays of gold rings, bracelets, and seals. Otherwise you'll go daffy.

Museum summer hours are: weekdays from 8 a.m. to 5 p.m., and on Sunday and holidays from 9 a.m. to 4 p.m.; it is closed on Monday. Admission is 50 drs (50¢), except on Sunday when it's free (and when, of course, you'll have more competition for a close-up of Poseidon and Hermes).

There are three other museums adjoining the National Archeological Museum, mostly of specialized interest—the **Epigraphical Collection** (inscribed monuments from all parts of Greece), the **Numismatic Collection,** and the **Display of Plaster Copies of Antiquities** (both for display and for sale). The hours are similar to the National Archeological Museum and the same 50-dr (50¢) ticket will get you into all of them.

BENAKI MUSEUM: At 1 Odos Koumbari (corner of Vassilissis Sofias Avenue).

It is, of course, almost *de rigueur* to visit the National Archeological Museum in Athens, and if you're a classical scholar you'll be excited by its thoroughness. If you're not, it may stagger you with its size. The Benaki, on the other hand, is a manageable museum. It's more human, which is probably how its founder, the late Anthony Emm. Benaki, would have liked it. This mansion was in fact his home, and most of the exhibits are part of his own collection, which his family turned over to the state after he died. Judging by the exhibits, Benaki must have been a man of wide-ranging interests, because here you'll find relics of the Greek War of Independence, ecclesiastical treasures, textiles, ceramics, glass, costumes, and furniture of Greek, Turkish, and Islamic craftsmanship.

The museum's on three floors, and the room arrangement is rather odd, so buy the 300-dr ($3) guidebook in English. Some highlights: the portable writing desk of Lord Byron; antique pistols and rifles impeccably decorated with silver and engravings; an intricately carved wooden door from Baghdad (ninth century); a virtually complete 17th-century reception room from Cairo with mosaic floor, fountain, basin, and tiled pilasters; a pair of early works by El Greco; some fascinating Coptic fabrics and embroidery; a whole roomful of Egyptian, Roman, Mycenaean, and French silver and gold jewelry; one-third of the magnificent collection of Chinese art that once belonged to Georgiou Eumouphopoulos (the other two-thirds is in London)—Han, T'ang, Sung, Yuan, Ming, and Chin. There are also collections of household embroideries and festive costumes from the islands, golden embroidered coats from Epirus, liturgical seals, distaffs, and musical instruments.

The Benaki is well worth the short walk up from Syntagma, or down from Kolonaki Square. Open 8:30 a.m. to 2 p.m.; closed on Tuesday. Admission is 100 drs ($1), 50 drs (50¢) for students, and free on Sunday.

NATIONAL GALLERY: The **Ethniki Pinakothiki** and **Museum Alexandre Soutsos,** or National Gallery, is the gleaming new building at 46 Vassilissis Sofias Ave. opposite the Athens Hilton. The National Gallery was established in 1900; its new home was inaugurated, however, in May of 1976, and it's a beauty. The collection includes a Goya (*Fiesta*), Correggio (*Guardian Angel*), Poussin (*The Holy Family* and *St. Anne*), van Dyck (*Portrait of a Nobleman*), and half a dozen El Grecos. Unfortunately, they're not always on view. A large gallery is given over to temporary exhibits, and there's a sculpture garden at the rear. Open from 9 a.m. to 3 p.m., on Sunday and holidays 10 a.m. to 2 p.m.; closed on Monday. Admission is 20 drs, or 20¢ (free on Sunday and Wednesday).

BYZANTINE MUSEUM: At 22 Vassilissis Sofias Ave., the museum is at the far end of a pleasant courtyard lined with fountains and sculpture fragments, rather like a Florentine palazzo. It has two floors of mosaics, sculpture, fragments, altars, garments, archbishop's staffs, and Bibles. The descriptive signs are in French and Greek only. Open from 9 a.m. to 3 p.m., on Sunday and holidays to 2 p.m.; closed Monday. In summer, open weekdays from 9 a.m. to 3 p.m., on Sunday and holidays from 10 a.m. to 4 p.m. Admission is 100 drs ($1), free on Sunday.

MUSEUM OF GREEK FOLK ART: At 17 Kidathineou St., Plaka. Folk art here includes vestments, embroidery, pastoral wood carving, icon stands, reliquaries, carnival costumes, and a roomful of murals from Mitilini. Open daily from 10 a.m. to 2 p.m. year round; closed Monday. Admission free. The museum's collection of folk ceramics is displayed in a former mosque at 1 Areos St., Monastiriki Square (but currently closed for repair).

NATIONAL HISTORICAL MUSEUM: Kolokotroni Square. Modern history's equivalent of the National Archeological Museum —the story of Greece from the Balkan Wars through more or less the present day. Summer hours are 9 a.m. to 2:30 p.m. on weekdays, to 3:30 p.m. on Sunday and holidays; closed Friday. Admission is 20 drs (20¢).

THE WAR MUSEUM OF GREECE: At 2 Rizari St. (corner of Leoforos Vassilissis Sofias). "War" in this fabled corner of the world means Achilles vs. Hector, Neoptolemos vs. Paris, Greek vs. Persian, Alexander the Greek vs. the rest, and continues all the way through recorded history to World War II and the Korea Campaign. The collection includes Neolithic cudgels, obsidian hammers, Corinthian helmets, diagrams of ancient battlefields, paintings, uniforms, ship models, a glittering armory of swords and sabres, and in the courtyard, an exhibition of howitzers, torpedos, and antique fighter planes. Refreshment corner in the basement. Open daily, except Monday, from 9 a.m. to 2 p.m.; admission free.

CENTER FOR FOLK ART AND TRADITION: At 6 Angeliki Hatzimichaeli St., Plaka. Opened in 1981, the Center is in the refurbished town house of a wealthy Athenian family—and feels lived-in, as though the family had just left to vacation on Skiathos. Door frames, mantels, and window seats are of dark wood, elaborately carved in classic and folk designs of ships, birds, and mythical creatures. Exhibits include tiled fireplaces, Skyros plates, handwoven fabrics, stained-glass windows, and family portraits. Free admission. Open Tuesday through Saturday from 9 a.m. to 1 p.m. and 5 to 8 p.m., on Sunday from 9 a.m. to 1 p.m.

KANELLOPOULOS MUSEUM: In the Plaka, at the top of Panos Street (near the Taverna Nefeli). In a private neoclassical house, this private collection of classic Greek artifacts includes kraters and figurines, Byzantine ikons, religious embroideries, and Persian *objets* in gold and crystal. Admission 35 drs (35¢). Open weekdays, except Monday, from 9 a.m. to 9 p.m., from 10 a.m. to 3 p.m. on Sunday and holidays.

CITY OF ATHENS MUSEUM: On Klafthmonos Square, halfway along Stadiou Street. Another newcomer, this time in a refurbished "palace" once occupied by King Otto I. You'll see paintings, prints, royal memorabilia—and a striking scale model of Athens as it appeared in 1842. Open Monday, Wednesday, Friday, and Sunday from 9 a.m. to 1:30 p.m. Admission is 25 drs (25¢).

SOME NOTES ON MUSEUMS: The following notes should be of interest to the serious museum-goer.

Hours

Subject to change. If you can, check with the Tourist Organization or your hotel receptionist.

Admission

Admission to all state museums is *free* on Sunday (but again, double-check). Naturally, this means that museums are busiest on those days, and if you want peace and quiet you'd better be prepared to pay some drachmas.

Public Holidays

Museums and archeological sites are *closed* on New Year's Day, March 25 (the National Holiday), Good Friday (after noon), Easter Sunday, and Christmas Day. For other holidays check with the Tourist Organization.

Free Passes

People who can prove they belong to the following categories are allowed into museums free of charge: directors of studies and students of foreign archeological schools; foreign archeologists, architects, and artists on a study visit; foreign interpreters and guides; foreign professors of classical studies; foreign students of classical studies (high school or university level). Foreign students of classical studies *not* accompanied by their professors will get a 50% reduction. To get your free pass you have to go to the office of the **Directorate of Antiquities and Restoration,** Department of Museums, 14 Aristidou St. (tel. 3243-015). The office is open Monday and Friday from 11 a.m. to 1 p.m. only. Take along your passport, plus proof of who and what you are. On second thought, it might be easier just to pay.

Cameras

There are some curious rules here: (a) if you pay the equivalent of the general admission charge you can take pictures, *provided* you don't use a tripod; (b) you can use a tripod in museums if you pay a fee of 100 drs or $1 (for amateurs), 200 drs or $2 (for professionals), extra if you're going to use electric current, and whether or not the object to be photographed will have to be removed from its case; (c) you can use a tripod in archeological sites if you pay a fee of 250 drs or $2.50 (amateurs), 400 drs or $4 (professional) (*Note:* The Acropolis is classified as an archeological site); (d) if you're using a tripod you may not photograph "a person or persons together with an antique object."

Minor Sights of Athens

Two of the more popular destinations for tour buses are the **Olympic Stadium** and the **Presidential Palace,** both within a couple of blocks of each other, beyond the National Gardens. The stadium was built on the site of the ancient Panathenaic Stadium, but this version was completely rebuilt in white marble for the first modern Olympic Games in 1896. The Royal Palace was the home of King Constantine before he went into exile; it's a handsome, French-style château, but you can't see much of it behind all the trees. Most people go there to see the evzones' changing-the-guard ceremony. Don't expect to see anything like the ceremony at Buckingham Palace. In fact, don't bother visiting the Royal Palace and the Stadium unless you have oodles of time.

Surrounding the Parliament Building, back at Syntagma, is the **National Garden** (often referred to as the Royal Garden). It's a formal garden, with a remarkable mixture of trees, lots of shady nooks, swan lakes, duck ponds, terrace cafés where orchestras play Viennese waltzes, and a beautiful palace-like building called the **Zappeion,** which is used occasionally for temporary exhibitions and EEC meetings.

One place you should visit, though, even if only briefly, is the **Cathedral of Athens,** or **Mitropoleos,** halfway between Syntagma and the Plaka, a red pile in Byzantine style, its interior draped with icons which in turn are draped with silver votive offerings like necklaces on an ample-bosomed dowager. The votive offerings are usually small effigies of people who have been blessed or cured by the particular saint. The cathedral genuinely *looks* like a place of worship, even to the black-garbed priests shuffling around in the rear.

The baby cathedral right next to it, the **Church of Aghios (or Saint) Eleftherios,** a tiny church dating from the 13th century, is as austere as the cathedral is ornate. This is a gem of Byzantine architecture, but it was built from marble and stone filched from pagan temples of the classical period. There are many of these venerable Byzantine churches around Athens. Your favorite will probably be the minuscule 11th-century **Church of Aghias Dynamis** (Divine Power), squatting in the middle of the sidewalk, beneath the arcade of the modern Ministry of Education, on Mitropoleos Street, or **Aghias Kapnikareos,** in the middle of the street halfway down Ermon.

The View from the Top

Athens has a couple of vantage points, besides the Acropolis, from which you can get superb views of the city. **Lycabettus Hill** is really a limestone rock reaching almost 1000 feet into the once-crystalline Athenian sky. In the evening the top half is floodlit, and from the Acropolis it looks something like a giant soufflé. By day it's a green-and-white hill topped by a tiny, glaringly white church, **Aghios Georgios.** It's a nagging challenge, and sooner or later you're going to want to climb it. Don't try to walk up (pilgrims used to, but it's an Everest for the faithless), and don't try to take a cab, because it only goes halfway and you still have quite a hike to get to the top. Take the two-minute funicular up the southeast flank. To get there follow the "télépherique" signs to the corner of Kleomenous and Ploutarchou Streets, between Kolonaki Square and the Athens Hilton. The fare is 20 drs (20¢) round trip. The panorama from the top is priceless—all the way to Mount Parnes in the north, west to Piraeus and the Saronic Gulf, with the Acropolis sitting like a ruminative lion halfway to the sea. There's also a café/restaurant up there, which you've read about in the chapter on dining out.

Philopappos Hill is the big hill west of the entrance to the Acropolis. It gets its name from the monument to a versatile fellow who was a Syrian prince, Roman consul, and Athenian magistrate which was erected sometime between A.D. 114 and 116. On some maps you'll see a sign on the northwest flank saying *Prison of Socrates.* It's a cave, and maybe it was and maybe it wasn't the philosopher's prison.

Lower down this great outcropping of rock you come to the hill known as the **Pnyx** (pronounced p-nicks). You may visit it some evening because it's now used as the auditorium for the Son-et-Lumière show, but you may not have time to reflect on what a hallowed spot this is. Free speech was born here. During the days of Pericles the Assembly met here; the Assembly, or Ecclesia, was nothing less than a quorum made up of as many of the city's 150,000 free citizens as felt like attending. The Ecclesia gathered here about 40 times a year, and listened to the great orators who addressed them from the speakers' podium (which you can still see). The amphitheater seated 18,000, and just to make sure it was well filled even when the Ecclesia was discussing something tedious, the police went around with ropes dipped in wet paint and herded the citizens up the hill to the Pynx. Some of the most fateful decisions in Athenian history were made right here, on this beautiful hillside; some of history's most rousing speeches were delivered right here on this speakers' podium.

Still another historic hill, to the northeast of the Pnyx, closer to the Acropolis, is the **Areopagus.** The name means the "hill of Mars," and according to legend this is where Ares (that is, Mars, the god of war) was tried for murdering one of Poseidon's sons.

He was acquitted. So was Orestes, when he was tried here for murdering his mother. And it was probably on this hill, in the spring of A.D. 54, that St. Paul delivered his sermon to the Athenians. Nowadays, when you walk past here on a soft Athenian evening the great hill is suffused with the silhouettes of young lovers and travelers.

How do you get to these hills? You can, of course, take a taxi, but to absorb the full significance of paths which have known the footfall of so many Olympian personalities you really have to walk. Slowly.

Three Walking Tours of Athens

Athens isn't really such a big city, and most of the places you're likely to be visiting, at least by day, are grouped in clusters. Many of the clusters are within walking distance of each other. The best way to get around is undoubtedly to walk. For one thing you'll be able to experience the exotic sights, sounds, and smells of the city as you go along. You'll *feel* the city.

From Syntagma, the cathedral, the Plaka, the Temple of Olympian Zeus, the Benaki Museum, and the Byzantine Museum are all five to ten minutes on foot. Even the Acropolis is not insurmountable on foot.

However, strenuous walking is really only possible in the early morning, late afternoon, or evening. And you can't always plan things that neatly, especially if your visit is short. Fortunately, public transport is inexpensive (see Chapter IV for details on buses, taxis, etc.).

Anywhere you stroll in Athens you'll find the unusual, the exotic, the surprising, the ancient, or the elegant. The three tours below will give you some idea of the possibilities. The first tour is a general sightseeing tour, the second could be called a shopping tour, the third is a museums tour, but of course all three overlap. They all begin in Syntagma.

TOUR A—THE SIGHTS: From Syntagma, stroll down Mitropoleos Street (it's the one on the southwest corner) down past the shops to the cathedral and the Church of Aghios Eleftherios; when you leave the cathedral or the church, turn left, walk one block, then turn right onto Pandroussou Street and enjoy the Oriental bazaar atmosphere of its leather, antique, souvenir, and jewelry shops.

When you get to the square at the bottom of the street you're in Monastiriki; go left and you're at the **Library of Hadrian**, then round the curving street to the left until you come to the **Tower of the Winds** and the **Roman Agora**. Now walk down Pikilis Street and you're at the archeological site with the **Stoa of Attalos**, the **Agora**, and the **Temple of Theseus**. From there you can walk up the hill to the Acropolis, or double back to the nearest taverna in the Plaka.

TOUR B—SHOP-AND-STOP TOUR: From Syntagma, leave by Mitropoleos Street; before you reach the cathedral, turn right and walk one block to Ermou Street, the main shopping street in this area. Continue up Ermou to Nikis, then turn left to Karageorgi tis Servias Street, go through the shopping arcade and into Stadiou Street, cross at the lights and walk up Amerikis Street to Venizelou Avenue, where you can stop for a coffee or lemon juice at Zonar's or Floca.

When you've built your strength up, continue up Amerikis Street to Akadimias Street, turn right and walk one block to Voukourestiou Street, then back to Venizelou Avenue. If you're bushed you can call it a day here and scramble over to Zonar's, or, better still, you can go left one block to Kriezotou, walk up the hill via Pindarou Street, to Tsakalof Street, then go right past the boutique shops there and so down the hill to the nearest café on Kolonaki Square.

Check this itinerary against the list of shops (see "Shopping in Athens"), and mark on this page which streets you really want to visit. That way you can probably shorten this tour. How long it takes depends on how much window shopping you do. It could last a whole day, in which case you'd have lunch in Zonar's or Floca, or one of the cafés on Kolonaki.

TOUR C—MUSEUM TOUR: From Syntagma, take Stadiou Street (between the tourist office and the NJV Meridien Hotel) to the **Historical and Ethnological Museum**. From there, cross Stadiou, walk up Amerikis Street to Akadimias Street, where you turn right, then bear left at Kanari Street and walk the one block to Kolonaki Square. Leave Kolonaki Square in the bottom right-hand corner (Koumbari Street), and at the corner with Vassilissis Sofias Avenue you're at the **Benaki Museum**. When you leave the Benaki, continue up Vassilissis Sofias to no. 22, the **Byzantine Museum**. (If you're still feeling energetic after that, walk up the hill to the funicular and take a two-minute ride to the top of Lycabettus Hill, or walk back to Syntagma via the Parliament Building and the National Gardens.)

Sightseeing Tours of Athens

One of the simplest, most relaxing ways to get around the sights of Athens, is to call one of the tour operators, make a reservation for the next morning, and have the bus come and pick you up at your hotel.

A company like **American Express, Key,** or **CHAT,** will pick you up in an air-conditioned coach, a comfortable 52-seater with a guide who'll speak English plus one other language. Both companies offer a choice of four or more sightseeing tours in Athens.

The **Morning Half-Day Tour** (9 a.m. to 1 p.m.) includes the National Archeological Museum (except on Tuesday when they substitute the Benaki), National Library, University, Academy, Royal Palace, Stadium, Temple of Olympian Zeus, Hadrian's Arch, the cathedral, and Aghios Eleftherios. Price: 1700 drs ($17).

The **Afternoon Half-Day Tour** (3 p.m. to 7 p.m. in summer) takes you via the House of Parliament, the Tomb of the Unknown Soldier, Theater of Dionysus, Philoppapos Hill, Odeon of Herod Atticus, the Acropolis, Theseum, and the Agora. Price: 1300 drs ($13).

The remaining tour is the **Athens By Night Tour,** which in Athens is more fun than usual because it includes a drive past the floodlit Acropolis, then along the edge of the sea to Castella (Piraeus), with a visit to a taverna for dinner and a floor show. During September, the tour may include a visit to the Wine Festival at Daphni instead of the taverna. These tours last from 8:30 p.m. until 1 a.m., and cost from 2700 drs ($27).

An alternative evening choice is the Sound-and-Light spectacle (English-language commentary) plus Greek folk dances. This tour, available nightly from May 1 to September lasts from 8:30 till midnight; the cost is 1700 drs ($17).

SHOPPING IN ATHENS

PEOPLE DON'T GO to Athens for a shopping spree as they might to London or Amsterdam or the Caribbean. But there are stores enough and temptations enough in Athens to lure you from ogling the antiquities, so be sure to bring along some spare cash for gifts and souvenirs—especially since there are so many attractive items that you can buy only in Greece.

What are the favorite buys in Athens? That's hard to pin down, but generally speaking Americans are impressed by the jewelry (especially gold items, and the reproduction of the patterns and designs of antiquity), flokati rugs, hand-knit sweaters (made by village women in winter, priced in some cases less than the wool back home), leather goods, hand-woven and hand-embroidered blouses and dresses, local pottery from the islands, tagaria (beach bags of cotton or wool), furs, and icons. There are many more, as you'll see when you wander around the streets of the city—or when you skim through the roundup below.

WHEN, WHERE AND HOW TO SHOP: The stores in Athens open early, at 8 or 8:30 a.m. Between 1:30 and 2:30 p.m. the doors are locked tight for siesta. They open again at 5 or 5:30 p.m., and close finally at 8 or 8:30 p.m. There are many exceptions to this rule, however. The stores are closed on Sunday, of course, and on Monday, Wednesday, and Saturday they're nearly always open in the mornings only. Summer hours may differ slightly, so plan your day accordingly: mornings, shopping; afternoons, museums. As for the kiosks and the Flea Market, they're nearly always open; and shops in the Plaka usually stay open late to catch the revelers.

The main shopping centers in Athens are concentrated in the streets around Syntagma Square, around Kolonaki Square, and the side streets between Stadiou and Panepistimiou, the two generalize, you might say that the gift and souvenir stores were more numerous around Syntagma; that the Athenians' everyday shopping was done around Stadiou and Patission Avenues (this is where some of the major department stores are to be found); and that cosmopolitan Athenians shopped in the streets between Syntagma and Lycabettus; but these are only generalizations, and you'll find quality shops in the most unlikely neighborhoods.

Of course, the most interesting shopping streets can change from year to year; right now, for example, **Tsakalof Street** running off Kolonaki Square is turning out to be one of the most interesting shoppers' streets in Athens. At no. 42, the end farthest from Kolonaki Square and opposite an old church, **Market 42** is a town house containing six small boutiques offering clothes that try to be as trendy as the names—Toothpick, Lotus, Bombita, and so on. If you don't find what you want, there's also a Coffee Bar to compensate you for the hike (if you can put up with the incessant music). Heading towards Kolonaki Square, Tsakalof will unveil a steady procession of boutiques (for men and women), jewelry, furniture and fabric stores, pastry shops and restaurants. Other browsers' streets in Kolonaki are Anagnoa stopoulou (parallel to Trakald and Patrarchouloakim)—but many of these Kolonaki streets, even the steep ones, are worth the stroll.

Traffic, in fact, has been banished from one of the city's most fashionable shopping streets, **Voukourestiou** (two blocks from Syntagma, between Panepistimiou and Lycabettus), which, with a few adjoining streets, has been transformed into a mall with potted plants and globe lamps.

BARGAINING: Should you bargain in Athens? Before you run out and start haggling, be warned that not all the city's shopkeepers take kindly to it. You can tell by the look of the place whether you can or cannot. Save your bargaining for the streets, especially the Flea Market—but when you do it, do it with gusto.

Some rules: Take your bargaining seriously—don't have the family gawking in the background. Totally disregard the vendor's first offer; reject out of hand his second. If you have a Greek friend, let him do the bargaining for you. And never rush. If you like something with a special passion, begin bargaining for the item next to it, then "settle" for the one you want. When in doubt, don't buy. It's cheaper next door.

KIOSKS: If you can't find it anywhere else in Athens, you'll probably find it at one of the numerous sidewalk kiosks, a unique Greek institution. They're open 18 hours a day, and sell an incredible assortment of goods: chocolates, magazines, newspapers, dolls, postage stamps, cigarettes, cakes, pharmaceuticals, chewing gum, films, pens, lightbulbs, detergents, cosmetics, books, and on and on and on. And you can use their telephones for 5 drs.

ATHENS MARKETS: Centering on Pandrossou Street, and spreading out to surrounding streets, the Flea Market is just what you'd expect it to be: a monumental assortment of cast-offs, some of it junk, the treasures or otherwise from the attics of Attica. You might like some of the brass and copper ornaments, jewelry, 1930 Victrolas, icons, lamps, woven bags, or old used clothing. Make a special point of visiting the crafts shops in the restored arcade at 15 Pandrossou (watch for the Hermion Café sign). A visit to the Flea Market can be quite exciting, especially if you try your hand at bargaining. Save this trip for a Sunday.

If the Flea Market should put you into a general market mood, then head as well for the **Meat Market,** at 81 Eolou. A tiny entrance beckons the unsqueamish into a passageway of butchers' stalls, with red meat hanging everywhere. Twenty steps in, the passageway is transformed into a giant cross of stalls. The **Fish Market** is here too.

On the other side of the Meat Market is **Sofokleous Street,** home to dozens of little cheese, olive, and grocery stores. Go there for a lunch of feta cheese, black/brown olives (they're loaded with vitamins A and C), a loaf of bread, and your choice of wine.

There is another, more "neighborly" flea market in Piracus, **Ta Paliatzidika tou Pirea,** just off Ippodamias Square (near the subway terminal); good for copper and silver, pottery, lamps and hand-embroidered bedspreads, and so on. Sunday mornings only.

In addition to these two flea markets there are several street markets (called *laiki*), following a tradition that dates back to the Middle Ages. Stalls are piled high with fruit and vegetables as well as clothing and country wares brought into town by itinerant merchants. These markets are held in different neighborhoods on different days (invariably from early morning until

2 p.m.); ask at the hotel reception desk for the day or location of the market nearest to your hotel.

Handicrafts and Souvenirs

You'll find the handicraft/jewelery/souvenir/"Greek Art" type of shop everywhere in Greece, and it often doesn't make much difference exactly which one you step into. The prices and merchandise, all "typically Greek," are similar at most of them. In this section, however, the listing concentrates on shops selling handicrafts that are of better quality than the usual souvenir-type trinket.

Before you start racing from store to store, however, you might first take a look at what's available by stopping off at the exhibition of Greek handicrafts at 9 Mitropoleos St., two blocks down from Syntagma. Here you'll find examples of ceramics from the islands, silverwork, hand-painted wooden utensils, leather desk accessories, embroidery, dolls, necklaces made from ahatis stone and various types of traditional rugs. If you have any questions about where to buy individual items, the staff will help you, although they're really there to help *commercial* clients since this is officially the Hellenic Organization of Small and Medium Size Industries and Handicrafts, or **Hommeh,** for short.

The **National Welfare Organization** channels the work of poor families and schoolchildren from all over Greece; it supplies the designs (invariably adapted or copied from museum pieces) and the families do the rest. Their handiwork makes excellent gifts, easy to pack, easy to carry, easy on the wallet: a package of two embroidered linen guest towels for under 840 drs ($8.40), embroidered silk evening bags for $15 and up, sets of four napkins and placemats for 2000 to 4000 drs ($20 to $40), hand-embroidered tablemats for 2000 drs ($20) and up. These prices are about one-third less than you'd pay for the comparable articles in New York, and all profits go to charity. The N.W.O. has a shop at the Athens Hilton, 24a Voukourestiou St., 135 Vasilissis Sofias Ave., and 6 Ipatias St. Open daily, except Sunday, from 8 a.m. to 9 p.m., with no lunchtime break.

Leshki at 19 Pindarou St., is the kind of hole-in-the-wall shop you miss if you blink, but in fact its worth a detour if you're interested in bookbinding, unusual leather wall plaques depicting characters from traditional Greek shadow theatre at prices from 3000 drs ($30). Everything here is done by hand (two hands only—the proprietor's), ranging from hand-painted note cards for less than $1 to oxidized gold-and-silver necklaces in one-of-a-kind designs at 2800 to 12,000 drs ($28 to $120).

One of the most delightful handicraft shops in Athens is **To Anoyi** at 1 Sotiros, one floor up in a quaint little Plaka house with a bookbindery in the basement. When you climb the stairs to iconographer Katherine Apostolou's workshop you may find her painting to the strains of Mahler. Her dazzling display of crafts includes attractive enamel rings, enamel ashtrays with delicate designs of boats and animals, bronze candle holders, hand-blown glass, cotton scarves with traditional regional designs, decorative wooden eggs in traditional designs. Something here for every taste and every budget, including the most modest.

Deros, 4 Stadiou St., is located in a large corner building, three floors of which are bulging with china, glassware, housewares, and crystal chandeliers. You'll find the prices reasonable enough, even though the store is the exclusive importer of some of Europe's leading crystal, porcelain, and tableware.

Other handicraft and "Greek Art" shops include **Stathis** at 2 Palaealogou Venizelou St. (just off Cathedral Square); **Cleo's** in the Hilton arcade (bags, dresses, necklaces, bracelets, leather pitchers, rings); **Mati** at 20 Voukourestiou St., where you can buy "mati" stones for keeping the evil eye away, as well as old monastery lamps, candlesticks, glass and silver, and all sorts of *unexpected* things; **Greek Corner** (Sam Pessah and Son), 10 Karageorgi tis Servias St., bursting with every sort of "authentica" available, including hand-woven blouses and dresses from 1000 to 18,000 drs ($10 to $180), as well as silver and gold jewelry.

ADC, short for Athens Design Center, is a small outlet for the works of a group of designers in ceramics, silver, and pottery. It's at 4 Valaoritou St., and its displays include saucers, cups, plates, bowls, flowerpots, and one-of-a-kind ceramic sculptures. Unusual pottery pieces include turtle doves, spoons, dolls, an interesting collection of silver-and-bronze jewelry, and unusual pottery candleholders for as little as 750 drs ($7.50).

Tanagrea, 15 Mitropoleos, at the corner of Voulis and Mitropoleos Streets (near the little church in the middle of the sidewalk), sells "Les Faïences de la Grèce, all handmade items," in classic and contemporary designs from all the islands and areas of Greece.

Cantoros, at 28 Voukourestiou, specializes in ceramic lamps and ceramic bangles. It's an unusual shop and prices are reasonable.

Pandora, 12 Voukourestiou St., is one of the more attractive shops selling artifacts, jewelry and gifts; it's clean and well laid out, and its owner, Mr. Sakellaridis, quite clearly takes pride in the place. Among the interesting items on sale here are silver-plated and silver/gold- plated brooches from antique Creto-Mycenaean and Byzantine original jewelry exhibited in various museums from 990 to 1950 drs ($9.90 to $19.50); attractive gold-plated brass paperweights that are copies of old coins, at 730 drs ($7.30); brass gold-plated paper clips and letter openers featuring the owl, symbol of Athens and wisdom, also 730 drs ($7.30). Among Mr. Sakellaridis's strikingly original knicknacks are superb heavy-sprung paper holders (almost like clothes pegs) made of gold- plated brass with engraved designs from Delphic friezes, 730 drs ($7.30).

Myconos at 10 Mitropoleos St. is two floors of jewelry, and terracotta wall plaques. Their own factory produces cotton caftan-like dresses with traditional Greek designs, from 1200 to 2100 drs ($12 to $21); they also have some chunky modern silver bracelets at 2500 to 3500 drs ($25 to $35), and their rugs featuring the famous Greek key design (black on red) are made from heavy wool but feel soft to the touch, priced from 9500 to 15,000 drs ($95 to $150).

Museum Shops: Greek arts and jewelry are also available in several museums; including the **National Archeological Museum** (reproductions of vases, figures, and statues) and the **Benaki Museum** (table linens, prints, matchbooks, etc.) Both of them, of course, also sell books, which are useful as souvenirs and gifts.

Dolls in Greek costume are one of the most popular sovenirs of a trip to Athens; you can buy them in most of the Greek art and souvenir shops, or you can go direct to the factory and buy them for a few drachmas less. The place to go is **Koumparoulis,** at 2 Diogenou St. (near the Roman Agora and the Tower of the Winds), where you can watch Mrs. Koumparoulis make the dolls in her tiny workshop. The dolls are all dressed in exact copies of authentic Greek costumes, from all parts of Greece, and if they don't have the one you want on display, they will make it for you in 24 hours. Best of all, you get wholesale prices—evzones for 600 to 1200 drs ($6 to $12), dolls of all sizes from 1000 to 2000 drs ($10 to $20). The firm will ship your dolls back to the States (delivery time is about 30 days).

Additional suggestions for handicrafts and gifts: for hand-woven, hand-knitted sweaters, **Helen de Luca** at 4 Aghios Hatzimhali St. (two doors down from the Hotel Nefeli); for hand-woven fabrics for upholstery, cushions, or bedspreads, priced from 800 to 3500 drs ($8 to $35), **Village Shop** at 30 Tripodou St. in the Plaka; and for one-of-a-kind textiles made into wall hangings, mats, and cushion covers, **Ilakat** at 46 Amalias, near the Royal Olympic Hotel (but open at odd hours).

Jewelry

This is one of the most popular shopping items in Greece, and the range of merchandise ranges from souvenir trinkets based on ancient designs to chic avant-garde creations in gold and precious stones. However, since the government, early in 1982, imposed a 20% luxury tax on jewelry, the advantages of a strong dollar have been cancelled out.

Voukourestiou Street might be the place to begin your expedition, since the city's finest jewelers are located at the corner with Panepistimiou, and the new mall is lined with reliable shops.

Some of the most original and imaginative gold jewelry in the world is designed by **Ilias Lalaounis** and handcrafted by his artisans in a workshop in the shadow of the Acropolis. Lalaounis introduces two new collections a year (sometimes more when he receives a special commission from a sheikh). A typical collection might include a dazzling array of gold necklaces, bracelets, and rings evolved from the shapes of aboriginal and prehistoric tools and statuettes, priced in the thousands of dollars. However, visit any of the Lalaounis stores and you'll find items costing as little as 5000 drs ($50). The main store is a 6 Panepistimiou, with branch boutiques in the lobbies of the Hotel Grande Bretagne, the Athens Hilton, and the Athens Tower, and on Corfu, Mykonos, and Rhodes.

Neck and neck, so to speak, with Lalaounis in quality and price is the other great name in Greek jewelery—**La Chrysothèque Zolotas** at 10 Panepistimiou, with branches in several deluxe hotels and museums throughout the islands and mainland. Charles Pentherondakis is at 19 Bucharest St., and on Voukourestiou Street itself you have **Adler** at no. 13, **Petradi** at no. 20, and **Petra Nova** at no. 19. The latter two feature *petradi,* or semiprecious stones (amethyst, tiger's eye, lapis, turquoise, and sodalite being the most popular here), set in imaginatively designed pins, necklaces, rings, earrings, pendants and what have you, at prices ranging from 3000 drs ($30) to well over 10,000 drs ($100). Petradi has a particularly interesting selection of gift items, such as ashtrays of petrified coconut.

At 10 Nikis St., **VIP** stocks Byzantine seals and brooches copied from originals in the National Archeological Museum, mostly from the Mycenaean and Alexander the Great periods, mostly priced above 10,000 drs ($100)—and the owners promise a discount to readers of this guide.

There are more museum copies at the showroom of archeologist **Maria Antoniades** (one floor up in the office building at 17 Voulis St.), as well as original modern designs in gold, silver, and precious stones. Prices ranges from a few hundred dollars to $4000. **Gold Coin Jewelry**, 17 Stadiou St., actually sells *you* money—a unique collection of unusual coins, some of it copies of ancient Greek currencies.

If you admire the Lalaounis concepts but cannot afford the price of gold, visit a store called **The 4 Lamda** in the Athens Tower skyscraper. It's actually another branch of Lalounis, with the same imagination and flare in design, but most of the items are crafted in silver, with scores of gifts in the $20 to $40 range, as well as more substantial items.

Women's Fashions

This is a subject you have to look at from two angles: local designs and fabrics on the one hand, high fashion and international chic on the other. Sometimes they overlap, but in general you will probably be interested in shopping only for local fashions—famous-designer clothes are even more overpriced than normal, and the trendy gear here is still panting to catch up with last year's trends in London, Paris, and New York.

Three designers are still setting the pace in Athen's fashion world these days, and all three of them turn enthusiastically to their Greek heritage for inspiration; yet they've all managed to attract international attention since their designs have been snapped up by various jet-set celebrities who shall go nameless.

Yannis Travassaros has his main boutique in the Athens Hilton. He designs virtually everything he sells, and in most cases he also weaves his own fabrics, or trims coats or dresses with old embroidery and authentic *bibiles* (needlework borders) from his own collection of old Greek costumes. Most of his creations are for dressy winter wear—pant suits, *zigouni* (sleeveless coats like jackets worn by Greek shepherds), evening coats, evening dresses. He has a sportswear boutique, also in the hotel lobby. Some prices: three-piece pant suits, 10,900 drs ($109); dresses, from 9000 drs ($90); one-of-a-kind silk blouses with antique appliquéd embroidery, from 35,000 drs ($350); zigounis, 2400 to 6000 drs ($24 to $60); batik patchwork vests, 1500 drs ($15); suits made of koukoulariko, a lovely raw silk made by the peasants of nothern Greece, 45,000 drs ($450).

Travassaros also designs leather hand-knit suits with wrap-around skirts at 21,500 drs ($215) and cotton hand-knit tops at 4000 drs ($40). Alterations within three hours.

The other two hot-shot designers work as a team—**Nikos & Takis**, two ex-painters who got fed up with people who expected to bargain a $2000 canvas down to $200, so they started designing clothes. Their boutique is at 10 Panepistimious Ave., near Syntagma Square (with branches at the Plaka in Athens, and in Corfu, Delphi, and Rhodes). The Plaka boutique is in a 250-year-old house at 5 Markou Avriliou St., at Aerides Square: the ground floor is taken up by handicrafts; high fashion (and air conditioning) is upstairs. Again, the inspiration for the designs comes from Classical Greek and Byzantine costumes and decoration. Since they're both designers and manufacturers, Nikos Takis offer reasonable prices, and they keep sizes 10, 12, and 14 in stock but can usually run up other sizes, or make alterations, within 24 hours. Their favorite fabrics are cotton, wool, silk, mohair, and raw silk.

For more ladies' fashions, less pricey than in the boutiques of Kolonaki, check out the windows of the following stores, all on Ermou Street: **Sinanis** at no. 9, **Tsantilis** at no. 23, **Papagiannis** at no. 47.

You'll find simpler items, like hand-woven and hand-embroidered blouses and dresses at some of the handicraft "Greek Art" shops—such as **VIP** (10 Nikis St.), where you'll find a selection of all-wool, hand-woven dresses from 9000 drs ($90), and hand-painted silk dresses with matching stoles for 12,000 drs ($120).

Lizard (14 Kriezotou St.) and **Gianari Gallani Boutique** (on the corner of Kolonaki Square and Skoufa Street) both have elegant selections of leather goods—including shoes, belts, and jackets.

Men's Fashions

If you want to look over suits, jackets, and shirts by Europe's top-flight designers (particularly Italian) the appropriate stores seem to be concentrated near the intersections of Akadimias Street with Pindarou Street, Voukourestiou Street, and Amerikis

Street. A few new men's boutiques have now set up shop in Kolonaki, mainly along Tsakalof Street.

Ascot, at 29 Nikis St. (just off Syntagma Square) and 6 Kapsali St. (just off Kolonaki Square) features a wide selection of suits, sportcoats, slacks, shirts, sweaters, ties, and toiletries. **Perla**, with a classy branch in the arcade at 5 Statiou St., also has a fine selection of menswear.

Sandals

Head up Pandrossou Street from Monastiraki Square to no. 89 and inside you'll find the "poet–sandalmaker" of Athens **Stavros Melissinos**. Look in the dusty window and you'll see several yellowing newspaper articles about this remarkable man, in among the sandals, straps, and tools of the trade; inside the small shop, you'll find up to 30 different styles of sandals ranging in price from 900 to 1200 drs ($9 to $12), in sizes 33 to 45. If your feet are bigger or smaller, Melissinos will make you a special pair. He counts among his clients various celebrities, such exalted figures as Jackie Onassis, and framed certificates above his workbench testify that Harvard College Library and Bodleian Library in Oxford, England, have copies of his books in their collections. An unaffected, gentle, and friendly man, Melissinos will chat about his poetry with you while helping you choose your sandals. His brother-in-law's workshop, **Tony's Sandals** at 52 Adrianou (near the Roman Agora), is the place to go when you want a comfortable pair of shoes or boots—casual style. A handmade pair of pale-tan leather boots is currently upward of 2500 drs ($25).

Furs

A high priority on your fur-stalking list should be **Voula Mitzakou** at 7 Mitropoleos, where the charming Mrs. Mitzakou herself runs the business her father founded over 75 years ago; her knowledgeable, British-trained assistant Stephanos will be happy to explain the entire process of making fur coats, and serious customers (with emphasis on the serious) will be treated to a tour of the workshops downstairs. (Mitzakou employs 25 people, each an expert in one specific stage of the process.) Mink jackets here will cost you anything from $650 to $2300 (six different qualities of mink are involved), a full-length multicolored mink coat from $750, Persian lambs from $600, and Greek red fox jackets are $950 or thereabouts. You can take your pick from 25 to 30 varieties of fur (from Greek wolf to French rabbit to sable) and get Mitzakou to design a coat specially for you (in which case you add a minimum of 10% to the off-the-peg prices). Mitzakou has full cold storage facilities, and exports fur coats to clients all over the world.

Old Established Company

The fur stores listed here are fine for most people, but if you have a chauffeured limousine waiting for you at the airport to whisk you to a suite at the Grand Bretagne, then you'll probably be able to persuade someone to take you to a rather special place—**J. A. Sistovaris & Sons, Inc.,** at 14 Voulis St. (up one flight), 4 Ermou St., or 9 Venizelou. This old, established company, now in its fourth generation, uses only the finest quality furs (no slap-together remnant here) for the finest quality clientele. Expensive, naturally.

George M. Trahos & Sons, 7 Filellinon St. (tel. 3228-256). Everyone refers to it as the Fur House, so the Fur House it is. It's been in business for over 100 years, it has its own expert fitters. Pick your favorite fur—Persian lamb, natural Greek stone marten, autumn haze natural mink, tourmaline natural mink, or palomino mink. Indian lamb is particularly popular because it combines lightness with warmth. Pick your favorite style—full-length, three-quarter-length, cape-stole, bolero jacket, or straight stole. You'll have a choice of hundreds of coats, stoles, jackets, hats, and scarves—and prices that will make you feel you've got a bargain, from $150 up for coats (but, of course, it pays to know something about furs and prices before you buy). And, if you produce this book, you will receive a 30% discount. Mailing service is available.

Antiques, Music, Art

Antiqua, 4 Amalias (tel. 3232-220). This is a proper, elegant antique shop owned by a man who both knows and loves his wares. John Yannoukos, an English-speaking Greek who seems always to be polishing his treasures, has filled his store to the brim with clocks, jewelery, paintings, ancient Greek votive dishes, ivory statues, icons, Chinese vases and carvings, and French and Venetian furnishings. The shop is a bit off Syntagma, and the prices range from 210 to 300,000 drs ($2.10 to $3000).

Mr. Yannoukos has a second antiques gallery at 2 Messoghion St., Athens Tower.

Tassos Th. Zoumboulakis, 7 Kriezotou St. (tel. 3634-454) and 20 Kolonaki Square (tel. 3608-278). Founded at the beginning of the century, the gallery (it's air-conditioned, by the way) collaborates with several of the finest art dealers in Europe and the United States, so it's not restricted to works by Greek artists. Nevertheless, those are the ones that will probably interest you most, and here you'll find a selection of the works of Greek artists who are known only within their homeland, and others who have earned reputations abroad. Among them are Tsazouchis, Chryssa, Matta, Alan Davie, and Fassianos. Also occasional works by Calder, Max Ernst, Rauschenberg, Magritte, and other contemporary artists. Zoumboulakis also specializes in Greek folk art and the jewelry of Greek national costumes (brooches, pendants, rings, and thins) from 1200 to 18,000 drs ($12 to $180), as well as embroideries from the native dresses (mostly 17th, 18th, and 19th century) of Attica, Crete, Naxos, Rhodes, and Patmos (they make exquisite wall hangings, but you'd better talk directly to Mr. Zoumboulakis about prices).

C. Haritakis Antiques, 7 Valaoritou St. (tel. 3621-254), has a fine collection of silverware, copperware, furniture, prints, porcelain, and icons.

Les Amis de Livres, in a short passageway at 9 Valaoritou, is everything its name promises to lovers of books—rare books, prints, engravings of Greek scenes. Open 9 a.m. to 3 p.m. Monday through Saturday in winter, closed Saturday in summer.

Collector, in the lobby of the Hilton Hotel, is an antique shop specializing in pewter, brass, copper, and wrought iron—a 150-year-old gunpowder holder in hand-hammered pewter with silver plating, old copper cooking molds, belt fasteners in brass or silver, antique rings, new ceramic necklaces in earthy colors. Reasonable prices.

Gallerie Antiqua, Queen Sophias and 2 Messoghion (tel. 7705-881), is an elegant shop housing the works of noteworthy Greek and foreign painters, exquisite art objects, and furniture of high quality and good taste. Near the American Embassy.

Three other galleries where you will see temporary exhibits of works by local and international artists: **Athens Gallery,** 4 Glyconos in Kolonaki (tel. 713-938); **Desmos,** 28 Akadimias (tel. 3609-449); **Jean Bernier Gallery,** 51 Marsails (tel. 723-5657, in summer by appointment only at 735-657); **Hydrohoos Art Gallery,** 16 Anapiron Polemon St. in Kolonaki (tel. 7223-684).

Rugs

There's a bewildering choice of designs and colors in Greek rugs—Horassa, Hamadan, the Lobanof with its playful lions, Greek designs from the Acropolis, blue-and-yellow Byzantine designs, the Sykrion (based on motifs taken from a village cemetery near Corinth), the Greek classical designs with their stark blues and whites and subtle flecks of ochre, some Oriental designs that look like woolen Jackson Pollocks (and beautiful enough to hang on a wall).

Two stores with good selections of rugs and carpets are **Arts and Crafts,** on the corner of Voukourestiou and Valaoritou Streets, a branch of the National Welfare Organization specializing in Greek designs—Cassandra, Mistra, Didoni, and Ionia; and **N. Rossopoulos & Co.,** at 18 Panepistimiou, which features only Oriental designs. The main enclave of carpet stores is on Patission Avenue, beyond the National Archeological Museum.

Flokati rugs are among the most popular purchases for visitors to Greece, and most visitors flock to one of two showrooms just off Syntagma—**Karamichos Flokati** on the corner of Voulis and Apollonos and **A. Kokkinos** at 3 Mitropoleos St. These flokatis come from the city of Trikala in Central Greece; they're made from a combination of wools (from Greece for wear, from New Zealand for softness), softened under fresh spring waterfalls in Trikala before being woven by hand or machine to make thick, close piles. Both showrooms display a variety of flokatis in natural tones or kaleidoscopic patterns. Prices from 2400 drs ($24) for a two- by five-foot rug in natural colors. Karamichos and Kokkinos will pack, insure, and mail your purchases.

Miscellaneous

If you didn't pack adequate shoes for clambering over all those ruins and archeological sites, try **Mouriades** at 4 Stadiou St., which most people consider the best shoe shop in the city (prices from 4500 drs, or $45, including some Bally models). On the other hand, if you've ruined your most stylish pair sightseeing you may be able to find a replacement at the **Charles Jourdan/Petrides** shop at 10 Ermou St. (where prices are fairly close to what you'd pay in Paris—and they have American-size lasts).

When you want to bone up on your Greek history and need *English-language books* and paperbacks, go to the **American Bookstore** at 23 Amerikis St., **Pantelides** at 11 Amerikis, **Eleftheroudakis** at 4 Nikis St. around the corner from Syntagma and the best bookshop in town), or the bookstand in the **Athens Hilton.** Newspapers you can buy almost anywhere, especially at the ubiquitous kiosks.

For **gifts** for sons, daughters, grandchildren, nephews, nieces, head for one of these toy shops: **Panhellinios Agora,** 9 Stadiou St.; **El Greco,** 67 Adriannou St.; or **Tsokas,** 52 Aiolou St. For children's colorful, smart clothing, check out **Free Kit,** at 19 Anagnostopoulou in Kolonaki.

Peau d'Ange, at 21E Voukourestiou St., has a fine collection of small **leather goods**—wallets, picture frames, purses, bags, desk sets, diaries, and calendars—in unusual designs. A good spot for gifts. More leather—wallets and luggage—at **Magasin Scourletis,** 8 Speusippou, in Kolonaki.

In the same neighborhood, **Laura Ashley** has opened a cheery boutique at 28 Irodston St.

Argaliou means loom and *Brailas* is the name of a family that looms, so **Argaliou Brailas,** at 7 Filellinon St., is the place to head for top-quality hand-woven silks. *Even the threads are hand-spun.* Priced by the yard (30-inch widths)—3500 drs ($35) and up. Hand-woven wool is 2600 drs ($26) and up. Made-up items include hand-woven capes from 4800 drs ($48), and reversible hand-woven handbags with shoulder straps (hand-crocheted finish) for less than 4000 drs ($40). They'll also make up anything for you, carefully tailored, within three to five days.

Worry beads are another popular souvenir. The *komboloia,* as they're called in Greek, are Greece's answer to tranquilizers, but try twiddling them yourself and you may find they have just the opposite effect—it's not as easy as it looks. Fortunately, they don't cost a fortune. You'll find selections in most "Greek Art" shops.

Sponges might seem an unlikely purchase, but they're on sale on street corners all over the city. These are natural sponges fetched out of the nearby sea by hardy divers. They come in all sizes, from 80 drs (80¢) all the way up to somewhere around 1000 drs ($10)—but you'd pay three times the amount back home.

Department Stores and Supermarkets

The three major emporia (at least, those that come closest to the American concept of a department store) are the **Athenee,** halfway along Stadiou Street, at nos. 33-35 to be precise; **Lambropouli** at Aiolou and Lykourgou Streets; and **Minion,** "the

Macy's of Greece," at 10 September St., near the National Archeological Museum. The **Pris-Unic-Marionopoulou** stores are a combination department store and supermarket, where you can buy Marks & Spencer's knitwear or pick up some useful inexpensive items and the makings of a great picnic; these stores are identified by a large orange M, and the closest one to Syntagma is at 9 Kanaris St., just off Kolonaki Square.

Tax-Free Shopping

The tax-free shop at the airport is very limited in its choice: don't put off serious shopping until you get there, other than small gifts, jewelry, perfume, and souvenirs.

Academy of Science

Chapter X

THE ABC'S OF ATHENS

THIS CHAPTER will serve as a reference guide to all the essential miscellany of travel in a strange city. These are the simple things you don't think about back home that can become major when you're away: buying stamps, finding an all-night drugstore, changing money, getting the news. So here is an alphabetical listing covering emergencies, and also some of those "uncategorizable" items I couldn't slip in elsewhere.

AIRPORTS: Plural, please note—there are two airport terminals in Athens. If you're flying a foreign airline, you'll arrive and depart from **Hellinikon East Terminal,** which is for international flights by overseas airlines. If you fly anywhere via Olympic Airways, internationally or to the islands or some other city in Greece, you'll leave from the **Hellinikon West Terminal** (sometimes referred to as the Olympic Terminal). Make sure you tell your driver which one you want. There is also a shuttle service between the East Terminal and West Terminal, every hour from 8:30 a.m. to 8:30 p.m. It's a ten-minute drive, but can take much longer.

AIRPORT BUS: There's airport bus service to and from Amalias Avenue, near the corner of Syntagma. Number 18 Express yellow buses leave for the East Terminal every 20 minutes; the ride takes 30 to 45 minutes, the fare is 45 drs (45¢) each way; there is no charge for luggage. But if you're not on a tight budget, the taxi fare is around $6 or $8, including luggage, direct from your hotel to the airport. Olympic Airlines buses leave from the Olympic downtown terminal at 96 Syngrou and go direct to the West Terminal at Hellinikon. The ride takes 20 minutes, costs 45 drs (45¢) and leaves every half hour from 4 a.m. to 10 p.m.

AIRPORT INFORMATION: East Airport, tel. 979-9466; West Airport, tel. 9814-093; Olympic Airways only, tel. 9616-161.

AMERICAN EMBASSY: 91 Vassilissis Sofias Ave. (tel. 7212-951, any time of the day or night).

AMERICAN EXPRESS: Constitution Square (tel. 7220-201; Travel Division, tel. 3244-975; Banking Division, tel. 3234-781). For changing money, buying travelers checks, making travel arrangements, booking sightseeing and escorted tours, receiving mail, meeting people. Open 8 a.m. to 2 p.m. Monday to Friday.

BABYSITTING: Ask your hotel concierge.

BANKS: Open weekdays from 8 a.m. to 2 p.m. The National Bank of Greece on Syntagma is open for currency exchange until 9 p.m. weekdays, until 8 p.m. on Saturday and Sunday. There are Athens branches of a number of American and Canadian banks: American Express, Bankers Trust, Chase Manhattan, First National Bank of Chicago, Bank of Nova Scotia, Continental Illinois National Bank, Bank of America, Manufacturers Hanover Trust, and First National City Bank.

BEAUTY PARLORS: No problem. They're all over the place, but you'll probably feel most comfortable in one of the hotel beauty parlors that cater to an international clientele. Try **Costi and Taki** at the Hilton—1000 drs ($10) for a haircut and 1300 ($13) for a shampoo and set. For men, a haircut will cost about 500 to 600 drs ($5 to $6).

BUSINESS HOURS: Athenians have a five-day work week. In winter, the hours are 8 or 8:30 a.m. to between 1:30 and 2:30 p.m., then from 5 or 5:30 to 8 or 8:30 p.m. (although most offices will close at 1:30 p.m. on Saturday); in summer, June through October, the hours are 8 a.m. to 1:30 p.m., then 5 to 8 p.m. All government offices (and many private companies) work from 8:30 a.m. to 2:30 p.m. in winter, 7:30 a.m. to 1:30 p.m. in summer, and in fact there's a movement afoot to make those the standard hours for everyone to avoid the extra lunchtime traffic rushes. Stores follow roughly the nongovernment hours, but close on Saturday afternoon all year round (except for grocers, barbers, and hairdressers, which close on Wednesday afternoon). However, these figures are liable to vary with the day of the week, so call ahead for specific hours.

BUSINESS ORGANIZATIONS: Athens Cosmopolitan-Lions Club (tel. 3601-311); **Rotary Club,** 3 Kriezotou St. (tel. 3623-150); **American Hellenic Chamber of Commerce,** 17 Valaoritou St. (tel. 3636-407).

CAMPING: Inquire at National Tourist Organization (see below). There are a dozen sites in and around Athens, and more than 100 throughout Greece. You can now rent fully equipped campers for around $460 a week in summer. For details, contact **Camper Caravans,** 4 Nikis St., Athens (tel. 3230-552).

CANADIAN EMBASSY: 4 Ioannou Gennadiou St. (tel. 7223-511).

CAR RENTALS: For full information, see Chapter XIII on "Touring the Hinterlands."

CASINOS: There are casinos at Mount Parnes (just north of Athens), and on the islands of Corfu (Casino Achillion Palace) and Rhodes (Casino de Rhodes). Roulette, baccarat, chemin de fer, blackjack, and slot machines. Take your passport with you.

CHURCH SERVICES: The main churches are St. Dennis Roman Catholic Church, on the corner of Panepistimiou Avenue and Omirou Street; St. Paul's Anglican Church, Filellinon Street; St. Andrew's American Church (interdenominational), 66 Sina St; the Synagogue, 6 Melidoni St.

CIGARETTES: A pack of American regulars costs around 70 drs (70¢); filters and king-size, about 111 drs ($1.11) Greek filter cigarettes, on the other hand, are only 50 drs (50¢) for 20.

CLIMATE: Summers are dry and hot, hovering around 90°F. It's cooler, of course, along the coasts and in the mountains to the north. In winter, the temperature can go down to 40° in some areas (Athens has an average temperature of 55° in January), and rain can also be expected 12 or 13 days a month from October through April. But the sun shines 300 days a year.

CLOTHING: Specifically, sightseeing garb. For hiking up steep hills and steps (of which there are countless thousands in Greece), women will probably be happier in slacks rather than skirts (which can be too revealing). If you're planning to visit one of the sites where donkeys are the standard method of conveyance, slacks are again recommended to avoid a case of donkey chafe on your knees. For churches, women are expected to wear appropriate clothing. Heavy shoes are essential for all ancient sites—and not such a bad idea for some sidewalks in Athens. In casinos, men must wear jacket and tie, women should wear cocktail dresses or pantsuits.

CREDIT CARDS: Diners Club, VISA, and American Express are honored throughout Athens and major tourist centers throughout Greece. Decals identify cooperating merchants, but verify beforehand that the contracts are still in existence.

CURRENCY: The drachma, divided into 100 lepta (almost obsolete), is worth 94¢; U.S. 100 drachmas equal, more or less, $1. Coins come in 1-, 2-, and 5-drachma denominations, and a 50-lepta piece. Bills are the blue 50-drachma note, the red 100-drachma note, the green 500-drachma note, and the brown 1000-drachma note. *Note:* There are no facilities for changing currency in the airport departure halls; change your remaining drachmas before going through passport control.

CURRENT: Talk to your concierge before using any U.S. appliances. You will probably need anywhere from one to three adapters, which should be available from reception in the *better* hotels. However, in Athens and most of the mainland the current is 220 volts, A.C. Top hotels also have a 115V outlet for shavers.

CUSTOMS: U.S. and Canadian nationals may travel freely anywhere in Greece for up to three months. On entering the country, you may bring in one liter of alcoholic beverage or two liters of wine, 200 cigarettes or 50 cigars—and five boxes of matches. There is no restriction on the number or value of travelers checks on either entry or exit. Be very careful about antiques you buy in Greece. The laws protecting Greek antiquities are very strict and no genuine antiquities may be taken out of the country without prior special permission from the Archeological Service, 13 Polygnotou St., Athens.

DOCUMENTS: All you need (as an American or Canadian citizen) is a valid passport. Customs and passport control are fairly quick on arrival; the latter can slow you down on departure—so leave yourself a few extra minutes. Your arrival automatically gives you permission to stay three months; if you want to stay longer, you have to apply for a special permit.

DRINKING WATER: Safe to drink in hotels and restaurants, but beware of well water. If you get bottled mineral water, make sure the cap is tightly fixed.

DRIVING: The **International Drivers' License** is officially recommended, but not usually required when renting a car. However, it's useful in emergencies since it's easier for the local constabulary to understand. For information, contact the **Automobile and Touring Club of Greece** (ELPA), Tower of Athens, 2-4 Messogion St., Athens (tel. 779-1615). For ELPA road assistance, dial 104.

DRUGSTORES: In an emergency, dial 107 for all-night service.

ELEVATORS: Greek elevators are reliable, but they don't operate on the same principles as in the U.S. Except in modern places, such as the Hilton, doors don't open automatically; you have to watch for the elevator arriving at your floor, then quickly pull the door open before someone else presses a button on another floor and the elevator shoots off. Others signal their arrival with a "ping." Also, in many cases the button doesn't register the floor you want to go to until *after* the door is closed tight; so you may have to press your number a second time after the door has closed. Some elevator floors seem to fall out from under you when you step onto them; don't be alarmed, they're simply registering the weight.

EMERGENCIES: For all kinds of emergencies, dial 171 for the Tourist Police; 100 for emergency police service; 104 for help with your car; 107 for all-night drugstores; 150 for ambulance and 166 for first aid; 199 for the fire department; 7212-951 for the American Embassy and 7239-511 for the Canadian Embassy.

EXECUTIVE SERVICES: For the business traveler who needs a temporary office base in Athens, an organization called Executive Services will provide telephone, Telex, secretarial, translating, and interpreting services; fully furnished, air-conditioned offices, equipped with phones and Telex lines, can be rented by the day, week, or month. For details, contact Lorraine Batler in the Athens Tower (tel. 7783-698, Telex 214227 EXSE GR).

FILM: Expensive. Bring supplies with you.

GUIDES: If you want to hire your personal guide, the rates are 3000 drs ($30) for a full day plus all expenses. Call the association of tour guides at 3229-705.

HOLIDAYS: Most shops are closed on the following days—New Year's Day, January 6, March 25 (National Day), Shrove Monday, Greek Orthodox Good Friday, Easter Sunday and Monday, May 1, Whit Monday, August 15, October 28, Christmas Day, December 26. In reality, the Orthodox Easter (one or two weeks after Christian Easter) is a four or five-day holiday.

HOSTELS: There are two types: youth and student. In Greece, call or apply to the **Greek Youth Hostels Association,** 4 Dragatsaniou St., Athens (tel. 3234-107 or 3237-590).

LAUNDERETTES: In the Omonia Square area, the self-service Maytag at 46 Didotou (near Zoodochou Pigis, and three blocks back from Akadimias) charges 250 drs ($2.50), soap included, for a full-service wash. Other launderettes in the Plaka are **Nakopoulos** at 9 Erechtiou and **Golfinopoulos** at 24 Kythathineon, with approximately the same rates.

LIQUOR: You can buy it by the bottle or take your own bottle to the grocery store and get a refill—the cost depends on the amount. Famous brands of scotch whisky cost about 500 to 800 drs ($8.33 to $13.33), but you can also buy bottles at supermarkets for around 350 to 400 drs (say $6 to $8).

LUGGAGE: Pacific Ltd., a travel agency at 26 Nikis St. and the *East* Terminal at the airport, will store excess luggage while you tour the hinterlands or islands. Call 3236-851 for more details.

MASSAGE, SAUNA: The Hilton's resident masseuse charges $22 for sauna and massage. Call 7220-201, ext. 381, from 11 a.m. to 9 p.m. Or try the Intercontinental (tel. 9023-666).

MEDICAL ATTENTION: For doctors and dentists trained in the U.S. or fluent in English, contact the **Tourist Police** (tel. 171); the **American Embassy** (tel. 7212-951), or the **State Hospital of Athens** (tel. 7778-901). Dial the Athens emergency medical and ambulance service is 166 (English spoken). Taxis are often faster than ambulances, and they are permitted to function as emergency vehicles by flashing their lights and honking their horns.

MEDICINES AND TOILETRIES: American brands are available in most pharmacy-type stores in Athens and other major tourist centers. But at a price. Bring your own supplies in the interests of economy. European brands are usually less expensive—but reliable. For names of all-night pharmacies, dial 107.

MONEY CHANGING: Best bets are the 8 a.m. to 8 p.m. or 9 p.m. service of the **National Bank of Greece,** 2 Karageorgi tis Servias, right on Syntagma (the tourist office is in the same building), and the **General Hellenic Bank,** also on Syntagma.

NAMES, SPELLINGS: You'd think that after all these centuries they'd at least know the names of their streets. But no, as you've already learned, several places and streets in Athens have one or more names, and in most cases each name has one or more spellings. Thus Syntagma Square, also Constitution Square; Venizelou Avenue, also Panepistimiou Avenue; Octovriou, also Patissiou; Mitropoleos, Metropoleos Street. Outside of Athens, the situation becomes even more confused. So you may have to check every street, restaurant, and town on your maps twice.

NATIONAL TOURIST ORGANIZATION: The **E.O.T.** Information office is at 2 Karageorgi tis Servias St., Athens (tel. 3222-545), right on Syntagma in the National Bank of Greece. In the U.S.A., it's at 645 Fifth Ave., New York, NY 10022; 611 West 6th St., Los Angeles, CA 90017; 168 North Michigan Ave., Chicago, IL 60601; and 31 State St., Boston, MA 02109; in Canada, at 2 Place Ville Marie, Montréal, Québec H3B 2C9; and 80 Bloor St., Suite 1403, Toronto, Ontario M5S 2V1.

NEWSPAPERS: English-language newspapers and magazines can be bought throughout Athens. Check with your kiosk around 6 p.m. for that day's edition of the *International Herald Tribune;* British papers arrive around 8 p.m. *The Athens News, 30 Days,* and *The Athenian* are local papers serving the English and American communities, and are worthwhile for restaurant, concert, and theater listings.

POLICE: For emergencies only, dial 100 on the telephone. The Tourist Police will handle your travel-connected problems. The address is 7 Syngrou, Athens (office number: 9239-224 or 9236-968; add the prefixed area code 01 if you're calling from outside Athens). Dial 171 for Tourist Police Information in five languages, 24 hours a day.

POSTAGE: An air mail postcard to the U.S. costs 25 drs (25¢); a letter, 32 drs (32¢) per 20 grams weight. Don't even consider surface mail: it could take up to two months. The central post office is on **Kotzia Square** at 100 Eolou St. (opposite Omonia Square). There are branches at 4 Stadiou St. (only for parcel post, and located in the Spyromilios Arcade), in the lower level of the subway station at Omonia Square, on Syntagma Square at the corner of Mitropoleos Street (open to 10 p.m.), and in the main lobby of the Athens Hilton Hotel. There is also a Central Philatelic Service of the Hellenic Post Office on the first floor above the Central Post Office of Athens at 100 Eolou St., open in the morning, in order better to serve the requirements of stamp collectors. *Note:* Packages should be left unwrapped until they've been inspected at the post office.

PRICES: As I've noted elsewhere in this guide, prices are liable to change. Probably up. It's nobody's fault, it's just the way the world is these days. So please, *please* check the rates of hotels, tours, and meals with your travel agent.

RADIO AND TV: The American Armed Forces Radio provides 24 hours of programming each day, including music, hourly newscasts, and excellent sports reporting. Hotel *television* usually costs a minimum of 250 drs ($2.50) additional per night, but features lots of English and American programs and old movies, with Greek subtitles.

SECRETARIAL SERVICE: There's an efficient, multilingual secretarial service in the **Athens Hilton.** They'll arrange contacts with local businessmen, fix you up with stenographers and interpreters, handle mail and phone messages, set up appointments. Call Elly Economopoulo-Hadziotis or the appointment secretary at 7220-201. Also, see under "Executive Services."

SHOESHINE: Shoeshine boys wait on the sidewalks at the thoroughfares with heaviest traffic. The cost is 50 to 70 drs (50¢ to 70¢), including tip and the quality is excellent. For 70 drs (70¢) you can flop down in one of the four stools of the shoeshine parlor on Filellinon Street, corner of Syntagma, where you can also have shoes repaired. Many hotels have free service.

SIESTA: They take it seriously in Athens, to the point where the police announce official siesta hours each spring (usually 2 to 5 p.m.) and will take appropriate action against anyone disturbing the Athenians' postlunch bliss.

STATIONERY: Pallis, on Ermou Street opposite the Electra Hotel, probably has the best selection, but as in all stationery stores in Athens, procedures are antiquated and service is slow. You can also have photocopying done here.

STUDENT DISCOUNTS: Valid student identification will get you discounts: to 50% on state railway travel; at a number of lodging spots (see "Hostels," above); to the Son-et-Lumière shows; at the Herod Atticus Theater; on island tours; on bus and train travel to the rest of Europe; at theaters; at all antiquity sites; in some restaurants; at a number of museums and other entertainment facilities. Two important addresses are: **Vikings's Travel Bureau,** 3 Filellinon St., Athens (tel. 3229-383), and **Lotus Student Travel,** 7 Filellinon St. (tel. 3221-680), for information on special travel rates.

SUNBATHING: The Greek sun is hot and piercing. If you overdo it and catch a burn, rub on—**yogurt.**

SWIMMING: There are no public pools in town (you can pay to swim at the Hilton or Caravel). Your best bet is to head directly for the Apollo Coast and establish a base of operations there. Smart Athenians *never* swim in the Saronic Gulf this side of Vouliagmeni because of the pollution (remember, Piraeus is a very busy port); moreover, at Glyfada and Vouliagmeni you have the problem of aircraft noise. The place Athenians head for is **Varkiza,** which is about an hour by bus from the city (it leaves from Leoforos Olgas, near the Zappeion, but you may be able to join another couple and share a taxi inexpensively). At all the beaches along the shore where you pay an admission fee you will find changing facilities and showers, and the beaches themselves are cleaned every morning; most of them also have snackbars and/or restaurants. Rates range from 45 drs (45¢) near the airport to 120 drs ($1.20) at the deluxe Astir Palace Hotel; Varkiza is in the middle range and costs less than 80 drs (80¢). *Note:* If you swim from rocks rather than sand, beware of sea urchins.

TAXIS: The rates are 20 drs (20¢) to begin, then 17 drs (17¢) per kilometer within the Athens/Piraeus area. Extras are 10 drs (10¢) for every piece of baggage, 30 drs (30¢) for any ride between midnight and 7 a.m. There is an additional charge of 20 drs (20¢) when going to or from the airport or harbor. Theoretically, there are taxi stations on or near every major square, but that doesn't necessairly mean there are any taxis at the stations. There is no telephone service for radio-controlled cabs (you have to go all the way up to a limousine for that kind of service); a recent law allows would-be passengers to flag down taxis that already have passengers and share the trip if they are going in the same general direction. This is intended to spread the taxis around, but in practice it makes a taxi more difficult to find than ever. Athenians have more money these days, and one of the ways they spend it is by taking taxis instead of buses. There's no easy answer, other than appearing on the doorstep of a deluxe hotel and tipping the doorman handsomely.

TELEGRAMS: The office at 85 Patission St., Athens, is open 24 hours a day. Another at 15 Stadiou St. has hours from 7 a.m. to midnight. There's also an office in the Athens Hilton. Daily rates to the U.S. are around 25 drs (25¢) per word, plus tax. Evening rates are half price; "urgent" is 100% more.

TELEPHONES: Public telephones are attached to the sides of kiosks, for local calls only; the cost is 5 drs (5¢), and you pay the kiosk owner. Phone booths with blue trim are for Athens calls only, with orange trim for calls outside of Athens; in either case, before dialing, the appropriate coin must be inserted. (Athens is in the process of changing its six-digit telephone system into a seven-digit system. If you dial the six-digit number and get no answer, call the operator for help.)

TELEPHONE SERVICE FROM GREECE TO U.S.A. (mainland): **Via the operator:** Station calls (first three minutes) cost 738 drs ($7.38); person-to-person calls (first three minutes) cost 1000 drs ($10); each additional minute for personal and station calls is another 132 ($1.32). The total amount of the call is subject to 8% tax.

Automatic service: From public telephone offices and coinboxes the cost is 245 drs ($2.45) per minute.

You can place telephone calls at OTE offices—85 Patission St. (open 24 hours a day), Omonia Square (open 24 hours a day), 15 Stadiou St. (open from 8 a.m. to midnight)—or dial 161 from any telephone to get the long-distance operator. When you want to communicate by I.D.D.D. system you have to dial the International prefix (00) then U.S.A. country code (1) and then the national number.

Please note that when dialing, all digits should be dialed without any pause, and there is no special signal between groups of digits. Dial 169 for recorded instructions for making international calls.

TIME: Athens time is Greenwich Mean Time plus two hours in winter, three in summer—or seven hours ahead of New York time, most of the year.

TIPPING: Porters at the airport and train station receive a fee of 50 drs (50¢) per bag minimum. Taxi drivers expect you to round off the meter in their favor. Leave chambermaids 50 drs (50¢) per day for an average stay of two or three days. Tour guides expect 100 drs ($1) or up, but *never* coins, although the tourist authorities say they don't have to be tipped at all. Theater ushers traditionally get 25 drs (25¢) for showing you to your seat. Barbers get from 20% to 30%; public room attendants get 5 to 10 drs (5¢ to 10¢); hatcheck girls get 5 to 10 drs; busboys in restaurants get the loose change.

TOILETS: Most public toilets have symbols on the doors that quite clearly distinguish between the sexes. In case they don't, however, and instead have the appropriate words in Greek, remember—the Greek word for men has six letters, the word for women has eight.

TOURIST POLICE: Dial 171 for information (hotels, shops, sports, nightclubs, etc.) in five languages, 24 hours a day.

TOURS: A great variety of organized tours is offered, from sightseeing in Athens and environs to complete tours of the Greek mainland, to air tours and cruises to the many islands. A few of the leading tour operators are: **American Express,** Constitution Square (tel. 3230-603); **Viking's Tours,** 3 Filellinon St. (tel. 3229-383); **Key Tours,** 2 Ermou St. (tel. 3232-520); **CHAT Tours,** 4 Stadiou St. (tel. 3223-137).

TRAVEL AGENTS: Here are two reliable organizations besides American Express and Viking's **American Travel,** 11 Patriarchou Ioakim, Kolonaki (tel. 733-863); **Wagons-Lits/Cooks,** 2 Karageorgi tis Servias (tel. 3242-281).

ATHENS BY THE SEA

Piraeus, Glyfada, Vouliagmeni, Sounion

THE ACROPOLIS is five miles from the sea, and in the days of Pericles it was quite a hike across the countryside to reach Phaleron Bay. Now it's a short bus ride, and the suburbs of Athens reach all the way to the edge of the sea. But the entire coast—from Piraeus in the north all the way south past the airport to Glyfada, and even as far as Lagonissi—is virtually an extension of Athens. In summer, the downtown nightclubs move out there, Athenians go to the seaside for dinner, wealthy Athenians flock out to the luxury hotels and beach houses—and stay put until September.

So, you're not really seeing Athens until you see something of its seaside satellites. In fact, if you're planning to be in these parts in midsummer you might even consider checking into a hotel by the sea and making your sightseeing excursions into town from there. Glyfada is only 20 minutes by car from downtown Athens; Vouliagmeni is 30 minutes; Piraeus, about 15 minutes.

Piraeus—Even on Sunday

The port of Piraeus is about six miles from Syntagma. In 461 B.C. Themistocles linked the two cities by his "Long Walls," but now they're intertwined by their sprawling suburbs.

Two outstanding events have taken place in the history of Piraeus. Themistocles chose the site as the home port for the Athenian fleet he was about to build—the "wooden walls" predicted by the oracle. After the Peloponnesian Wars it slumped back again to a fishing village, and when Greece became independent and Athens became the capital in the 19th century, Piraeus was a ragtag hamlet on the edge of the water.

After the turn of the century it slowly emerged as one of the major ports of the Mediterranean, thus preparing it for its second outstanding event—when Melina Mercouri made a movie called *Never on Sunday,* which has since introduced the waterfront of Piraeus and its boisterous bars to the whole world. The waterfront still looks like the movie here and there, but Piraeus has blossomed in recent years and on your way to or from your cruise ship you may want to spend an hour or two among its flower-decked boulevards and terrace cafés.

The dedicated archeologist can find many remnants of antiquity here, including traces of the Long Walls (the subway track follows roughly the same route). The city's museums of archeology and naval history are worth peeking into.

In the past few years, the city's gung-ho council has pushed ahead a rejuvenation program that included new beaches, new beach facilities, and especially the big new marina at Zea. You may be coming here at some point to catch a small ferry or hydrofoil to some of the islands, but if not, come anyway and take a look at the luxury yachts and three-masted schooners and other toys of the Mediterranean jet-set. There's a new, completely equipped marina here with restaurants, hairdressers, ship brokers, ship chandlers, and other appurtenances of seagoing. The large cruise ships, by the way, leave from the docks around Akti Miaouli and Akti Xaveriou in Piraeus port, over the hill, or around the bend.

On the opposite side of the bay is the hilly peninsula known as **Castella** (which was the site of ancient Munichia and another acropolis). It's mostly residential (very desirable, with views over the harbor and the Royal Hellenic Yacht Club next door), and there are several good restaurants and cafés up here.

Round another bend and you're into another bay and a circular harbor bobbing with more yachts and sailboats, the entire waterfront ringed with blue, yellow, and red awnings of the restaurants across the street. This is **Mikrolimano,** which you read about in an earlier chapter. In the morning it's a typical little fishing village, with the fishermen mending their nets and drying them in the sun; in the evening it's Athens's dining hall. It's one of the most romantic places for dining out along the entire coast (yet only 20 minutes by car from Syntagma, or by subway from Omonia Square to the Neon Phaleron, or New Faliron, stop). There are tables all along the waterfront, their matching restaurants across the street. After dinner you can take a half-hour trip around the harbor with a gnarled old Greek seafarer in his caique. Around midnight you still won't want to head back into town, so take your car or a taxi farther down the coast to one of the nightclubs by the sea.

THE APOLLO COAST: The next spot along the shore, known by the tourist authorities as the Apollo Coast, is **Faliron**, which away back used to be *the* harbor of Athens; then comes **Kalamaki**, which is a continuation of the nightclubs, restaurants, and tavernas of Old Faliron. The blue bus (no. 132), marked Edem, will take you from Syntagma to Faliron, and the no. 103 bus, marked Aghios Cosmas, will take you to Kalamaki, both for less than 20 drs (20¢).

Aghios Cosmas is a new beach development and sports center —two soccer fields, eight basketball courts, eight volleyball courts, two tennis courts, and a beach for 3000 bathers.

Glyfada

Glyfada is the first of the big resorts, and it's only ten miles from Athens (you can catch a no. 129 bus from Vassilissis Olgas Avenue, and the fare is only 20 drs). The main road to Sounion passes through the center of town, but turn off at the big green nightclub, Dionysios, onto the marine drive and you pass an unending stream of cafés, restaurants, tavernas, hotels, and marinas. The café/restaurants on the beach side are mostly modern places where you can have anything from pizzas to freshly caught mullet, and your dinner bill needn't go above 800 drs ($8).

One of the most famous restaurants along here is **Psaropoulos** (telephone for a reservation—8945-677), popular with politicians and high society, but rather expensive by Greek standards —say, 1200 drs ($12) and up per person, with wine.

All the way at the end of this marine drive, you'll come to a restaurant on both sides of the street, with tables right at the edge of the marina. This is **Antonopoulos** (tel. 8945-636). An order of prawns here (big ones, but only three of them) costs about 450 drs ($4.50); mullet is about 400 drs ($4). Right next to it, behind the trees and right on the beach, is the **Asteria** nightclub and taverna (tel. 8945-675). It's part of the big Astir Beach development that includes restaurants, snackbars, a bookstore, public beach ($1 admission) with pedalos and canoes (100 drs an hour). This area is also the best place to stay in Glyfada.

The **Astir Beach Bungalows** curve around one side of the bay, in groves of lemon, orange, and pine trees. The bungalows have kitchens, refrigerators, showers, closets, beach towels, 24-hour service, beach chairs, patios for dining or sunning—and all a step from the cool, clear water. In other words, you have your own private little beach house. It's classed as a deluxe hotel, so the rates in summer are 8500 drs ($85) and up for a double—but that includes breakfast, lunch or dinner, and tips. Come in April, May, September, or October, however, and you can have the same room for two-thirds the price. The complex has 120 one-room bungalows, seven two-room, and seven three-room bungalows, so it's a great place to bring the family, although its proximity to the airport may be a drawback for some people.

There are two more public beaches, with entrance fees of 50 drs (50¢), in the next village, **Voula**, but keep going another five miles to two of the stars of the coast. . . .

Kavouri and Vouliagmeni

These two are the liveliest and loveliest of the resorts within 15 miles and a 20-dr (20¢) bus fare from Athens.

They're on either side of a cape covered with pine trees, separating the bay, one half facing the ocean, the other half on the bay. The ocean beach faces a flotilla of gleaming white yachts (there are still more of them tucked away in a marina farther down the cape); the restaurants are stacked above the beaches with terraces overlooking the sea, and new hotels and apartments are stacked up behind the restaurants. There are so many new hotels going up there's no point in saying which is the best place to stay.

Except for the **Astir Palace Hotel**—one of the grand resort hotels of Europe, the playground of the shipping tycoons. The original Astir Palace Hotel has 147 rooms and 34 penthouse suites, all tastefully furnished, a palatial glass-and-marble lobby, an enormous terrace overlooking one of three private coves and its 77 relatively secluded bungalows (where the wealthiest of the wealthy Athenians idle away their summers), shaded by trees and cooled by terraced lawns. In 1979 an additional 165 rooms opened in a spectacular new wing, called the **Nafiska Astir Palace Hotel**, built into the hillside, and decorated in a lavish contemporary style. Yet another 165-room wing opened in 1984. This one, called **Aphrodite Astir Palace**, faces out to sea, all the rooms have balconies, and comes fully serviced by indoor and outdoor restaurants, boutiques, hairdresser, news ticker, and 100-car garage. In summer (June through September), a one-room suite (with bedside buttons to summon your groom or your maid, switch on the Don't Disturb sign, and dim the lights) for two costs 27,240 drs ($272) a night with breakfast and dinner; a regular deluxe room or one-room bungalow for two is 15,120 drs ($151), half board. (Prices are higher in the new wings.) But in April and October you have the accommodations for 20% to 25% less, and from November through March for 45% to 50% less, and the luxury remains, the armies of servants are still there, and even if it's too cold to swim it's perfect for playing tennis and hiking on the cape. This is certainly class, Greek style.

In the same deluxe league but newer, the **Apollon Palace Hotel** towers nine stories above the beach at Kavouri, just before Vouliagmeni. Its 284 guest rooms are decorated in Scandinavian modern, with air conditioning, marble bathrooms, and balconies overlooking the bay; sporting facilities include three swimming pools (including one indoors), bowling alley, waterskiing, windsurfing, pedalos, and tennis court. (*Note:* This hotel was closed during 1984, but is likely to be functioning again under new management in 1985. Check with your travel agent.)

SOUTH TO SOUNION: But the best is yet to come. From Vouliagmeni to Cape Sounion (about 40 miles from Athens) the coastline twists and turns around beaches and rocky coves; a beautiful scenic highway winds alongside, sometimes by the edge of the sea, sometimes up on the cliffs. This is the true Apollo Coast. And from the point of view of sunning and swimming, it's worth the extra miles and minutes from Athens, because here you'll find less pollution and less noise from the aircraft landing at Hellinikon Airport. Try, for example, the town of **Varkiza**, where the beach has small bungalows rentable by the day (about $8, no resrevations required), and a good, inexpensive, self-service cafeteria. For a hotel, try the 32-room Class B **Varkiza** or Class A **Glaros.**

South of Varkiza there are half a dozen small towns, most of them being spruced up and "resortified," and you now have a choice of about a dozen hotels in these parts. The most popular of these towns is **Lagonissi,** 25 miles from Athens, where you'll find one of the complete tourist villages set up in recent years by the Greek government—hotels, bungalows, chapel, kindergarten, tavernas, open-air cinema, sauna, beauty parlor, shopping center, beaches, tennis courts—all carefully landscaped to disguise any hint of concrete overkill. You can sunbathe here on any of five beaches, waterski, and snorkel in the clearest of waters. The rate structure at the **Xenia Lagonissi** needs a computer to figure out the variations for the complex's 99 rooms, 15 suites, and 243 bungalows (in three sizes). In summer you're obliged to take half board, which will set you back 6256 drs ($63) or thereabouts in a double room or bungalow; from November through mid-March, rates are about 30% less. *Note:* There's a free, direct service by private coach between Athens and Lagonissi (a taxi or limousine, on the other hand, will cost you about $15).

Another up-and-coming resort along this stretch is **Anavyssos**, where the Class A **Alexander Beach** and the B Class **Eden Beach Hotel** have practically taken over the town (almost 400 rooms between them); but your final goal is Cape Sounion, specifically, the romantic Temple of Poseidon, perched on top of the cliff.

Cape Sounion

You get your first glimpse of the temple from the coastal road, several twists and bays before you actually get to the cape. First you see it, then you don't. Finally you're there. The **Temple of Poseidon** was built in 444 B.C., probably by the architect who designed the Temple of Theseus in Athens, and only 15 of its original 34 Doric columns remain. But it's still one of the most dramatic sights of Greece. Lord Byron was so carried away by it that he carved his initials on one of the columns (you try that today and *you'll* be carried away). The site is closed on Tuesday. Admission is 50 drs (50¢). After you've tramped around this sea-girt acropolis, go down to the bay for a swim (the beach is nothing special but the water and the view are), or lunch at one of the waterfront tavernas.

If you decide to stay overnight, you have a choice of three Class A hotels in Sounion: the 90-room **Belvedere Park** (2775 drs, or $28, for two with half board), the 45-room **Egeon** (3691 drs, or $37, for two with half board) and the 152-room **Cape Sounion Beach Hotel** 5080 drs, or $51, for two with half board); the largest resort in the area is the Class B **Surf Beach Club** with beds for over 500 guests (2953 drs, or $49, for two with half board).

Note: There's an alternative, picturesque route back to Athens from Sounion, following the valleys and wine villages of the interior. It's a tough decision which to take—coastal or inland.

Bets are you'll want to enjoy the constantly changing shore, the sparkling water that changes from deep blue to turquoise from bay to bay, the islands and sailboats and fishing boats along the way. In any case, most people want to stay at Sounion until the sun sets beside the Temple of Poseidon, so you may be driving back in the dark anyway. In which case, stop off at the Astir Palace in Vouliagmeni for dinner, or one of the fine seafood restaurants and beachside tavernas along the coast if you're less than impeccably dressed.

Greek fishing boats

DAY TRIPS FROM ATHENS

YOU'LL BE AMAZED how many trips to how many historic sites you can make from Athens. Many of them can be completed in one day—there and back. To get some idea of the choices you have, skim through the catalog of the CHAT tour people: half-day tours to Cape Sounion and the Temple of Poseidon, half-day tours to Ancient Corinth and the Corinth Canal, half-day tours to Attica and Marathon, one-day tours to Mycenae, Nafplion, Epidaurus, Thebes, and Delphi. You can even make one-day mini-odysseys to the Greek islands—and still be back in Athens in time for a night on the Plaka.

You've already read about Cape Sounion and the Apollo Coast in the preceding chapter. Now here's a quick briefing on some of the other sights. Although I have grouped them here as *day* trips, you may decide (wisely) to stay overnight, so I've included some comments, where appropriate, on accommodations.

Daphni

Daphni is so close to Athens (five miles to the northwest) it doesn't really merit a tour on its own, so it's often included in the itineraries of other tours, especially during the **Wine Festival** held every summer (July through September). You pay the small admission charge (around $1), then sample as many local wines as you can handle. With a deal like that, your best idea is to take the special bus, no. 864, rather than go by car—the bus fare is only 20 drs (20¢), and the bus leaves from Koumoundouros Square.

The other attraction in Daphni, year round, is the medieval monastery dedicated to the **Dormition of the Virgin Mary**. It was built on the site of an earlier temple, in a grove of laurel trees, dedicated to the laurel-bearing god Apollo. The present church, which dates from the 11th century, is noted for its inlaid mosaics on a golden background, and for its cloisters, cells, and sarcophagi. Opening hours vary with time of the year and day of the week, but as of press time it was temporarily closed—check with the Tourist Organization before you leave Athens.

Kaisariani

A half-hour ride in the opposite direction on bus 234 from downtown Athens and a pleasant half-hour walk from the bus terminal brings you to the delightful 11th-century mini-monastery of Kaisariani, or Caesariani. You can cheat and take a taxi for the last stage rather than walking, but then you won't appreciate the ice-cold water that gushes from the fountain in the monastery wall. In ancient times these waters were believed to cure sterility, and they are still believed to have healthful if not magical qualities. It's quite safe to drink, and you will see many Greeks filling huge containers from the fountain. You can visit the monastery's mill, bakery, bath house, refectory, and church, all in 20 minutes, if you wish; but it's much better to sit and relax in the peaceful surroundings for a spell before strolling back to the bus terminal. Kaisariani lies almost at the base of Mount Hymettos, so quiet and peaceful it's difficult to believe you are just beyond the suburbs of Athens. Buses run every 15 minutes, more or less, from Polygonon, but there's also a stop on Kaningos Street, near Omonia. Since there seems to be some doubt about when the monastery closes officially (2, 3, or 5 p.m.), make this a morning excursion.

Delphi

The famous city of the oracle is in that richly historical part of Greece known as Boeotia. Thermopylae and Thebes are not far off. Delphi itself is 110 miles from Athens, and the combination of ruggedly grand scenery and the haunting quality of the ruins makes it one of the most dramatic sights in all of Greece.

For centuries the story of Delphi was the story of Mediterranean politics. Hardly a decision was reached without consulting the oracles at the Apollon Temple. Evidently, the mountain exuded strange fumes (now considered water vapors or carbon monoxide), which put shepherds and peasant women into trances and led to prophetic pronouncements. In the magnificent setting of Mount Parnassos, with eagles soaring from peak to peak, it was easy to believe that here you stood in the presence of the gods.

Initially the name of the site was Pytho, and the Earth Mother known for her prophetic powers lived here. Later, seafarers from Knossos introduced the cult of Apollo Delphinius. The story starts with Apollo disguising himself as a dolphin. He jumps into the water and captures a Cretan ship, returning both booty and prisoners to Delphi. The prisoners become "priests" in his sanctuary and Delphi's reputation for wisdom and prophecy is consolidated.

Nearby personages came to consult with the gods. And as was the custom, they brought gifts. From the eighth to the fourth centuries B.C., before an envious Nero looted the temples after Rome's conquest, the gift-giving and advice-seeking rose to such proportions that Delphi became a huge complex of treasuries and temples, all laden with works of art and riches.

Today, Delphi consists mainly of a theater, a sanctuary, an athletic area surrounded by a wall, and an excellent museum. But it is more than a ruins-cum-museum site: it is a total environment. Start your exploration from the main road, which leads both to the town and the ruins. Gaze toward the ruins, noting the distant views, the colors (especially at sunset and sunrise), the sheer valley below. Then amble through the ruins, starting with the **Marmaria** and the **Castalian Spring**, both of which are located below the main road. The ancient Greeks regarded springs as a gift of the gods. Steps leading to the water can be seen carved into the solid rock surface. Then walk up the hill beyond the road, onto the main site.

The **Sacred Way** is a path leading from the entrance to the stadium. Follow it as it zigs and zags between half-columns, perches, stones, and the **Treasury of the Athenians**. The Treasury is easy to recognize: it is almost completely reconstructed, using the original blocks of Parian marble. Look for the inscription written on the marble: "The Athenians dedicate to Apollo the Persian spoils from the Battle of Marathon."

At the top of the ruins site is the **theater**, built for an audience of 5000, a model of engineering and aesthetic brilliance; and farther up the hill there is a fifth-century stadium almost 200 yards long.

Returning from the ruins to town, stop at the **museum** near the entrance to the site and go immediately to the *Charioteer*, the famous bronze sculpture from the fifth century B.C., and one of the great masterpieces of Greek art. The museum's art pieces are mainly from the Mycenaean period (1600 –1100 B.C.). Note particularly the Roman *Statue of Antinous*, a column of *Acanthus Dancing Girls*, and the *Wingless Sphinx of the Naxians*, a characteristic work of the sixth century B.C.

For at least six centuries Delphi's priests held most of the known world in thrall. Their ambiguous interpretations of the unintelligible ramblings from the "oracle" changed the course of history many times—and brought riches and incalculable power to a canny bunch of priests in a tiny mountainous village.

How it all began doesn't appear to be on record, but from the seventh century B.C. onward, the god known as Phoebus Apollo was heard to be speaking through the mouth of an old woman known as the Pythia, and what she said, after being placed into neat hexameters by the priest-interpreters, made kings tremble and emperors lose their sleep.

Ordinary people consulted the oracle too, of course; the gods were willing to answer the question of anybody who brought money. More often than not, important people brought silver, gold, precious stones, and other gifts, and Delphi soon built up considerable treasure.

There was a set routine for the Pythia to follow on pronouncement days (which at first took place only during February, the month of Apollo's birthday), and it was strictly adhered to by one Pythia after another through the centuries.

First, the woman had to fast for three days and then, on the set day, bathe in the nearby Castalian Spring, burn laurel leaves at the altar, drink some water, and take up her place beside the copper-and-gold tripod which was set up over the fissure in the ground from which came "intoxicating vapors." Working her way into a trance she would then mumble garbled replies to questions asked of her. Sometimes the questions concerned banal personal problems and sometimes they concerned matters of state. But all got answers, usually so cryptic that they could be construed to mean anything at all, and seekers invariably went away happy.

A king, who was told that if he crossed a certain river a great empire would be destroyed, was chagrined to discover that the empire was his own. A man who came to ask about his stammer was instructed to go live in another country. The Roman emperor Nero was warned to "beware 73"—and died well before he reached that age at the hands of Galvus, who was 73.

Naturally there were some skeptics, among them Aesop, but

the Delphi city fathers had providentially anticipated that by instituting formal trials for those they charged with sacrilege, and the sentence was usually to be tossed off a high cliff onto the jagged rocks below.

That well-known heretic Socrates may well have been thinking about Delphi when he announced that "the augur should be under the authority of the general and not the general under the authority of the augur."

This advice should have been taken to heart in 480 B.C., when Xerxes prepared to invade Greece with the combination of a massive army and fleet of ships. Athenians consulted the Delphic Oracle to find out what to do. They were told:

Wretches why sit ye here? Fly, fly to the ends of creation.
Nay, not alone shall ye suffer, full many a town shall be leveled;
Many a shrine of the gods will he give to fiery destruction
Get ye away from the Temple and brood on the doom that awaits you.

Athens, and most of Greece, was naturally in a panic. The message, for once, hardly seemed ambiguous, and some were ready to take it at face value and flee in panic. But wiser counsels prevailed and the Athenians and their Spartan allies held the northern passes until Themistocles built up the navy (here the Delphic Oracle redeemed itself somewhat with a prediction that the city would be saved by its "wooden walls") and eventually repelled the invasion attempt.

Delphi never entirely recovered from this erroneous taking of sides, however, and although the world rallied with contributions after an earthquake almost destroyed the town in 373 B.C., the oracle's influence continued to decline.

But worse was to come. In 356 B.C. a band of Phocians from the west suddenly invaded the town and captured the shrine along with all its wealth. For a time they terrorized their neighbors by raising an army of mercenaries paid with their newfound treasure, but eventually the shrine was restored to the priests to continue their prognostications for three centuries more.

The coming of the Christian era was the beginning of the end, and in A.D. 381 the emperor Theodosius outlawed "paganism" and Delphi passed into history.

HOW TO GET TO DELPHI: The simplest way is to take a one-day coach tour, in air-conditioned comfort, with a guide to explain the ruins and sights along the way. **Key Tours, American Express,** and **CHAT** operate one-day tours (8:30 a.m. to 6:30 p.m.), costing 3050 drs ($31) including lunch (2500, or $25, without lunch), admission fee, and a visit to the nearby monastery of Ossios Lucas. The two-day tour is much better if you can afford the time, because you can spend more time among the magnificent ruins and see them (and photograph them) at sunrise or sunset; this full 34-hour tour costs 4020 drs ($67), with half board, in air-conditioned hotels. The cheapest way to reach Delphi is by regular bus service—only 840 drs ($8.40) round trip, with a choice of five departures daily from the bus terminal on Liossion Street, a three-hour trip each way. The most convenient way to get to Delphi is undoubtedly to rent a car and drive; for the first third of the trip you'll be driving on the relatively fast but tricky Athens–Thessaloniki National Highway, then after an hour you turn off at the Delphi sign and start heading up into the mountains (where the roads are being improved enormously). This is a tough trip, and you should either leave very early in the morning to get to the site before the museum closes for siesta, or arrive in time for a leisurely lunch, an afternoon visit to the ruins and the museum, lingering there through sunset, then facing the after-dark drive back to Athens (allow four hours in this case). Better still, stay the night in Delphi and drive back the next day, stopping at the quaint hilltop town of Arahova and the monastery of Ossios Lucas along the way.

HOTELS IN DELPHI: For a tiny town (population 800), Delphi certainly offers visitors a vast selection of accommodations, but then it's had a long time to practice being a host. The main street alone has over a dozen hotels, most of them inexpensive; those on the left side as you walk into the town are the most interesting, because they're perched on the edge of a cliff looking all the way across the plain to the Gulf of Corinth. Try the **Iniochos** (Class B, 15 rooms with private baths) or **Hermes** (Class C) for reliable accommodations around 1500 drs ($15) double. The **Castalia,** also on the cliff side of the street, is an elderly Class B hotel with a large dining terrace overlooking the valley. The three most interesting hotels in Delphi are the 61-room **Vouzas** (closest to the ruins), a Class A hotel built in tiers *down* the side of the cliff; the 50-room Class A **Xenia**, and above all, literally and otherwise, the handsome Class A, 185-room **Amalia**, a spacious affair of granite, marble, polished wood, modern and comfortable furniture, and well-equipped guest rooms that rent for around 3200 drs ($32) for a double per night. The Amalia, Delphi, Vouzas, and Castalia all have attractive dining rooms (the Amalia most of all), but you'll probably want to sample one of Delphi's tavernas with large, sometimes windswept terraces, overlooking the gulf and the plain (all that greenery you see down there, by the way, is the topside of something like 3 million olive trees); you can dine on these terraces for less than 600 drs ($6).

Marathon

This, of course, is where the famous battle was fought in 490 B.C., when the Athenians trounced the Persians and the messenger ran the 26 miles back to the city, gasped out the news of victory, and flopped down dead. The site of the battle is now marked by a barrow in which the Greek soldiers were buried, and a white marble column. Buses leave Athens (from the terminal at 29 Mavromateon St.) to the Marathon battlefield approximately every half hour—one hour and 100 drs ($1) each way.

The Peloponnese

The next batch of destinations are all on the peninsula known as the Peloponnese ("the land of Pelops"), the almost-island chunk of land that makes up the southwestern corner of Greece. It's a region of mountain scenery highlighted by an incredible collection of ancient monuments and brightened by flashes of beach and sea.

CORINTH: The first landmark you come to in the Peloponnese is the city of Corinth, or rather the **Corinth Canal.** This channel, 3½ miles long and 75 feet wide, makes the peninsula an island, and chops 185 miles from the voyage between Italy and Piraeus. It was built between 1882 and 1893, but it was originally conceived way back in the days of Nero and Hadrian. In fact, Nero got so far as to dig the first shovelful—with a golden spade. But it didn't get much beyond Nero's first shovelful, and shipowners had to continue hauling their ships overland, over the *diolkos,* a stonepaved track, traces of which you can still see here and there.

This suited the Corinthians fine, because they supplied the hauling power and collected the fees. They also collected tolls on all cargos heading between the peninsula and the mainland, and between the Gulf of Corinth and the Saronic Gulf. Their wealth made them self-indulgent, and at one point the city could boast 1000 "sacred prostitutes" who plied their trade in the name and to the honor of Aphrodite. No wonder St. Paul came along and gave the Corinthians a tongue-lashing. The tribune where he delivered his sermon is still there in Ancient Corinth. There are now two Corinths. The new city was destroyed by an earthquake in 1928 and an even newer one was built after that. Its main interest for visitors is as a base for excursions to the fascinating surroundings. The more fascinating of the two is **Ancient Corinth.** It too was completely destroyed—by the Romans in 146 B.C.—and most of what you see today dates from 44 B.C. when Caesar set up a colony there. The principal sites are the sixth-century Temple of Apollo, Saint Paul's tribune, the agora, and the Pirene fountain.

Acrocorinth is a mighty citadel towering over the town. This was originally the site of the Temple of Aphrodite. The citadel was built by the Byzantines, and at various states subtracted from or added to by Crusaders, Venetians, and Turks. Today you get a great view from the top. You can drive to the entrance up a precipitous dirt road, and both the view and the citadel justify the effort. There's a coffeeshop at the top of the hill.

How to Get to Corinth

The full-day sightseeing tours leave Athens at 8:30 a.m. and return at 7 p.m., after stops also at Mycenae, Nafplion, and Epidaurus, and cost 2500 drs ($25) without lunch, 3050 drs ($31) with. You can also get there by diesel train, rail, or bus from Athens (check with your hotel concierge for times and fares); or in roughly 1½ hours by car, on the National Highway.

Hotels

The new **King Saron** (156 Class A rooms) at Isthmia, the **Kalamaki Beach** (Class A, 66 rooms) at Paleon Kalamaki, and the 48-room Class B **Almyri Beach** at Almyri are all a short drive from the center of town; downtown, the Class B **Kypselos** has

18 rooms, all with private bath and larger-than-usual beds, about 990 drs ($16.50) double.

EPIDAURUS: This town, 20 miles from Nafplion, but on the Saronic Gulf, is famed for two things. In the sixth century it was a place of pilgrimage, a sort of Lourdes, where sick people journeyed to find a cure in the **sanctuary of Asclepius,** the god of healing. There was more than faith involved, however, and you can still see inscriptions of prescriptions in the sanctuary, and in the nearby **museum,** as well as the votive offerings brought by the people who had been cured. (*Note:* There's a whole room of the National Archeological Museum in Athens devoted to friezes and statues on this subject—always with an oversize god-doctor seated nonchalantly at his desk, while Hygeia his nurse collects the loot from the patients, who are usually depicted as small and humble. Sound familiar?)

Other sights at Epidaurus include the **Greek Bath** (where the sick washed themselves), the **Abaton** (the so-called portico of incubation), where the sick slept on beds waiting for an apparition of the god who would cure them in their sleep, the **Roman bath, the stadium,** and the **museum** (admission: 100 drs, or $1, but free on Sunday and Thursday; closed Tuesday).

The other great sight of Epidaurus is the ancient **theater** with its circular "orchestra" and 50 tiers for 14,000 spectators. It was built in the fourth century B.C. by Polycleitus the Younger, who ought to be around today to teach acoustics to his successors: despite its size and its age, the acoustics of Epidaurus are so perfect you can hear the performers' gowns trailing across the stage. Fortunately, you can still enjoy the benefits of these acoustics, because performances are given here every summer during the **Epidaurus Festival** (it's in June and July, and the National Tourist Organization can give you details of dates and plays).

How to Get to Epidaurus

You can get to Epidaurus by regular bus service from Athens via Nafplion, about 500 drs ($5) one way. During the festival, there's a special pullman bus service from Athens direct to

Epidaurus on days of the performance only (but you'd better have your hotel concierge make a reservation in advance).

MYCENAE: Identified on some maps, signposts, and guides as Mikine. Either way it's the mountain palace-fortress of Agamemnon, "lord of the many islands and all of Argos" (this part of the Peloponnese, including Nafplion and Epidaurus, is in a region known as the Argolis). This is the place that gave its name to an entire civilization that was cock-of-the-walk in the 14th century B.C., although some of the archeological digs have uncovered evidence that the area was inhabited as early as 3000 B.C. What you see here today are the impressive entrance (the **Lion Gate**), and the remains of granaries, reservoirs, and the **shaft graves** that sheltered the golden treasures of Mycenaean art (Homer's "Golden Mycenae") for all those thousands of years, before they were carted off to the National Archeological Museum in Athens. Just outside the fortress walls, you can see nine **beehive tombs,** one of which is thought to be the tomb of Clytemnestra (who, you'll remember, bumped off her husband, Agamemnon, before she in turn was disposed of by her son, Orestes); one of the others is probably the tomb of Agamemnon himself. Admission to the site is 100 drs ($1); closed Tuesday; open to 3 p.m. in summer, 3:30 p.m. in winter, 4 p.m. on Sunday and holidays all year.

How to Get to Mycenae

Take the regular bus from Athens to Nafplion and get off at Argos, where you catch a local bus to Mycenae; there's also a train service from Athens to Fichtia, a couple of miles by bus from the ruins.

Corinth, Mycenae, Nafplion, and Epidaurus are included in one-day (one-crowded-day) sightseeing tours from Athens, leaving at 8:30 a.m. and returning at 7 p.m., and costing 3050 drs ($31), including lunch at Nafplion.

NAFPLION: I've kept this one to the end of the Eastern Peloponnese group because although Nafplion is an easy day trip from Athens, it also makes an ideal tour center if you want to stay overnight (or nights) and do a series of morning and afternoon excursions to Mycenae, Epidaurus, and other attractions such as the ruins of ancient Tiryns, or for longer trips, to Porto Heli and the island of Spetsai.

Depending on your first impression, Nafplion is either a holiday resort, or a medieval fortress town, or a picturesque little port. A walk around town tells you it's all three. Nafplion was also at one time the capital of Greece, right after its liberation from the Turks. The tiny island fortress, **Bourtzi**, out in the bay, was built by Venetians; the **Acronafplion** citadel towering over the town's south side was built on the site of an even more ancient acropolis; and the town's third fortress, **Palamidi**, is actually seven fortresses in one, built by the Franks and added to by several later conquerors. Nafplion is now a pleasant resort, its waterfront lined with cafés and tavernas, with steep stairways leading to narrow streets lined with more tavernas, some boutiques, and a few boîtes. If you walk past the cafés, you'll find a narrow pathway by the sea running around the base of the Acronafplion; at the opposite end it leads up to the fortress itself, where you can take the elevator of the deluxe Xenia Palace Hotel back down to town.

How to Get to Nafplion

You can get there by regular hourly bus service from Athens, and it's also included on most of the one-day and two-day coach tours to the Peloponnese.

Hotels

If you decide to stay overnight there's a wider selection of hotels here than in other towns in the region. However, since it's also one of the most popular spots in Greece at any time of the year you must always make reservations in advance; you may have to pay a half-board rate; and the attitude of the hotel personnel, especially in the two Xenias, tends to be off-hand.

The 154-room deluxe **Xenia Palace** is the most interesting hotel in town, built right on top of the Acronafplion, with all its rooms overlooking the bay and Bourtzi (doubles with half board at 5640 drs, or $56); its namesake, the 58-room **Xenia Hotel** is nearby, on the shoulder of the acropolis with half its rooms facing the bay, half facing the gulf and the fortress of Palimida, possibly the more interesting view of the two (doubles with half board at 4488 drs, or $49).

In town itself, the top hotel is the Class A **Amphitryon**, with 46 rooms, many overlooking the bay (doubles at 3597 drs, or $36); the 40-room Class B **Agamemnon** is right on the waterfront with a roof taverna for summer dining (doubles at 1854 drs, or

$19); and the popular 70-room Class C **Dioscouri** is alongside one of the stepped streets (doubles at 1300 drs, or $13).

A new deluxe **Amalia Hotel** opened in 1983, which is giving some much-needed competition to the Xenias. The new hotel is in the neoclassical style, near the waterfront, with 175 air-conditioned rooms, pool, and stylish restaurant. Doubles here cost about 5000 drs ($50), with half board.

And there you have a cluster of some of the most famous spots in history, and I've covered only one small corner of the Peloponnese; but you'll learn about Arcadia, Sparta, and Olympia in a later chapter, since they are too far from Athens to be accessible on one-day trips (but not too far from Nafplion).

The $25 Mini-Odyssey

Everybody wants to see the Greek islands, but not everyone has the time to be away from Athens for a few days. No problem. You just take the subway down to Piraeus, hop on a ferry, and sail across to an island with pine-clad hills, valleys of vineyards and pistachio trees, and a ruined temple overlooking a bay; or an island with a harbor ringed by restaurants and surrounded by a hillside of small palazzos; or an island with no cars where the only way to get around is by horse-drawn carriage or the back of a donkey. Better, call CHAT, Viking Tours, Key Tours, American Express, or some other tour operator, have them pick you up at your hotel, drive you to Paleon Phaleron—and leave everything else to them.

"Everything else" will add up to a memorable day that's part Mediterranean cruise exploration, part sightseeing, part sunning, and wholly relaxing. Say you decide to take the cruise—a bus will collect you, transfer you to a second bus and drive you down to Paleon Phaleron, a new marina at the end of Syngron Avenue, where you'll board your cruise ship and head out of the harbor past the private yachts and the three-masted schooners waiting patiently for busy shipping tycoons to come and take them out for a sail.

There are currently half a dozen ships operating this three-island cruise of the Saronic Gulf—some as big as 3000 tons, some with cabins you can rent by the day. All of them have swimming pools, plenty of deck space for sunning, as well as dining salons, lounges, bars, hostesses, and boutiques for souvenirs and film.

Your first port of call, 1¼ hours out, is the island of **Aegina**.

This is the closest island to Athens, and consequently one of the busiest on weekends. Aegina is a hilly little island, with a precipitous town perched above the dock, with a few cafés, a bakery shop, a souvenir shop or two, and a movie house.

You can go to the beach here, or you can join a tour up through the pistachio plantations and vineyards to the almost mystical **Temple of Aphaea**, "a very ancient local deity," with a hexastyle Doric temple built of local limestone. Back on board it's time to have lunch (a simple tray-lunch). An hour later you come to one of the most interesting parts of the cruise as the ship squeezes through the Strait of Poros.

Poros is a conical island with a tiny village (also called Poros) that's a classic of its kind—a jumble of whitewashed buildings piled above the harbor, which is also the roadway which is also the sidewalk which is also the plaza, and is totally hidden under a mass of awnings and café tables that come right down to the edge of the water. Unfortunately, some of the ships don't stop here, so you may want to mark Poros down in your diary as one of those places you have to come back to some day.

Next stop is **Hydra**, a bleak, rocky, undulating island, until you get into the harbor which you immediately recognize from a thousand photographs. It's unique. The ship sails right into this small bowl-like haven, almost right into the nearest café, next to the fishing boats and the tiny ferries that shuttle cargo and people back and forth to the Peloponnese. Hydra had its heyday in the time of Napoleon, when more than 30,000 people lived here; now the population is down to a little more than 2000, and most of them are the artists or writers or gallivanting jet-setters. The town is different from any other in these parts because it's terraced with a type of house, or rather mansion, known as the Hydriot palazzo, dating from the 18th century. It's one of the prettiest harbors you'll find anywhere, complete with a cathedral, belfry, the School for Training Merchant Navy Officers, and dozens of stores selling souvenirs and some of the niftiest handicraft bargains in the islands. You have an hour and a half here, so you can either flop into one of the cafés and admire the harbor, or wander around to the rocky cove on the other side of the bay and join the artists, writers, and jet-setters in the unbelievably clear rock-bound sea. (*Note:* Some of the ships reverse this itinerary, giving you longer on Hydra.)

By the time you sail for home the sun is low in the sky and glistening on the sea, and you can enjoy a comfortable cocktail on deck; by the time you get to Piraeus and the waiting buses, the sun has settled behind the mountains of the Peloponnese. You've cruised on the Mediterranean, you've seen three islands, and you've probably had a swim in the "Med." Not a bad day for 2500 drs ($25) or thereabouts. (The sightseeing trip on Aegina costs an extra 350 drs, or $3.50.)

INDEPENDENT TRIPS: If you don't feel like following an organized itinerary, you can easily get to any of these islands by ferryboat or hydrofoil. That way you get to go ashore at Poros too, and you'll also be able to visit the fourth and farthest island of the group, Spetsai (the one with no cars), and maybe catch a glimpse of Spetsopoula, the private island of Stavros Niarchos, the *other* shipping tycoon. There's plenty to see on all of these islands—ruined temples, monasteries, picturesque fishing villages with almost as many tavernas as houses—but most people come over to find a secluded stretch of beach (and there are hundreds of those).

Aegina

Perhaps the most interesting, as well as most accessible, of these islands for a one-day excursion is Aegina, mentioned above. To get there independently, you go down to Zea Marina as early as possible in the morning and take the first available regular ferry, express ferry, or hydrofoil (the hydrofoil takes only 35 minutes; the ferry, 75 minutes). When you arrive at the main town of Aegina, find out when the next bus leaves for Aghia Marina; while you're waiting, stroll along the front and have an ouzo with a small platter of freshly grilled octopus. The bus takes you right across the island through fig and pistachio plantations, past vineyards and across the mountains to your first stop, the Temple of Aphaia, a sixth-century B.C. marvel in limestone perched at the top of a steep hill above Aghia Marina, a temple which some people rate alongside those at Delphi and Sounion. Pause and marvel. Have a coffee or soft drink, while you decide on your next move. If you opt for sunbathing and swimming, take the bus on down to Aghia Marina (or follow the path down through the fields and vineyards, a 20-minute hike). During the summer months, incidentally, you can catch the boat back to the mainland from Aghia Marina.

If, instead, you opt for more sightseeing, get on a bus heading back to the town of Aegina and ask the conductor to put you off at Paleochora (if the bus is crowded, sit near the driver and keep reminding him). At Paleochora (rough translation, "old town," it was once the ancient capital), leave the bus and strike off right, up the hillside, until you come to a hill dotted with numerous tiny churches and monasteries. Right at the top of this hill there's also a ruined castle. Peek inside some of the churches along the way to admire the Byzantine frescoes, some of them barely visible. You should allow yourself a good two hours for this visit (and wear sturdy walking shoes). In springtime the hillside is a riot of red and yellow flowers; in midsummer it's a good idea to take a bottle of water with you as the nearest café is opposite the bus stop, back down by the main road. A word of advice: Before setting off into the hinterland of Aegina, check the times of the last ferries back to Piraeus, but don't wait for the last one, and buy your ticket in advance. All Athens, it seems, heads for Aegina on weekends in summer.

Ferry Services from Piraeus

To	No. of departures		One-way fares
	Weekdays	Weekends	(third class)
Aegina	32	48	222 drs
Poros	12	12	320 drs
Hydra	4	4	352 drs
Spetsai	4	4	462 drs

Fares are subject to change, and may be 20% higher. All will be under $9, round trip. For further information, phone 4120-808.

Flying Dolphins

During the summer months (and on calm days in spring and fall) you also have the choice of a **hydrofoil** trip to these islands aboard the Flying Dolphins of Ceres Flying Hydroways. They're Russian-built hydrofoils; they tend to be noisy; there's very little deck space on top and no air conditioning below; the fares are almost double those of the regular ferryboat; and the ride can be unpleasant on choppy seas. Nevertheless, the hydrofoils do get you to the islands quickly (just two hours all the way to Spetsai), so they're popular with Athenians. The Flying Dolphins now also serve four locations on the Peloponnese coast (Porto Heli, Leonidion, Nafplion, and, Monemvassia), getting you there in much less time than by car (but if the sea is rough you may prefer the traffic jams).

For full details of all schedules to these islands, check with the reception desk of your hotel, or with the National Tourist Organization information services at Syntagma; don't be discouraged if they hedge their answers, because the published schedules don't always tally with reality. In addition, double-check your ticket as soon as you pay for it, to make sure it's for the correct shipping company and correct vessel and correct destination; mistakes have been made, and it's usually impossible to have your money refunded. But don't let these words of caution dissuade you—your trip to the Saronic islands can be one of the highlights of your vacation.

Sample Flying Dolphin fares from Zea Marina

Zea to Aegina	316 drs	($3)
Zea to Hydra	812 drs	($8)
Zea to Spetsai	907 drs	($9)
Zea to Monemvassia	1516 drs	($15)

Fares are subject to change without notice. For further information, phone the Flying Dolphins at 4527-107.

Sounion, Temple of Poseidon

TOURING THE HINTERLANDS

BACK IN Chapter III you read a basic outline of what constitutes the nation known as Greece; now I'll fill in some of the details of the country beyond Athens. You can get to most parts of mainland Greece relatively easily and relatively quickly from Athens by car, bus, train, or plane, and there's certainly plenty to see once you get out there. In fact, there may be too much, and you may find it almost impossible to decide how to fit everything into one short vacation.

The Western Peloponnese

In the chapter on one-day trips from Athens you read about the highlights of the eastern part of this peninsula (Epidaurus, Mycenae, and Corinth); the *Western* Peloponnese is a shade too far to be tackled on a one-day round trip—yet the chances are that you will want to visit Sparta, Olympia, and the district known as Arcadia, where Pan and the nymphs frolicked.

Arcadia is a region of rugged mountains rising to 3500 feet or thereabouts, with many pleasant drives along winding roads through ancient villages and fir forests. Two of the most interesting towns in the Western Peloponnese are **Sparta,** which was the seat of the great military power that battled Athens in the Peloponnesian Wars, although not much remains of its former glory; and **Mistras** (or Mystra), where there is more to see—scores of Byzantine monasteries, palaces, and citadels in an extraordinary setting.

The main goal of visitors to this part of Greece is **Olympia,** where you can still see traces of the stadium where the first Olympics were held. Olympia was dedicated to Zeus, and at its peak was an impressive collection of temples, altars, statues, and treasuries. It survived for over ten centuries, until A.D. 426 when Theodosius II commanded that the temples be destroyed. The games, which were also in honor of Zeus, were held for the first time in 776 B.C., and then every fourth year thereafter, from June until September. They were heralded each time by messengers setting off in every direction to announce the start of the sacred truce, during which all warfare and squabbling among the city-states had to be suspended: for four months, the gods and heroes and everyone else in the neighborhood concentrated on running, wrestling, chariot races, horse races, the pentathlon, and, eventually, artistic and literary contests. The names of the victors in each contest were recorded alongside the date of each Olympic Games. You can still see traces of the stadium and temples, the monuments and statues, and the starting block for 20 runners. The **museum** of Olympia houses many intriguing finds unearthed during excavations, but its most famous exhibit is the famed *Hermes* of Praxiteles, standing nobly in a room all by itself.

There are other virtually unknown spots you might want to include on a tour of the Western Peloponnese: **Kyllini,** set among forests of wild oak and eucalyptus, was famous for centuries as a spa and is currently one of the largest holiday complexes in the Peloponnese; **Pylos,** built in tiers at the southern end of the Bay of Navarino, is a historic town in its own right but it is also close to the more famous ruins of the **Palace of Nestor** and the two formidable Venetian fortresses at **Methani** and **Koroni.**

Central Greece

Take the National Highway from Athens to the north and you come to the regions known as Boeotia, Thessaly, and Epirus, none of which means a great deal to the average visitor until they discover that these are the lands of Delphi (which you read about in an earlier chapter), Thermopylae, Meteora, Ioannina, and Missolonghi, all names ringing with myth and history.

North of Delphi, the National Highway follows the outline of the Gulf of Evoikos (which separates the Greek mainland from the island of Evia) and the Gulf of Pagasitikos, past the port of Volos, and across the plain to Larissa. The capital of Thessaly, **Larissa** has several fine hotels, which make it a convenient base for exploring, but the main attraction in these parts is almost 70 kilometers to the west—Meteora.

Long before they reach **Meteora,** visitors can see what the place's fascination is all about—great columns of rock soar almost 2000 feet into the air, and topping them off are precariously perched monasteries. In all, there are 24 of these eyrie-like monasteries at Meteora; only two of them are still functioning as monasteries, but several of them are open to visitors. Inside (once you make it up the hill), you can tour the refectories and cells arranged in rows with balconies and galleries, the chapels with their ikons and frescoes dating from the 14th century.

To the west of Meteora, the magnets for tourists are **Ioannina**, capital of the region known as Epirus, noted for the baronial mansions that dot its narrow streets; **Nikopolis**, which was built by Octavius Caesar to honor his own victory over the combined fleets of Antony and Cleopatra at the Battle of Actium in 31 B.C.; and **Missolonghi**, which has gone down in the annals of Greek history because of its stubborn resistance to the Turks during the War of Independence—and because Lord Byron died there.

The major landmark between central Greece and the northern provinces is **Mount Olympus** itself, the very eyrie of the gods and the highest point (9793 feet) in Greece. Here you'll see some of the most spectacular, and beautiful, scenery in Greece.

If, on the way north to Meteora or Olympus, you detour to the east, around Pagasitikos Gulf, you come to the port of **Volos** and the ancient land of the Argonauts. Today's Volos is a substantial town and resort, its spacious waterfront lined with cafés and restaurants, and it's hard to conjure up images of Jason and his crew there. The hills beyond Volos are another matter. The wild peninsula that separates the gulf from the Aegean Sea is dominated by the peaks of the Pelion range, their flanks covered by forests of beech and chestnut at the upper levels, with groves of olive, peach, and apple trees on the lower levels. On the eastern shore the mountains dip directly into the sea, dented here and there with tiny bays lined by narrow spits of beach.

There are a few modest one-taverna resorts along this coastline, but the main appeal of the Pelion range is its hill towns—**Portaria, Makrynitsa, Vizitsa, Kissos, Tsagarada**—clinging precariously to the slopes, their mule-wide cobbled streets winding between attractive balconied homes with russet roof tiles and traditional painted woodcarvings. The two hill towns most popular with sightseers are probably **Makrynitsa** and **Vizitsa**, both of which have historic buildings being preserved by the National Tourist Organization. Skiers head for **Hania** in winter. But lovers of solitude head for tiny towns like **Tsagarada**, teetering on its hillside, its town square dominated by an 800-year-old plane tree with church bells hanging from its massive limbs: there's a taverna up the hill behind the church, cobbled goat paths lead up and down and across the hillside (you can spend hours hiking here, but be sure you get back before dark), and the views from almost any outlook are breathtaking. There are Class B **Xenia Hotels** at Tsagarada (fashioned from the local stone and timber) and Portaria. The roadways are well engineered, but winding, narrow, and at times hair-raising; if you're heading for the Aegean side of the mountains, the easiest drive is not the most direct route on the map, but the seemingly longer one along the shores of the Pagasitikos Gulf and then across the mountains where they're narrower and lower. It's a trip of some five hours, and you can drive straight there, since there's little to see along the way—unless you're a devout archeology buff.

Northern Greece

This is where Alexander the Great was born (in the town of **Pella,** now noted for its recently excavated pebble mosaics, dating from Alexander's time) and where Marc Antony and Octavius defeated Brutus and Cassius in the battle fought at **Philippi** (the ruins of the ancient agora and acropolis can still be visited). At the village of **Vergina,** archeologists have unearthed a fabulous fourth-century royal tomb, believed to be the grave of Philip II of Macedonia. Many of the gold funerary objects found there are now on display in the Archeological Museum of Thessaloniki.

The capital of ancient Macedonia and Greece's second-largest city, **Thessaloniki** is a bustling modern city, with a sweeping promenade curving around the harbor; the old quarter of the city is built in tiers against the flank of Mount Hortisti, and between the mountain and the sea you can visit a wealth of Byzantine churches, Roman agoras, and triumphal arches.

But perhaps the most dramatic sight up in the north is **Mount Athos,** a mountainous finger of land on a three-pronged peninsula known as **Chalkidiki.** This "Holy Mountain," or Aghios Oros, has long been an isolated monastic community with its own republican government and police force of gowned monks. The flanks of the mountain are lined with spectacular, if sometimes crumbling, medieval monasteries, which can be visited only by men, only by special permission. The easiest way to see them is from a sightseeing boat, on a pleasant two- or three-hour cruise along the coast. The Chalkidiki Peninsula is one of the newest "in" spots in Greece, and there are several striking resorts where you can sport and play between serious excursions to Vergina, Pella, Philippi, or Mount Athos. Two of the grandest Class A hotels are the lavish and tastefully handsome 600-room **Athos Palace** on the Kassandra peninsula-within-a-peninsula and the dramatically sited, 166-room **Eagle's Palace** at Ouranoupoulis (near the entry point for Mount Athos).

The Amazing Porto Carras Resort

The most spectacular resort up here (or anywhere in Greece, for that matter) is the five-year-old Porto Carras development, a self-contained 4500 acres that produces its own wines (some of them highly regarded in Athens), olive oil, feta cheese, and fruit. The resort's three hotels—Meliton (deluxe), Sithonia (Class A), and Village Inn (Class B)—have hosted princes, presidents, and ballet super-star Rudolf Nureyev; and Zubin Mehta and the Los Angeles Philharmonic regaled guests in the resort's open-air theater. There's also an indoor theater, plus two discos, a range of restaurants, and cafés. Its sports facilities, the most complete in Greece, include lighted tennis courts, pro shop, a championship golf course, a stable with 35 horses, a marina for 100 yachts, and all water sports from day-sailing to para-sailing. If it all sounds rather crowded, it isn't: the Porto Carras shoreline runs for eight miles, and beyond the marina guests can bicycle along a dirt track to their choice of 34 secluded sandy coves.

Perhaps the resort's most attractive feature is its rates: *the deluxe Meliton costs roughly half what you'd pay in a comparable hotel elsewhere in Greece.* Porto Carras is 65 miles from Thessaloniki and the resort's motorcoach will drive you from and to the airport. (*Note:* Your air fare to Athens will probably include the jet flight to Thessaloniki, if you let the airline know in advance, and if you continue north within 24 hours of arriving in Athens.)

Getting Around by Bus and Train

There's now an efficient network of bus routes fanning out from Athens through the country to 66 cities and towns. The buses are big, comfortable, mostly pullman-type, and the fares are remarkably low. Athens to Naoussa in the north is less than 1800 drs ($30) round trip. Athens to Corinth is less than 300 drs

($5) round trip. The services operate several times a day—for example, 13 departures daily to Missolonghi, eight a day to Pyrgos (for Olympia), six a day to four different towns in Thessaly.

Greek State Railways operates diesel trains to the Peloponnese and the north, and supplements them with pullman coaches into the smaller towns. There are five trains daily to Pyrgos and Patras (665 drs, $6.65, one way, first class) and to Thessaloniki (955 drs, $9.50, first class; 640 drs, $6.40, second class, one way). These are the least expensive ways of getting around in Greece.

Sightseeing Tours by Coach

Most of the tour companies in Athens also offer a choice of conducted tours of the hinterlands lasting for anywhere from three to nine days. Check with your hotel concierge for details of tours by CHAT, American Express, and Key Tours, and by Viking's for budget-priced tours. Meantime, here are some samples of the *range* of tours and typical prices available.

Four-Day Classical Tour: Corinth, Mycenae (lunch), Epidaurus, Nafplion (overnight), Tripolis, Vytina, Olympia (lunch, dinner, overnight), Patras, ferry ride from Aegion to Itea, Delphi (lunch, dinner, overnight), Ossios Lucas. Cost: $222, with half board.

Five-Day Archeological Tour: Corinth, Mycenae (lunch), Epidaurus, Nafplion (dinner, overnight), Tripolis, Sparta (lunch), Mystra, Sparta or Tripolis (dinner, overnight), Vytina, Olympia (lunch, dinner, overnight), Patras, ferry ride Aegion to Itea, Delphi (lunch, dinner, overnight), Ossios Lucas. Cost: $297, with full board (CHAT only).

Five-Day Classical Tour plus Meteora: Same itinerary as Classical Tour (above) with an additional day spent in Meteora, Kalambaka, Trikala, and Thermopylae. Cost: $311, with half board.

Six-Day Northern Greece Tour: Thebes, Arakhova, Delphi (lunch, dinner, overnight), Amphissa, Lamia, Trikala, Kalambaka (dinner, overnight), Meteora, Larissa, Valley of Tempi, Platamon, Thessaloniki (dinner, overnight), Amphipolis, Philippi, Kavala (dinner, overnight), Thassos (lunch), Kavala, Thessaloniki (dinner, overnight), Pella, Larissa (lunch), Thermopylae, Kammena, Vourla. Cost: $375, with full board (CHAT only).

Nine-Day Grand Tour of Greece: Corinth, Mycenae (lunch),

Epidaurus, Nafplion (dinner, overnight), Tripolis, Sparta (lunch), Mystra, Sparta or Tripolis (dinner, overnight), Olympia (lunch, dinner, overnight), Patras, ferry ride from Aegion to Itea, Delphi (lunch, dinner, overnight), Amphissa, Lamia, Trikala, Kalambaka (dinner, overnight), Meteora, Kalambaka (lunch), Larissa, Valley of Tempi, Platamon, Thessaloniki (dinner, overnight), Amphipolis, Philippi, Kavala (dinner, overnight), Thassos (lunch), Kavala, Thessaloniki (dinner, overnight), Pella, Larissa (lunch), Thermopylae. Cost: $550, with full board (CHAT only).

Note: Not all of these tours leave every day of the week, and not all of them operate year round; your travel agent can find the tour and operator that best suit your schedule.

Touring Greece by Car

In the end, if you have the time, the cash, and the inclination, the best way to tour Greece is by car. The Greek government has been forging ahead with its road-building program, and although there are only limited stretches of expressway, there are now good, comfortable roads linking all the major tourist areas.

There's an expressway of sorts, National Highway 1, all the way from Athens, along the eastern shores of Attica, through Lamia, Larissa, and Kateria to Thessaloniki—a distance of just over 300 miles. And another from Athens, around the Gulf of Saronica to Corinth, and along the northern shore of the Peloponnese to Patras (where you can catch a ferryboat to Italy). There's also a new extension of the expressway that goes from Corinth south to the city of Epidaurus. These highways are considered expressways in Greece, and you have to pay tolls (trifling amounts) on some stretches, but don't zoom onto them expecting an interstate highway or you'll be disappointed—in addition to which you'll have your timetable thrown for a loop. The stretch of National Highway 1 from Athens to Thebes (the turnoff for Delphi) is a four-lane highway, without dividers and with an unmarked shoulder on the right, so that most drivers seem to position themselves halfway between the right lane and the passing lane. Also, the standard of driving in Greece is probably the most immature this side of the Middle East. This doesn't mean that you shouldn't drive in Greece—it's simply a warning to drive with extra care, and not to plan on averaging more than 40 miles an hour.

But you don't need an expressway to enjoy some pleasurable

driving. The coastal road from Athens to Sounion, for example, is a well-engineered corniche-type highway with many bends but no tricky corners, and there are some fine, scenic roads in the mountains of Arcadia and around Olympia.

Distances in Greece are manageable, and you can cover a lot of territory even with leisurely driving. Here are three suggestions for car tours from Athens:

1. A three- to five-day tour could include Corinth, Epidaurus, Nafplion, Mycenae, Arcadia, Sparta, Kalamata, Pyrgos, Olympia, Patras (from which you can head across to Italy or return to Athens). How long you spend on that tour will depend on how much time you spend snooping around the ruins, or nipping off to the beach for a dip.

2. A five- to seven-day tour could take you up through Delphi and Amphissa to Missolonghi, Agrinion, and Arta to Ioannina in Epirus, then back via Trikala and Karditsa to Lamia, where you pick up the expressway to Athens. That itinerary gives you a nice mixture of antiquity, resorts, and scenery.

3. This itinerary, again for **five to seven days,** would take you along the old scenic road through Boeotia to Delphi and Lamia, then to Karditsa and Trikala, over a stretch of less than first-rate highway to Grevena and Kozana, with a sidetrip to Naoussa on the way to Thessaloniki, and returning via Alexandria, Katerina, and Larissa, to Lamia and Athens—on expressway all the way back. Again, a mixture of antiquity, scenery, and resorts.

Car rentals

Greece may well be the most expensive country in Europe both for car rentals and gas. It always seems to cost more to rent than you think it will, so the following tips may help.

There are several reliable companies renting cars and you'll have a fairly wide choice of cars—German, French, Italian, Japanese, from Ford Fiestas and Volkswagens to a luxury Mercedes with air conditioning and automatic transmission. You'll recognize a few old faithfuls among the list of companies, such as Avis and Hertz, both of which have desks at the arrivals hall in the airport, but there are also several local European or Greek organizations. Rates vary considerably; for a Ford Fiesta, for instance, they fluctuate between $15.50 a day and $20 a day, with kilometer charges from 17¢ to 23¢, and for a Mercedes 200 between $53 and $61 a day. Your best bet is to pick out a selection of the rate sheets that seem to be stacked in most hotel lobbies, make a few calculations, and then choose the price that comes closest to your budget. My experience is that most of the local companies are reliable, and I've had particularly good service from an organization called Batek (see below).

Some Sample Car-Rental Rates*

	Peak Season		Off-peak season
	Per day	Per Kilometer	Weekly, unlimited mileage
VW Polo	$15	16¢	$175
Ford Fiesta	$12.50	15¢	$224
Fiat Ritmo	$19.50	21¢	$240
Datsun 1200	$19.50	21¢	$318
Mercedes 200	$53	51¢	(not available)

*Prices are subject to change; some companies may quote lower rates; peak season is generally July 1 through September 30; all rates subject to 20% tax.

If you are unfamiliar with European cars and wonder which one to select, several rental brochures include photographs and descriptions of the cars; but in my experience, the VW Polo is a reliable workhorse for the type of driving you'll be doing in Greece—it accommodates four people comfortably (provided they don't have too much luggage), and it is light on gas, which can cost as much as $2.50 a gallon. Some additional tips: Read through the insurance information included in each brochure; considering the general standard of driving in Greece, it is recommended that you take full insurance coverage. If you pay with cash, you may be able to get a discount of 6% or 10%. When you return the car, stop into a gas station near the rental depot and fill up the tank; otherwise you will pay (a) a higher rate for the gas, and (b) the 20% tax on the cost of gas, since the tax applies to every item on the rental bill—including insurance and gas.

Top Car Rental Companies in Athens

    Avis, 48 Amalias Sofias Ave. (tel. 3224-951)
      and several other locations
    Hertz, 12 Syngrou Ave. (tel. 9220-102)
      and several other locations
    Batek, 43 Syngrou Ave. (tel. 9215-795)
      and several other locations
    Autorent, 118 Syngrou Ave. (tel. 9232-514)
    Kosmos, 9 Syngrou Ave. (tel. 9234-698)
    Hellasacars, 7 Stadiou St. (tel. 3233-487)

Distance by Road from Athens to Various Points in Greece

The figures below are in kilometers, the measurement used on Greek maps and road signs. A kilometer equals five-eighths of a mile, but the simplest way to translate kilometers into miles is to multiply by 6 and divide by 10. It's not a precise figure, but close enough for most purposes.

From Athens to:	Kilometers
Corinth	84
Ioannina	444
Kalamata	283
Karditsa	302
Katerina	440
Lamia	215
Larissa	356
Missolonghi	248
Nauplia	145
Naoussa	533
Patras	217
Thessaloniki	539

Some General Comments on Driving in Greece

The wearing of seatbelts is now compulsory throughout Greece, for both the driver and front-seat passenger. The police conduct frequent spot checks, and the fine for non-use is 1000 drs ($10), payable at the local public treasury office.

When parking in Greek cities, make doubly sure you're not infringing regulations; if you park illegally the police may remove your license plates (rental cars are not exempted), in which case you have to trot off in Athens, to the police station on Aghiou Constantinou Street, near Omonia Square, to fight your way through layers of bureaucracy to retrieve your own plates and pay a 1300-dr ($13) fine (remember to take along your parking ticket). If you happen to arrive at your car as the plates are being removed, under no circumstances try to talk your way out of the dilemma with offers of money or you'll be in real trouble. If you park somewhere really dumb and block other traffic, your car will be towed away.

The speed limit in Greece is 62 m.p.h., and you would be well advised to stay well within that limit. Signs are in Greek with phonetic English.

Outside of Athens, the majority of accidents are head-on collisions caused by careless or foolhardy overtaking on bends or on two- and three-lane highways. When it's time for you to pass, always alert the driver in front by signaling, honking your horn, and/or flashing your lights. *Never* rely on the driver to look in his rear view mirror to see what other cars are doing. On narrow roadways you may drive temporarily on the hard shoulder to allow other cars to pass. Be doubly alert for mammoth coaches and trucks.

Traffic on main roads has priority over traffic on side roads; except that there is also the basic principle of "priority on the right." Most of the time this is not a problem, since most main highways are clearly defined—but never take it for granted. *Always observe traffic on your right with extra caution.*

Never let your tank get too low since gas stations can be few and far between out in the country, and most of them close around 7 p.m. If you do get into a tight spot out in the country, head for the nearest village café, which frequently keeps a can or two in reserve for forgetful locals.

All these dire warnings apart, Greece offers some of the most pleasant and interesting driving in Europe, especially off the beaten track. But take along a reliable map. Your car-rental company will probably offer you a basic map, but it may not be completely up-to-date. The most reliable map is considered to be the one published locally by Efstathiadis.

Chapter XIV

THE ISLANDS

And How to Reach Them from Athens

GO DOWN TO PIRAEUS any day of the week and you can take your pick of a score of cruise ships or ferryboats waiting to take you to some offshore Elysium. Or go to the airport and hop on a jet to any of a dozen islands. In some cases, you can fly over and back in the same day. So your vacation in Athens can easily include a day or two on the Greek islands as well. The question is: Which one? That's an impossible question to answer. Start with the numbers.

There are 1425 Greek islands. Of these, 166 are inhabited, including the privately owned islets such as the Niarchos family's Spetsopoulos and the Onassis family's Skorpios, but only about three dozen are visited regularly by tourists from abroad.

Within that three dozen you have a choice of highly sophisticated, swinging resorts or unspoiled one-taverna-one-guesthouse-and-a-handful-of-fishermen islands.

The islands all have a few things in common. Sun. Torrential sun. About 300 days of sunshine a year, and many of the islands are warm enough for sunbathing or swimming in January. They all have their typically Greek villages, with whitewashed houses huddling around narrow alleyways leading to a tiny harbor confettied with the red, blue, and yellow awnings of cafés and tavernas. Many are dotted with remnants of antiquity—temple columns, Byzantine churches, Crusader fortresses; others have little besides secluded coves and beaches, and valleys filled with olives, lemon trees, and vineyards.

Whatever type of island you choose, they're all great places to be . . . day or night.

GETTING YOUR BEARINGS: It's no easy matter charting your way through all these islands, even on paper. Begin by breaking them down into groups.

There are eight groups—from west to east (more or less). They are the Ionians, the Saronics, the Sporades, the Cyclades, the North Aegeans, the Eastern Aegeans, the Dodecanese and Rhodes, and Crete (which is one island, but large enough to be ranked with the groups).

The Saronic Islands are in the Gulf of Saronica, just off Piraeus, and you've already read all about them in the chapter on one-day tours from Athens—Aegina, Poros, Hydra, and Spetsai.

Now here's a brief preview of the others. Very brief, because this is a book about Athens, and the islands really deserve a volume all to themselves, but you'll read about half a dozen island highlights in the next chapter.

The Ionian Islands

Greece's seven islands in the Ionian Sea (at the southern end of the Adriatic Sea) are Corfu (or Kerkyra), Paxi, Lefkas, Cephalonia, Ithaca, Zante, and Kythera (or Cerigo). Ithaca was the birthplace and kingdom of Odysseus, and Lefkas is the closest island to Skorpios.

But the island most visitors flock to is the largest in the group, Corfu. It's one of the most beautiful (unlike the Aegean islands, Corfu has lots of greenery), and one of the most interesting (it has been held variously by the French, the Venetians, the British, and the Greeks, and it's only a few miles from Albania). Turn to the next chapter for more details on Corfu.

The Sporades and Evia (or Euboea)

The islands known as the Sporades—Skiathos, Skopelos, Alonissos, and Skyros—lie to the northeast of Evia (or Euboea), which looks like a peninsula off the eastern shore of central Greece but is, in fact, the second-largest Greek island after Crete. It's joined to the mainland by a swing bridge over the Straits of Euripos, which are famous for an unusual tidal current that zips through in alternate directions roughly every six hours, at speeds that vary from four to six knots, depending on the moon. If you don't see it, you'll hear it.

Skyros is the island where Odysseus discovered Achilles, who had been hidden there, disguised as a girl by his mother to protect him from the ravages of the Trojan War; you can also see the tomb of Rupert Brooke, another of those English poets who died unheroically of fever or blood poisoning in Greece. There's nothing you really must see on these islands—you simply go there to lounge on the beach by day and live it up in the tavernas by night. All of them are acquiring new hotels and resorts at a rate to match that tidal current. Evia now has six Class A hotels. For more information on Skiathos, turn to the following chapter.

The Cyclades (or Kyklades) Islands

Next to the Saronics these are the islands closest to Athens, and therefore the most popular and the most developed. Some of their names are probably familiar—Mykonos, Delos, Kea, Serifos, Kimolos, Milos, Paros, Naxos, Kythmos, Siphnos, Ios, Sikinos, Andros, Tinos, Syros, Antiparos, Anafi, Santorini, Amorgos, Pholegendros. They get their collective name from an ancient Greek word meaning "wheeling ones," because they seem to whirl, like one of the islands' famous white windmills, around Delos.

Delos is accessible only by caique, or fishing boat, from Mykonos (unless it's included on a cruise itinerary); it was the birthplace of Apollo, the god of the sun, among other things, and was, therefore, a sacred island. Its most famous features are a line of marble lions, and three temples dedicated to Apollo and his twin sister Artemis. The island is now uninhabited—and because of a pronouncement from Delphi, no one has been born there or died there since the sixth century B.C.

Kea is the Cyclade closest to the mainland (a mere 13 miles from Cape Sounion), but because tourists have to catch the ferryboat from Lavrion, near Sounion, rather than convenient Piraeus, it's almost totally unspoiled, the way Mykonos was until it was discovered. Unspoiled maybe, but it can offer you fine accommodations in three Class B hotels; otherwise you can enjoy the beaches, the snorkeling, the walks, and the tavernas without being crowded out by tourists, Greek or otherwise.

Tinos was the legendary abode of Poseidon, the god of the sea, but in more recent years it has acquired a reputation as the island of the Virgin Mary, and Greeks come from all over the country on her feast day, August 15 (an interesting day to visit the island, but no time to turn up without a hotel reservation).

Syros was an old shipbuilding center, and is now the home for wealthy shipowners who can't quite afford a Skorpios or Spet-

THE AEGEAN ISLANDS

GREECE

TURKEY

To Istanbul

Marmara Sea

Thassos

NORTHEAST

Gallipoli

Samothraki

AEGEAN ISLANDS

Dardanelles

Canakkale

Limnos

TURKEY

Skiathos

Aegean Sea

Alonissos

Skopelos

Lesbos

Skyros

AEGEAN

ISLANDS

Izmir

Chios

GREECE

Andros

Samos

Ephesus

Delos

Tinos

Mykonos

Hydra

Siros

CYCLADES

Patmos

Spetsai

Paros

Naxos

Naxos

Kalymos

Santorini

Ios

Kos

Symi

Rhodos

DODECANESE

Rhodes

Sea of Crete

Karpathos

Rethymon

Iraklion

Knossos

Crete

N

sopoulos. **Andros, Naxos,** and **Paros** are all dreamy and idyllic, the way Greek islands are supposed to look, and still undiscovered. **Santorini** is, in many ways, the most fascinating of the Cyclades, and you'll read more about it, and Mykonos, in the highlights chapter that follows.

Santorini still has no more than half a dozen hotels, which is about par for most of the Cyclade islands—except Mykonos and Tinos which are well endowed with accommodations up to Class A hotels.

The Northern Aegean Islands

Sometimes called the Thracian Islands because they're way up north off the coast of Thrace: Samothrace, Thassos, and Lemnos. **Samothrace** is a mountainous island (5000 feet and more) which was the home of the *Winged Victory;* most of the island's hotels are now booked by archeologists who're busy digging up all sorts of fascinating relics from B.C. eras.

Thassos is just off the coast of Macedonia; this is where the Phoenicians got their gold, and where modern Greeks now spend their vacations (it's one of the up-and-coming resort areas). **Lemnos** is the island where Hephaestus, the god of goldsmiths, landed when his old man, Zeus, tossed him off Olympus, and where Jason and the Argonauts came searching for the Golden Fleece and found an island populated only by women who had killed all their men. The Argonauts stayed a year. You'll probably want to stick around too. Especially if you're staying in the island's sole deluxe-class hotel—the serene, 125-room **Akti Myrina.** Thassos is well supplied with budget-priced hotels; Samothrace has only a small number of beds for visitors.

The Eastern Aegeans

There are four of them, all tucked in close to the coast of Turkey—Samos, Ikaria, Chios, and Lesvos (sometimes spelled Lesbos, and sometimes called Mytilene after its biggest village). Sappho, the greatest poetess of antiquity, and Aesop, the greatest yarnspinner of antiquity, were both born on **Lesvos;** there are various ruins, galleries, and museums there, but it's really a place to go to lie on the beach and read Sappho and Aesop.

Chios (sometimes spelled Hios) is one of the larger Greek islands, with a population of 60,000, most of them descendants of generations of seafarers. Both **Samos** and **Ikaria** have been bypassed by history—ancient and modern. All four islands have a range of budget-priced hotels.

The Dodecanese Islands and Rhodes

Rhodes is the largest, and the others include Patmos, Leros, Astypalaea, Karpathos, Kassos, Nisyros, Castellorizo, Kalymnos, Kos, and Symi. **Kos,** the second largest, is the island of Hippocrates, the father of medicine, and you can still see the ruins of his school and the temple to Asclepius. This is another relatively lush island, plump with figs, pomegranates, bananas, mulberries, cherries, oranges, and lemons—and, of course, grapes. **Patmos** is sometimes called the Island of the Donkey because every family owns one (there are even some two-donkey families); most of the donkeys are used to carrying tourists up the hill to the 11th-century monastery of St. John, a unique fortress-like place with priceless manuscripts, and the Cave of the Apocalypse, where St. John wrote the divinely inspired Revelations.

Patmos, Kalymnos, and **Kos** are the only other islands with a wide range of accommodations. The others have hotels or rooms in private homes—but only in limited quantities. That's why they're unspoiled. Rhodes is featured in the "Islands Highlights" chapter that follows.

Crete

Crete is the fourth-largest island in the Mediterranean (technically, it's surrounded by its own sea, the Cretan), and it's full of ruins and historic sites from the days of the Minoan civilization right up to World War II. The main town is **Heraklion,** which has interesting museums and churches, but the goal of most visitors is the great palace at **Knossos** to see the royal apartments, drainage system, terraces, and traces of the dreaded Labyrinth where the Minotaur gobbled up its human prey. Knossos is one of the great sights of the Mediterranean, so you'll read more about Crete in the next chapter.

How to Get to the Islands

Olympic Airways, its subsidiary Olympic Aviation, and Greek

shipping companies operate "bus" services by plane or ferry to many of the islands, and between them they cover most of the islands tourists are likely to visit. However, some of the islands mentioned in the previous pages cannot be reached directly, either by sea or air from Athens, and if you have an urge to visit any of those spots, check out possible transportation with the National Tourist Organization.

BY SEA: In an area of the world where so much history was written by seafarers for so many centuries you'll probably want to sail from the mainland to the islands. That's no problem, as you'll see from the following table. There are plenty of boats, lots of departures, accommodations to suit every budget; an island like Mykonos, for example, is only six or seven hours away by sea, and you can get to the farthest islands, such as Rhodes, within 24 hours. Mykonos and neighboring Cyclades islands are now linked by regular hydrofoil service.

The ferryboats and ships that carry passengers from Piraeus to the islands vary considerably (some of them have been around for a long time), and it's not possible in these few pages to give you a listing of the best craft—you'll have to get that information from your travel agent, or the National Tourist Organization, or from someone standing in line at the American Express office on Syntagma. Generally speaking, you'll be able to choose between private cabins, shared cabins, bunks, lounges, or deck class (which may be rugged but in some ways is the most fun). Most ferryboats have some kind of snackbar on board, but to be on the safe side take along some kind of simple picnic.

Theoretically, the boats operate on a fixed schedule but since so many indirect factors may affect their performance (weather and cargo, to name two) you should never rely on precise timing. Getting around *between* the islands is strictly for people with time to spare.

There's a more reliable (and more comfortable) way of seeing the islands by boat, and that's by taking one of the dozens of cruise ships on three-day, four-day, or longer voyages, which you'll read about later. But the great advantages of ferryboats and inter-island boats are frequency of schedules and *economy*, as you can see from the chart below.

Ferryboat Services from Piraeus

To	No. of sailings per week	Duration of trip (hours)	One-way fares (drachmas)	
			Second	Tourist
Crete				
(Heraklion)	15	12	1900	1400
Hios (Chios)	7	10	1544	1114
Ios	9	8–10	1635	1221
Kos	11	15	2034	1522
Mykonos	15	5–7	1114	862
Rhodes	9	12–19½	2224	1687
Santorini				
(Thira)	11	9½	1394	1102
Siros	35	23½	934	739

* The Tourist Class fare is for the young and adventurous; most travelers will prefer the comfort of the more expensive class of accommodations—"expensive" in this case being a mere, say, $15 for the trip to magical Mykonos; first-class fares vary from vessel to vessel and they are usually 25% to 30% more expensive than second-class fares.

Again, always check details of shipping company, name of vessel, and destination before you leave the ticket office, otherwise you may have to pay again to get to where you really want to go.

BY AIR: Internal air service within Greece is operated by Olympic Airways and a subsidiary, Olympic Aviation S.A., the latter handling those domestic services involving light aircraft. However, all the services are listed together in the Olympic timetable, individual flights use Olympic codes, and all reservations are handled by Olympic Airways offices throughout the world.

On its domestic routes, Olympic Airways flies Boeing 707s, Boeing 720s, and a few Nihon YS-11As; Olympic Aviation now has a versatile fleet of Piper Aztecs, Britten-Norman Islanders, Alouette helicopters for rich Swiss who can't wait to get to their yachts, Skyvan SC-7s, and, latest addition to the fleet, the 30-seat Short SD-3-30. For island-hopping vacationers, the best news is that this augmented fleet offers service within the islands, so that travelers no longer have to double back to Athens to get from one island to another. Olympic Aviation operates several times a week between Rhodes, Santorini, and Crete; between Rhodes and Kos; between Rhodes and Kabathos; there are also additional services to and from Skiathos, Lemnos, Mytilene, and Kastoria, and between Athens and Volos, to name just a few. These new services make life much simpler for travelers with limited time; when it's time to plan your trip, ask your travel agent for the latest details of these and other new domestic services.

Flights to the Islands (summer schedules)*

From Athens to:	No. of flights weekly	Duration of flight	One-way fare*
Chios (Hios)	23	50 mins.	$25
Corfu (Kerkyra)	32	1 hr. 20 mins.	$38
Crete (Heraklion)	54	1 hr. 10 mins.	$33
Kos	21	1 hr. 10 mins.	$37
Lemnos	10	1 hr. 5 mins.	$26
Lesbos (Mytiline)	35	1 hr. 5 mins.	$29
Mykonos	22	55 mins.	$27
Rhodes	49	55 mins.	$43
Samos	21	1 hr. 5 mins.	$29
Skiathos	21	40 mins.	$27

* Subject to change (probably 15% higher in summer 1985); check with your travel agent.

Evzones (Greek soldiers)

ISLAND HIGHLIGHTS

AS I MENTIONED earlier, choosing which island to visit is a ticklish problem. They all have something to offer—antiquity, glamor, beaches, or in some cases, just plain isolation. If you're having trouble making a decision, here are some notes on half a dozen islands based on recent visits.

Corfu

This is the green Greek island. Because of its location in the Ionian Sea, a few miles from the coast of Albania, Corfu has much more foliage than most of the other islands. (It also rains more often here, but that still adds up to only a few showers in winter.)

The main town of Corfu, also called Corfu (or **Kerkyra** to the Greeks), has arcaded streets modeled on the Rue Rivoli, palazzos in the style of Venice, and cricket fields in the style of Eton—all holdovers from the centuries of conquerors from different parts of Europe.

It's an old town, relatively unchanged through the ages, and to this day its cobbled back alleys, or cantounias, are accessible only to pedestrians. It's a great place for walking and exploring (houses built in the style of Naples or Paris or London, Byzantine churches and fortresses), but once you get beyond the cantounias there's a lot to see on the island.

Corfu has its own patron saint, St. Spyridon, who lies in a richly decorated sarcophagus with his mummified, slippered feet sticking out; four times a year (Palm Sunday, Easter, August 11, and the first Sunday in November) his body is carried through the streets, and anyone who has a favor to ask whispers it to his slippered feet. St. Spyridon is credited with several miracles.

At **Gastori**, a few miles from the town of Corfu, you can see the remains of the Kaiser's Bridge, which crosses the main road and allowed Kaiser Wilhelm to walk from his royal yacht direct-

IONIAN ISLANDS

ly to Achilleion Palace; this sumptuous palace, which was built by Empress Elizabeth of Austria in 1890, is now a gambling casino. Mon Repos, a more modest villa built by a British governor in the 19th century, was the birthplace of Prince Philip, duke of Edinburgh.

But in the end, it's the natural beauty of the island that will probably make the most lasting impression on you. A spectacular spiral road will bring you to **Aghios Gordis,** one of the island's most beautiful beaches, surrounded by rugged almost spooky nature; readers of Henry Miller will know about **Paleokastritsa** even before they reach its beautiful beach—small tavernas where you can select a meal from tanks of live lobsters, the 13th-century fortress of Angelokastio, and the panoramic view from "Bella Vista," a natural balcony overlooking the town and the sea. The island has lots of seafood restaurants, of course, besides the tavernas of Paleokastritsa. One of the most famous is **Giannis,** which hangs over the edge of a cliff, in the aristocratic quarter of the island, Perama, about five miles from the town.

Before you go exploring the island, check out your plans with the tourist office in the new Government Building next door to the post office on Samara Street. They'll give you information on how to get around the island by scheduled bus, or by tourist boats to the various coves along the west coast. You can also rent a car (Fiat 127s for $25 a day plus 15¢ for each additional kilometer) and try to find your own way—no easy matter because the signposting is unreliable or nonexistent, and out in the countryside you won't find too many people who speak English.

HOTELS ON CORFU: When it comes to a place to stay, your only problem will be choosing among several attractive locations and hotels. You can stay in the town itself, or at some of the new hotels and resorts out on the island. In town, the top choices are the deluxe **Corfu Palace,** where the management is Swiss and most of the 110 rooms look out to the sea; swimmers have a choice of the hotel pool or the beach at the Miramare Beach Hotel (12 miles away but linked by free shuttle bus). Summer half-board rates are 8228 drs ($82) double. One of the loveliest hotels in town is the 50-room Class A **Cavalieri,** converted from a 17th-century nobleman's mansion (or what remained of it after it was hit by a bomb in World War II). Rates are around 3024 drs ($30), double without board, in season. The **Corfu Hilton International Hotel** is located in Kanoni a few kilometers south of the town; each of its 274 rooms and bungalows has balcony, well-equipped bathroom, telephone, individual controls for heating and air conditioning; resort facilities include two swimming pools (one indoors), bowling alleys, two tennis courts (with lights for night play), health club, and an 18-hole golf course a short shuttle-bus ride away. Summer rates are around 9840 drs ($98) double, with half board.

Other leading hotels on the island are the deluxe **Miramare Beach** (at Moraitike) with 149 beachside bungalows; the 122-room deluxe **Eva Palace** at Dafnila; the 72-room deluxe **Castello** at Dassia, a converted manor house with splendid antique furnishings; and the 308-room deluxe **Astir Palace Corfu;** the deluxe 260-room **Marbella Beach** at Aghios Ioanis Peristeron, about 12 miles south of town. Other Class A accommodations include a pair of Chandris hotels—the **Chandris Corfu** and **Chandris Dassia,** where summer room rates are around 6532 drs ($65) double, with breakfast and dinner. In addition, there are scores of Class B, C, and D hotels throughout the island, with new ones opening every year. *Room* rates are from 1500 drs ($15) double in summer, but in most cases you'll be expected to settle for a half-board rate.

HOW TO GET TO CORFU: The quickest way, of course, is by Olympic Airways—half a dozen flights from Athens every day in summer, the first one leaving very early in the morning to give you a full day on the beach. The slowest way is by car or bus across the mountains to Igoumenitsa, where you board a ferry for a short trip to the island. There is also ferryboat service once a week from Patras.

Skiathos

Think of a tiny island covered with wild strawberries and pine trees and rimmed with—wait for it—66 beaches. Beautiful beaches, most of them, particularly Koukounaries, a half-mile combination of dazzling sand and clear water, named for the stone pines which separate the sea from a freshwater lagoon. And so that you can enjoy this beach to the fullest, fortune has perched two luxury hotels there—one at each end of the beach. The **Skiathos Palace** has 200 rooms and 15 suites, heated swimming pool, disco, beauty parlor, and sauna. Guest rooms are decorated in white with cinnamon and turquoise highlights, and come equipped with two-channel radio, telephone, refrigerator prestocked with everything from ice and beer to cognac and créme de menthe miniatures. It's open all year. Rates are from 6740 to 7740 drs ($67 to $77) for a double, with half board, in season. The 32-room, Class B **Xenia** is open only during the summer, when doubles are from 3500 drs ($35), with half board. There are another half-dozen hotels in town, offering double rooms for less than $20 for a double in-season, with half board.

Nightlife on Skiathos consists of a couple of clubs, a couple of tavernas with bouzouki, and lots of waterfront cafés where you can watch the fishing boats in the harbor and the brightly colored nets hanging in the trees to dry.

Mykonos

Everyone has heard of Mykonos—and when you get there, you won't be disappointed—it's everything you've hoped for . . . maybe even more: whitewashed waterfront, disappearing in whitewashed cobblestoned alleys, lined with whitewashed houses and balconies with blue or yellow trim; tiny cobblestoned squares with whitewashed churches. There are no cars in this part of town, just hundreds of spindly tables and chairs, sun umbrellas, little old ladies in long black dresses, and tourists in next to nothing; take a bus and a boat to Paradise Beach (about 60¢) or Super Paradise Beach ($1) and you'll find yourself among tourists in nothing at all. Or wander around the island and admire its famed windmills (whitewashed, of course), or some of its 300-odd churches and chapels. Where to stay?

When you set foot on the island you'll probably be surrounded by dozens of those little old ladies in black offering rooms in their cottages, most of which are simply furnished but spotlessly clean and inexpensive; if you want to play it safe, go first to the Tourist Police office, right on the harbor, and ask them to recommend some rooms. Otherwise, you have a choice of pensions: **Philippi**, otherwise known as **Angelique Kontiza Pension** (tel. 0289-22295; 20 rooms, some with private bath) in the center of town, at 11 Kalogera St., is recommended; the Class C **Mykonos Beach**, where a double room with breakfast costs around 1956 drs ($20); any of the three Class B hotels **Theoxenia, Afroditi, Alkistis**—the latter two bungalow-style accommodations—or the Class A **Leto**. In any of the Afroditi's modern bungalows, room and half board for a single is 3940 drs ($39) in high season, 4340 drs ($43) for a double.

Try to avoid half-board rates if you can, because there are so many delightful little restaurants on the island—such as **Maria's** and **Zanni's**, both on the waterfront, the touristy **Taverna Mykonos** (also on the waterfront), and the **Taverna Antonini** (on the square).

Some of the best shopping in Greece is to be found on Mykonos: a branch of the famed jeweler **Lalaounis** (see Chapter XI on "Shopping in Athens"), **Galatis** (more jewelery), **George Konteous** (still more jewelery), **Nikis** for ladies' fashions, and **Panos** for superb hand-woven bedspreads, shoulder bags, and placemats—all with exquisite combinations of earth-and-sea-inspired colors.

HOW TO GET TO MYKONOS: Two or three flights daily in summer (45 minutes flying time), or 15 crossings a week by boat from Piraeus (six to seven hours).

Santorini

Alias Thira. Alias, perhaps, Atlantis. No island in the Mediterranean offers a more dramatic landfall than this one: you sail into what remains of the crater of the volcano created when, as you read back in the chapter on museums, "Enkeladus in the bowels of the Earth was roused with undescribable fury," past a flat island of brown-black lava to the towering cliffs of Santorini itself, topped by the gleaming, whitewashed churches and homes of the village. When you go ashore here you still haven't arrived—you still have to get up that almost-vertical 600-foot cliff. There's a zigzag path to the top, and most people negotiate it on the back of a donkey in about 20 minutes. Some foolhardy people, (like me) *walk* up (despite what the muleteers tell you, "one hour, one hour" it's only *half* an hour to the top, even with picture stops), but walking is not really recommended, especially if your ship has put lots of people ashore, in which case the 100-odd donkeys are working overtime and the path becomes the setting for a donkey stampede; the only reward for dodging the hooves and the droppings is that the muleteers assume that anyone who has reached the top has paid his 100 drs ($1) for the round-trip ride, so you can treat yourself to a free ride down. Once you get to the top, the thing to do is ignore the souvenir shops, find a cliffside taverna, and over a glass of Santorini white marvel over the history of this extraordinary, legendary island.

Scientists speculate that Santorini/Thira was destroyed by a gigantic earthquake, volcanic explosion, *and* tidal wave, which left only the tips of the volcanic cone behind. That became Santorini and its satellite islands. The tidal wave, according to some estimates, may have been as high as 600 feet, which would make it the largest natural convulsion in the recorded history of mankind; some scientists and archeologists speculate that this same convulsion wiped out the civilization of Knossos on Crete, caused the parting of the Red Sea (the same one recorded in the Bible), and sent that giant wave all the way to the Sahara where it gathered up some desert sands before sweeping all the way back to deposit the sands on Crete. (If this seems farfetched, compare it with history's most recent counterpart, the eruption of Java's Krakatoa in 1883, when so much red-hot pumice was forced into the air that skies turned red in *North America* . . . so red that fire departments in Poughkeepsie, New York, and New Haven, Connecticut, were called out twice because people thought those towns were on fire, and a Dutch ocean-going freighter was carried off by the tidal wave and dumped intact in the jungle *two miles away*.) Anyway, it's romantic to speculate that somewhere far beneath this gleaming, white clifftop village there may rest the lost continent of Atlantis.

As it happens, **Atlantis** is the name of the best of the town's hotels. It's Category A, has 25 rooms, and costs 4400 drs ($44) for a double, with half board, with a big terrace overlooking the town and the sea.

If you come to Santorini on one of the cruise ships, you will not (by the time you've made your way up the hill on donkey-back) be able to see much more than the whitewashed village at the edge of the crater—which for most people may be experience enough for one day, since it *is* such an extraordinary place. Visitors who stay for a few days may want to explore some of the quiet coves and beaches on the opposite side of the island, linger in the tavernas drinking the local wines (Vissanto and Nihteri), or explore the site of Ancient Thira—the agora, theater, temples, and shrines. On July 20, the feast day of the Prophet Elijah, the islanders celebrate at the monastery of the same name, and the evening is given over to the local dances—the syrtos and the repati. Join them. You'll soon learn the syrtos and repati.

HOW TO GET TO SANTORINI: There are daily flights (55 minutes) by Olympic from Athens, one or two a week from Rhodes or Crete, but really the only way to arrive in Santorini is by boat—either ferryboat (once a day from Piraeus) or cruise ship. If you come by ferryboat, make sure you get off at the right port—Thira (not Ia).

Crete

Zorba's island is the largest of the Greek islands, with half a million people. Its 3000 square miles are mostly mountains, which rise to 7500 feet at their highest peak. Crete lies equidistant from Europe, Asia, and Africa (which is only 200 miles to the south), another of those islands with a mishmash history—except that this one goes back farther than the others. As Cretans will constantly remind you, the *first* civilization in Europe was on Crete—the legendary Minoan kingdom with its bull-oriented culture that flourished here 3000 years before the birth of Christ. All that remains of this culture are the ruins of the **Palace of Knossos,** one of the outstanding archeological sites of Europe—what was once a five-story structure (4000 years ago!), with private bathrooms and flushing toilets (4000 years ago!). The most striking remnant of the civilization is the modest throne of the king, which still stands against the wall of the throne room after all these centuries, and which Cretans claim is the oldest throne in existence. The palace is only 20 minutes by bus from the town of Heraklion (where you'll probably arrive, whether you come by air or sea), but before you dash over to check out the ruins and the labyrinths, pay a visit to the downtown **Archeological Museum** first, because after you've inspected its exhibits (frescoes, artifacts, and models visualizing the original palace) you'll appreciate the ruins even more. The Palace of Knossos is open weekdays from 8 a.m. to 5 p.m., and on Sunday and holidays from 9 a.m. to 5 p.m.; admission is 100 drs ($1). The museum is open from 8 a.m. to 5 p.m. daily (except Monday to 11 a.m.); on Sunday and holidays, from 9 a.m. to 5 p.m.; admission is 100 drs ($1), which includes entry fees to other archeological sites (including the Palace of Knossos). Sightseeing tours to the museum and palace, with English-speaking guides, cost about 550 drs ($5.50), including admissions.

There are several other Minoan sites on Crete, most notably the secondary palace of **Phaestos;** otherwise the things to see are the natural beauties of the island, wild headlands and rugged mountains, valleys filled with olive trees and cypresses, a plain filled with windmills, and the whitewashed villages. Crete is the island of El Greco, who was born Domenico Theotokopoulos in the village of Fodele, before heading off for Italy, Spain, and immortality. Its second most famous son is Nikos Kazantizakis, who wrote many distinguished novels before one of them, *Zorba the Greek,* was made into a movie earning him international fame.

If you're coming to Crete mainly to see Knossos and wallow in the Minoan civilization, you'll probably want to stay in downtown Heraklion, where you'll find dozens of hotels, most of them built within the past ten years. But if you've come for a vacation, to mix the sand and the sea with the quest for culture, stay at **Aghios Nikolaos,** 40 miles east of Heraklion, a pretty resort town poised between the sea and a lake. There are several new hotels here too, in every price range, but top honors go to the deluxe bungalow-hotel **Minos Beach,** one of the finest resorts anywhere in the Mediterranean. Its nearest rival is the Class A **Mirabello Village,** where the 158 bungalow rooms rent for 6133 drs ($61) double, including breakfast and dinner—slightly less than the Minos Beach. At Elounda, the **Astir Palace Elounda Hotel** sprinkles its bayside site with 300 deluxe rooms, for 8700 drs ($87) and up for a double with half board. Elsewhere on the island there are scores of hotels in the A, B, and C categories, but you'd still be wise to make a reservation far in advance in summer.

HOW TO GET TO CRETE: Olympic Airways has seven or eight flights every day during the summer months between Athens and Iraklion (mostly Boeing 737s; flight time is 50 minutes and the fare is around $66 round trip); seafarers have a choice of two boats daily from Piraeus.

Rhodes

If you go to Rhodes by sea, so much the better, because that way you can more readily capture the flavor of this, one of the great crossroads of history. You sail into another dramatic harbor, past the 15th-century fortress/lighthouse of St. Nicholas, past three small stone windmills guarding the old harbor, almost right up to the turreted walls of the old city, which at this point is virtually concealed behind its battlements, except for its minarets and the magnificent **Palace of the Grand Masters.** The Grand Masters, that is, of the Knights of St. John, who built these fortifications so thoroughly that they were able to rule the island, behind those walls, for two centuries.

Rhodes is half a dozen Mediterraneans rolled into one—Saracen, Crusader, Turkish, Venetian, Ancient Greek, Modern European. It's the largest of the Dodecanese, and its recorded history goes back all the way to the 11th century B.C. It has one of the most pleasant climates in Europe, with warm days ten months of the year, which makes it a favorite winter resort for Europeans living in northern climes. Fortunately, it's a simple matter to enjoy both the historic and the resort side of the island. The old city of Rhodes is a delightful experience (alleys and courtyards, bazaars, tavernas, fountains, squares, wrought-iron balconies, ornate doorways, mosques, churches, mansions), with a couple of interesting museums, but it won't take you long to complete your tour. The only other sight on the island (but some sight) is **Lindos**—a circular harbor and a whitewashed village, topped by a Crusader fortress and an even more ancient acropolis which is today not much more than a few toppled columns and some well-trodden steps. You get to the acropolis either by donkey along a special path, or on foot (the best way) up through cobbled streets not much wider than your shoulders, and lined with a phalanx of handicraft and souvenir shops. It's quite a hike, but the view from the top is breathtaking—the town and the harbor on one side, an even tinier harbor on the other, with a pair of fishing boats and a toy-size chapel marking the spot where St. Paul came ashore to preach to the Rhodians.

Accommodations in Lindos, as of this date, are confined to rooms in private houses (or complete houses for longer stays), but elsewhere on the island you have a choice of almost a hundred hotels in every class, and more are being put up every year. The grandest of all is the renowned **Grand Hotel Astir Palace**, a vast, deluxe complex, with 380 rooms, a casino, a tennis court, and a new indoor swimming pool. In high season, doubles are 6942 drs ($69) and up.

HOW TO GET TO RHODES: Six flights every day from Athens in summer (60 minutes each way, about $80 round trip); five companies operate regular sea service to the island all year round (trips take 20 hours nonstop, up to 28 hours with intermediate stops).

CRUISES THROUGH THE GREEK ISLANDS

IN THE PREVIOUS two chapters you learned about the various Greek islands and how to get to them by scheduled ferryboat and plane, but there are two other ways of seeing these gleaming sunny islands . . . on island cruises by cruise ship or charter yacht. You board a luxury cruise ship in Piraeus and set off for a few days of relaxed island-hopping—without having to pack and unpack more than once, without having to dash out to airports to catch flights. These island cruises are a happy combination of touring and vacationing—you have a chance to see the sights, but you also get to lounge around the pool or sunbathe on the deck between ports of call.

Usually the longer stretches between islands are covered during the night, when you can't really do much sightseeing anyway, and the time you do have to spend on shore varies, depending on all sorts of factors—time of departure from Piraeus, availability of berths on tenders, arrangement of itinerary. Some stops you'll find too short—obviously on a three-day cruise, for example, you can't include everything. However, a stop on Crete will always allow you time at least to visit the Minoan ruins at Knossos, and in Rhodes you'll be able to visit the old walled city and its museums, and you'll probably have time also to take the four-hour coach tour to Lindos.

Here are some sample cruise itineraries:

3-Day Cruise

Friday	Piraeus			dep. noon
	Mykonos	arr.	7 p.m.	dep. 10 p.m.
Saturday	Rhodes	arr.	10:30 a.m.	dep. 6:30 p.m.
Sunday	Crete	arr.	8 a.m.	dep. noon

	Santorini	arr.	5 p.m.	dep. 8 p.m.
Monday	Piraeus	arr.	7 a.m.	

4-Day Cruise

Monday	Piraeus			dep. noon
	Mykonos	arr.	7 p.m.	dep. 11 p.m.
Tuesday	Patmos	arr.	7 a.m.	dep. 10:30 a.m.
	Ephesus	arr.	3 p.m.	dep. 8 p.m.
Wednesday	Rhodes	arr.	8 a.m.	dep. 6:30 p.m.
Thursday	Crete	arr.	8 a.m.	dep. noon
	Santorini	arr.	5 p.m.	dep. 8 p.m.
Friday	Piraeus	arr.	7 a.m.	

7-Day Cruise

Wednesday	Piraeus			dep. 6 p.m.
Thursday	Crete	arr.	8 a.m.	dep. noon
	Santorini	arr.	5 p.m.	dep. 8 p.m.
Friday	Rhodes	arr.	7 a.m.	dep. 9 p.m.
Saturday	Ephesus	arr.	7 a.m.	dep. noon
Sunday	Istanbul	arr.	2 p.m.	(overnight)
Monday	Istanbul			dep. noon
Tuesday	Delos	arr.	10 a.m.	dep. 1:30 p.m.
	Mykonos	arr.	3 p.m.	dep. 11 p.m.
Wednesday	Piraeus	arr.	7 a.m.	

Other seven-day itineraries include Santorini, Crete, Rhodes, Kos, Patmos, Samos, Kusadasi, Mount Athos, Chalkidiki, Delos, Mykonos; and Istanbul, Izmir, Ephesus, Delos, Mykonos, Rhodes, Crete, and Santorini. Beginning in 1984, "K" Lines began regular cruises to the northern islands—Skiathos, Skopelos—and Thessaloniki. The cruise season is from early April through November.

The Cruise Ships

There are half a dozen shipping companies operating cruises through the Greek islands to serve the one in six visitors to Greece who take cruises—a total of almost a million passengers each year. There are several newcomers to the flotilla of cruise ships for longer trips, such as the TSS *Atlas* of Epirotiki Lines, the MTS *Constellation* of "K" Lines, and the *Aquarius* and *Castalia* of Hellenic Mediterranean Lines; some of the ships you may recognize from their winter assignments in the Caribbean—

such as Sun Lines' fine *Stella Solaris*, *Stella Maris*, and *Stella Oceanis*. In addition, you can often board "international" cruise liners like the *Queen Elizabeth II* and *Vistafjord* of Cunard Lines for segments of longer itineraries passing through Piraeus. The largest single fleet, however, belongs to the Epirotiki Line, which was founded in 1919 and claims to have started the fashion for cruising the Greek islands two decades ago. It probably offers you the widest choice of cruises, ships, accommodations, and, most important, departures.

Most of these cruise ships are equipped with all the facilities you would find in a resort hotel—swimming pool, air conditioning, dining rooms that can usually seat the entire quota of passengers at one sitting, beauty salon, nightclub, bars and lounges, discos, and in some cases cinemas. On most of the ships, some or all of the cabins are equipped with wall-to-wall carpeting, private toilets and showers, telephones, and two-channel radios. Stewards, cruise directors, tour guides, and most other members of the crew who come in contact with passengers speak fluent or adequate English.

These seagoing cruises also give you the opportunity to broaden the scope of your vacation by including additional *countries* with the minimum of effort. Without the bother of repacking and unpacking, without having to stand in line for check-ins or boarding you can visit, say, Egypt, Israel, Turkey, the Black Sea, and Italy simply by stepping aboard a cruise ship in Piraeus. The schedules of cruise lines like Sun, Epirotiki, and "K" Lines–Hellenic include seven-day itineraries through the Greek islands and on to Ephesus and Istanbul, or a sampling of Greek islands with visits to such ports of call as Ashdod (for Jerusalem) and Port Said (for Cairo), or, in the opposite direction, by "K" Lines or Chandris to Corfu, Dubrovnik, and Venice. Rates for these cruises vary, of course, from line to line and ship to ship but generally fall within the ballpark range of $115 to $120 per day per person.

WHAT IT WILL COST: Rates vary enormously, of course, depending on the duration of the cruise, the size and facilities of the ship, the type of cabin accommodations. Your travel agent will be able to show you deck plans when you get around to choosing a specific cruise and a specific ship, at the same time giving you up-to-date details of the fares. Meantime, here are some guidelines.

Fares for a three-day cruise:
  with three or four passengers in a cabin, from $360
  with two in stateroom with private shower, from $470
Fares for a seven-day cruise:
  with three or four in a cabin, from $810
  with two in a stateroom with private shower, from $1,140

On a deluxe ship like the Sun Lines' *Stella Solaris,* of course, rates are higher—seven-day cruises cost from $1,200 per person to $2,000 per person for deluxe suites. The average prices on four-day cruises are around $650 per person, or roughly $125 a day for all meals, accommodations *and* transportation. On a seven-day cruise, the basic rates work out at only $120 a day for meals, accommodations, and transportation.

When deciding how much you ought to pay, keep these points in mind: You spend most of your time on deck or ashore, so the size and luxury of your cabin is of minor importance; most of these ships are modern and air-conditioned so you don't have to be on an upper deck, and you don't need an outside cabin (in most cases, you can't open the portholes anyway because of the air conditioning); even the least expensive accommodations have private showers and toilets. So don't think that you can't afford to take one of these cruises unless you can afford the most expensive cabins. In fact, in some cases cabins one deck down are a better value than cabins on the boat deck because that part of the ship is wider and the cabins have more space—but they may cost $30 or $40 less.

Remember also that these fares include all your meals for three or four days—a total of nine meals, for example, on a three-day cruise. The food is usually international fare, with a touch of Greek at most meals; at least one poolside buffet; and usually one Greek evening when the entire meal is Greek and the crew entertains you with folk music and dancing.

Shore excursions are extra (you don't have to take them if you don't want to), and tips for a three-day cruise usually add up to another $20—but, of course, that figure is up to you.

Think about it. A cruise is a great way to see several islands on a short vacation. It's a great way to get some sun. The sea is usually calm. *(Usually.)* You see the sights. You meet new friends. You eat heartily. Chances are, you'll probably find the three-day cruise too short and decide to stretch the trip to four days, at least.

SEVEN-DAY YACHT CRUISE: There's another way to cruise the Greek Islands, more in the spirit of the Argonauts but with much less effort. It's on one of **Viking's Tours'** seven-day "Fascinating Yacht Cruises," aboard an 85-foot motor-yacht, the *Viking of Kos.* This *Viking* is equipped with twin Rolls-Royce diesel engines; the cabins have showers and toilets, the main saloon doubles as bar and dining room, and there's ample deck space for sunning and lazing. One of these seven-day *Viking* cruises takes in the islands of Mykonos, Delos, Santorini, Ios, Paros, Tinos, and Naxos, with seven nights on the yacht. The fare, around $695, includes bed, breakfast, and light lunch (no dinner; most passengers prefer the option of dining ashore), services of an English-speaking tour leader (but not shore excursions), all port fees and transfers, round-trip steamer ticket to Mykonos. Your travel agent can give you full details, or write to Viking's Travel Bureau, 3 Filellinon St. (Syntagma, in the Arcade), Athens.

Cruising by Charter Yacht

You've seen it so many times in movies—jet-setters taking their ease, bronze bodies in skimpy bikinis, stewards in white, fetching drinks and serving sumptuous dinners by candlelight on the after deck. Maybe this is everyone's dream way of seeing the Greek islands, but for some people it's actually being lived every summer somewhere in the Aegean and Ionian Seas. (And not just by jet-setters either!)

In some ways this *is* the perfect way to see the islands. You set your own pace. You join the crowds or avoid them. You float past headlands with ancient temples, moor beside ancient monasteries, go ashore to mingle with the crowds, then escape when you feel like it. No packing and unpacking, no standing in line waiting for luggage or waiting to board. More and more vacationers are discovering the advantages of cruising by charter yacht, yet there's no feeling of crowded anchorages (how could there be, with 2000 islands to chose from); the sailing is easy too, with islands rarely more than two or three hours apart. And these days there's a wider choice of charter yachts than ever—everything from 25-foot sailboats without crew ("bare boat") to 200-foot luxury yachts with a crew of 20. You can charter yachts that once belonged to Mussolini or Prince Rainier—even, for $10,000 a day, the floating palace that appeared in the movie *The Greek Tycoon.* But don't get the idea that charter yachts are the special privilege of the rich—that 25-foot sailboat, sleeping six, is yours for around $150 a day, or less than $30 a head for accommodations *and* transportation.

Between those two extremes, there are charter boats for every taste and budget—with or without private facilities, with or without air conditioning, with or without wall-to-wall carpeting and wall-to-wall stereo. Charter boats all have certain things in common: by law they must carry adequate navigational and radiotelephone equipment; they must be drydocked once a year and inspected by representatives of the Ministry of Merchant Marine; with the exception of boats based in Rhodes, they must be Greek-registered and carry a Greek skipper; and their skippers must qualify for a Merchant Mariner's license.

I've checked out a selection of the charter yachts based at Zea Marina, and without exception they were in first-class condition, the crews obviously took a pride in them, and there seemed to be little reason to suspect any language problem under normal circumstances. Nevertheless misunderstandings could arise, as they could even with an English-speaking crew, and the charterers should determine in advance exactly the kind of trip they anticipate—whether or not they want to do a lot of sailing or whether they'd prefer to motor from island from island; whether or not they want to go ashore for dinner or dine aboard; whether or not they want to spend evenings in harbors and marinas or in some secluded cove; whether or not they want to do a lot of sightseeing ashore, which will affect the way the skipper plans the itinerary, and so forth. Above all, the charterers should know clearly in advance exactly what size of boat they need, what kind of facilities they expect (such as a dinghy for waterskiing, and how much extra that will cost). The people to give you this information are yacht brokers specializing in charters: several of the leading brokers in U.S. handle bookings for the Greek islands, and many of them (such as Sparkman and Stevens or World Yacht Enterprises in New York, and Nicholsons in Cambridge, Massachusetts) have personal experience of individual yachts.

In Greece, charters are handled by some 40 brokers, most of whom are members of the Hellenic Professional Yachting Association (64 Akti Themistokleous, Piraeus) which will send you a list of members. In the meantime, you might want to consider three typical organizations and some of the services they offer. The largest of these brokers (and indeed the largest owner and operator of charter yachts in Europe) is a company called **Valef Yachts** at 22 Akti Themistokleous in Piraeus. Their office is right at the marina in Zea Marina, and the rates of their 200-odd boats range from $130 a day to $6500 a day, from 25 feet to 188 feet overall. Bill Lefakinis, the owner, is a Greek-American applying Yankee ideas of marketing to the sometimes confusing business of chartering. He has a distinguished roster of clients, 80% of whom are Americans, and he now has an office in the U.S. to spread the gospel stateside—at 7254 Fir Rd., Ambler, PA 19002 (tel. 215/641-1624)—and to answer any questions you may have about what boats are available and how much they cost. Another reliable broker with a U.S. office is **Regatta Yachts** at 123 East 45th St., New York, NY 10022 (tel. 212/421-0389) or 11 Akti Montsoponlon in Piraeus.

Another major broker is **Hellenic Marine Consultants** (94 Skra St., Piraeus), which specializes in charters in the eastern Mediterranean as well as out of Zea Marina. Their yachts, from $100-a-day bare boat to $9000 a day with crew (but mostly in the $3000- to $4000-a-day category), are popular with experienced charterers who want to get off the beaten track and sail out of Rhodes to explore places like Izmir and Kusadasi on the Turkish coast.

Both of these companies list a selection of bare boats, but their main business is crewed vessels: a company that specializes in bare boats is **SeaHorse** (Marina 4, Glyfada), which was founded 12 years ago by two Dutch brothers called van Seggelen. Their roster of 40 yachts ranges from a 32-foot Baltic at $110 a day to a 76-foot Swan for $1270 a day. They're really interested in chartering to serious sailors (who must prove their ability before they hoist sail), but they can also arrange to have a skipper aboard for $60 a day, and a cook for $30 a day. Unlike most brokers, SeaHorse offers discounts in the off-season.

Please note that all these rates are subject to change; food, liquor, and fuel are extra, and there's an additional tax of 2½ %. Even so, a charter yacht can be a relatively inexpensive way for four, six, or eight people (even more, since many yachts are chartered to corporations for seminars), when you consider how much it would cost to fly four, six, or eight people around the islands, to say nothing of their hotel bills.

How much can you see, how far can you travel? That depends on all sorts of factors, of course, not the least being the wind, but a couple of sample itineraries, based on average cruising times by sail or power, will give you some idea of the opportunities. On a five- to six-day odyssey (in most cases seven days is the minimum rental, but you may not be able to, or want to, travel each of the seven days) you could cruise from Piraeus to Hydra, Monemvassia, Spetsai, Poros, or Aegina and back to Piraeus, a total of something like 185 to 190 miles. In seven days you could cover almost 300 miles, visiting Mykonos, Naxos, Ios, Santorini, Sifnos, and Kythnos, depending on how long you plan to stay in each.

The National Tourist Organization of Greece publishes a useful 54-page booklet called "Greece for the Yachtsman" which lists and describes a range of itineraries; copies may, or may not, be available from the NTOG in New York (645 Fifth Ave., New York, NY 10022; tel. 212/421-5777).

When is the best time to go? The most popular time is June, July, and August, when it may be blisteringly hot ashore but pleasantly cool among the sea breezes. Many Greek yachtsmen consider September the best month for cruising; May, June, and possibly October are good for *sailing,* if you don't want to do much sunbathing or waterskiing. The remainder of the year is really for enthusiasts.

Port of Athens, Piraeus

Appendix I

CAPSULE VOCABULARY
—And Calendar of Events

LEARN A FEW BASIC words and phrases in Greek before you go (you could memorize the following list, for example, on the flight over). You'll be amazed how much difference this will make to your reception in shops, restaurants, and hotels. Greeks *really* appreciate it when foreigners make an effort to speak a few words of their language. When you go into a shop, for example, say *"kah-lee-MEH-ra"*—good day (you can use it any time up to, say, 4 o'clock). Good evening is *"kah-lee-SPEH-ra."* When you are introduced to someone, say *"HEE-ro po-LEE,"* and at the end of that first meeting you say *"HAH-ree-kah,"* which means "pleased to have met you." Greeks are much more formal about such basic courtesies, as you can see.

Because the Greek alphabet is different from our own, I am including in this guide a phonetical vocabulary of useful expressions to assist you in your everyday dealings.

To aid your **pronunciation,** I have written the *accented syllable in capital letters,* the rest of the word in lowercase. As a general rule, in modern Greek the *accent* of the word is *on the middle or last syllable,* unlike English, where you usually find the accent on the first syllable of a word. This simple difference in pronunciation often determines whether or not you will be understood. Don't worry too much, though. So many people in Athens learn English in school that you may find you need this handy vocabulary only for courtesy or fun.

EVERYDAY EXPRESSIONS

Good morning	kah-lee-MEH-ra
Good evening	kah-lee-SPEH-ra

Hello or good-bye (informal)	YAH-sahs!
Hello or Good-bye (formal)	HEH-re-te
What is your name?	POSS-ssas LEH-neh?
I have enjoyed myself very much	HAH-ree-kah po-LEE
Yes	neh
No	O-nee
Excuse me	sig-NO-mee
Does anyone speak English?	mi-LEYE kan-EES on-glee-KAH?
Thank you (very much)	ef-hah-ree-STOH (PAH-rah-po-lee)
Please	pah-rah-kah-LO
You're welcome	pah-rah-kah-LO
Good health! (Cheers!)	stee-nee-YAH-sou (singular)
	stee-nee-YAH-sass (plural)
	stee-nee-YAH-mas (us)
I don't understand	THEN-kah-tah-lah-VEH-no
Please repeat it	PEH-steh-toh PAH-lee,
	pah-rah-kah-LO
What time is it?	TEE O-rah EE-neh?
How much is it?	PO-so EH-ee?
	PO-so KAH-nee?
It's all right	en-DAX-ee
It's not all right	THEN EE-nai en-DAX-ee
I'm sorry	li-PAH-mai
Men's room	AN-thron
Ladies' room	yee-NAI-kon
What?	TEE?
Why?	yah-TEE?
When?	POH-teh?
How?	POHSS?
How far?	POH-soh mah-kree-AH?
How long?	POH-soh ke-ROH?
Good	kah-LOH
Can you tell me?	boh-REE-teh nah-moo-PEE-tah?
I am lost	EH-khah-sah tah-THROH-moh
I am sorry	lee-POO-mee

TRAVEL EXPRESSIONS

I want to go to the airport.	THEH-loh na PAH-oh stoh ah-eh-roh-THROH-mee-oh
Please call a taxi for me.	sass parakaLO foNAXTeh EHna afhtohKEEnee toh

	toh
Show me on the map.	THEEK-steh-moo stoh KHAR-tee
Am I going in the right direction for . . . ?	pee-yeh-no kah-LAH YAH . . . ?
Please tell me where to get off.	pah-rah-kah-LO PEH-steh-moo poo na VGOH

SHOPPING

I'm just looking.	ah-PLOSS kee-TAH-zo
May I try this one?	boh-ROH na toh thoh-kee-MAH-so?
It doesn't fit me.	then moo YEE-neh-teh
Will this fade (shrink)?	thah kseh-VAH-psee (mah-ZET-see)?
Will you please wrap this?	moo toh tee-LEE-yeh-teh pah-rah-kah-LO
Where do I pay?	POO thah plee-ROH-soh?
My (mailing) address is . . .	ee (tah-khee-throh-mee-KEE) thee-EF- theen-see-moo EE-neh . . .

TELEPHONE

Where can I telephone?	POO boh-ROH nah-tee-lee-fo-NEE-so?
Will you telephone for me?	tee-lee-fo-NEE-teh ya MEH-nah?
Give me the long-distance operator.	THOH-steh-moh tohn tee-lee-fo-nee-TEE mah-KRASS ah-poh STAH-seh-oss
Hello	ehm-BRO HSS
May I speak to . . .	boh-ROH nah-mee-LEE-stoh . . .
Please speak more slowly.	pah-rah-kah-LO mee-LAH-teh PYOH ar-GHAH

CALENDAR OF EVENTS

The following is only a sampling of the hundreds of special events—folkloric, religious, festive, cultural—that take place throughout the year all over Greece. For a complete list, contact the National Tourist Organization of Greece.

JANUARY: Feast of St. Basil—a general celebration with traditional New Year's cake and national costumes (1st).

Epiphany—the "Blessing of the Waters" ceremony throughout Greece. The most spectacular spot to visit is Piraeus (6th).

FEBRUARY: In mid-February it's carnival time throughout Greece.

MARCH: Greek National Holiday, honoring the War of Independence with military parades throughout the country (25th).

APRIL: Sound and Light performances in Athens, Corfu, and Rhodes (through October).

Anniversaries dedicated to St. Spyridon, patron saint of Corfu (midmonth).

Easter Sunday in the Greek Orthodox church, a public holiday and the most important religious holiday in the Greek calendar (movable—April 14 in 1985).

MAY: Labor Day and Flower Festival, a public holiday (1st).

The anniversary of the union of the Ionian islands with Greece, celebrated mostly on Corfu (21st).

"Hadjipetria" Festival in Trikkali, in the province of Thessaly (end of month).

JUNE: Wine Festivals at Daphni (11 kilometers from Athens), Rhodes, and other locations—wine-tasting, tavernas, dancing.

JULY: Wine Festival at Alexandroupolis (mid–month).

Athens Festival—drama, concerts, opera, ballet at Herod Atticus Theater (through September).

Epidaurus Festival—performances of ancient Greek drama in open-air theater (through August).

Northern Greece National Theater performances of ancient Greek drama in the open-air theaters at Philippi and on the island of Thassos.

"Dionysia" Wine Festival on island of Naxos (mid–month).

AUGUST: Ancient Greek dramas performed in the open-air theater at Diou, near Mount Olympus (mid–month).

Art exhibition on Skyros island (first week of month).
Holiday honoring the Virgin Mary, celebrated on the island of Tinos (15th).

SEPTEMBER: Thessaloniki International Trade Fair.
Film Festival and Festival of Light Music, Thessaloniki.

NOVEMBER: St. Andrew's Day, celebrating the patron saint of Patras (30th).

OCTOBER: Demetrius Festival—music, opera, ballet—in Thessaloniki.
National Anniversary (28th).

The Alphabet

Aα	álfa	Nν	ní
Bβ	víta	Ξξ	xí
Γγ	gáma	Oo	ómikron
Δδ	thèlta	Ππ	pí
Eε	èpsilón	Pρ	ró
Zζ	zíta	Σσ	sígma
Hη	íta	Tτ	táf
Θθ	thíta	Yυ	ipsilón
Iι	yóta	Φφ	fí
Kκ	kápa	Xχ	hí
Λλ	làmtha	Ψψ	psí
Mμ	mí	Ωω	oméga

Last Word

As I said earlier, every care has been taken to check and cross-check prices, dates, opening hours, and other facts in this guide. Inevitably, some of them may change before you sit down to plan your trip; there's little the author or publisher can do about such variations, which are the responsibility of governments, economies, oil sheiks, and other quirky factors. Nevertheless, the prices should not be off by more than 10% to 15%, except in unprecedented circumstances; use the figures in these pages as a basic guide, and if precise dollar-and-cents calculations are a critical matter, check out the detailed prices with your travel agent before you leave home.

NOW, SAVE MONEY ON ALL YOUR TRAVELS!
Join Arthur Frommer's $25-A-Day Travel Club

Saving money while traveling is never a simple matter, which is why, over 22 years ago, the **$25-A-Day Travel Club** was formed. Actually, the idea came from readers of the Arthur Frommer Publications who felt that such an organization could bring financial benefits, continuing travel information, and a sense of community to economy-minded travelers all over the world.

In keeping with the money-saving concept, the annual membership fee is low—$15 (U.S. residents) or $18 (Canadian, Mexican, and foreign residents)—and is immediately exceeded by the value of your benefits which include:

(1) The latest edition of any TWO of the books listed on the following page.

(2) An annual subscription to an 8-page quarterly newspaper *The Wonderful World of Budget Travel* which keeps you up-to-date on fastbreaking developments in low-cost travel in all parts of the world—bringing you the kind of information you'd have to pay over $25 a year to obtain elsewhere. This consumer-conscious publication also includes the following columns:

Travelers' Directory—members all over the world who are willing to provide hospitality to other members as they pass through their home cities.

Share-a-Trip—requests from members for travel companions who can share costs and help avoid the burdensome single supplement.

Readers Ask . . . Readers Reply—travel questions from members to which other members reply with authentic firsthand information.

(3) A copy of *Arthur Frommer's Guide to New York*.

(4) Your personal membership card which entitles you to purchase through the Club all Arthur Frommer Publications for a third to a half off their regular retail prices during the term of your membership.

So why not join this hardy band of international budgeteers NOW and participate in its exchange of information and hospitality? Simply send $15 (U.S. residents) or $18 U.S. (Canadian, Mexican, and other foreign residents) along with your name and address to: $25-A-Day Travel Club, Inc., 1230 Avenue of the Americas, New York, NY 10020. Remember to specify which *two* of the books in section (1) above you wish to receive in your initial package of members' benefits. Or tear out this page, check off any two books on the opposite side and send it to us with your membership fee.

FROMMER/PASMANTIER PUBLISHERS Date_____
1230 AVE. OF THE AMERICAS, NEW YORK, NY 10020

Friends, please send me the books checked below:

$-A-DAY GUIDES
(In-depth guides to low-cost tourist accommodations and facilities.)

☐ Europe on $25 a Day	$10.95
☐ Australia on $25 a Day	$9.95
☐ England and Scotland on $25 a Day	$9.95
☐ Greece on $25 a Day	$9.95
☐ Hawaii on $35 a Day	$9.95
☐ India on $15 & $25 a Day	$9.95
☐ Ireland on $25 a Day	$9.95
☐ Israel on $30 & $35 a Day	$9.95
☐ Mexico on $20 a Day	$9.95
☐ New Zealand on $20 & $25 a Day	$9.95
☐ New York on $35 a Day	$8.95
☐ Scandinavia on $25 a Day	$9.95
☐ South America on $25 a Day	$8.95
☐ Spain and Morocco (plus the Canary Is.) on $25 a Day	$9.95
☐ Washington, D.C. on $35 a Day	$8.95

DOLLARWISE GUIDES
(Guides to accommodations and facilities from budget to deluxe, with emphasis on the medium-priced.)

☐ Austria & Hungary	$10.95	☐ Cruises (incl. Alaska, Carib. Mex.	
☐ Egypt	$9.95	Hawaii, Panama, Canada, & US)	$10.95
☐ England & Scotland	$10.95	☐ California & Las Vegas	$9.95
☐ France	$10.95	☐ Florida	$9.95
☐ Germany	$9.95	☐ New England	$9.95
☐ Italy	$10.95	☐ Northwest	$10.95
☐ Portugal (incl. Madeira & the Azores)	$9.95	☐ Southeast & New Orleans	$9.95
☐ Switzerland & Liechtenstein	$9.95	☐ Southwest	$10.95
☐ Canada	$10.95		
☐ Caribbean (incl. Bermuda & the Bahamas)	$10.95		

THE ARTHUR FROMMER GUIDES
(Pocket-size guides to tourist accommodations and facilities in all price ranges.)

☐ Amsterdam/Holland	$4.95	☐ Mexico City/Acapulco	$4.95
☐ Athens	$4.95	☐ Montreal/Quebec City	$4.95
☐ Atlantic City/Cape May	$4.95	☐ New Orleans	$4.95
☐ Boston	$4.95	☐ New York	$4.95
☐ Dublin/Ireland	$4.95	☐ Orlando/Disney World/EPCOT	$4.95
☐ Hawaii	$4.95	☐ Paris	$4.95
☐ Las Vegas	$4.95	☐ Philadelphia	$4.95
☐ Lisbon/Madrid/Costa del Sol	$4.95	☐ Rome	$4.95
☐ London	$4.95	☐ San Francisco	$4.95
☐ Los Angeles	$4.95	☐ Washington, D.C.	$4.95

SPECIAL EDITIONS

☐ How to Beat the High Cost of Travel	$4.95	☐ Marilyn Wood's Wonderful Weekends	$9.95
☐ New York Urban Athlete (NYC sports guide for jocks & novices)	$9.95	(NY, Conn, Mass, RI, Vt, NJ, Pa)	
		☐ Museums in New York	$8.95
☐ Where to Stay USA (Accommodations from $3 to $25 a night)	$8.95	☐ Guide for the Disabled Traveler	$10.95
☐ Fast 'n' Easy Phrase Book (Fr/Sp/Ger/Ital. in *one* vol.)	$6.95	☐ Bed & Breakfast-No. America	$7.95

In U.S. include $1 post. & hdlg. for 1st book; 25¢ ea. add'l. book. Outside U.S. $2 and 50¢ respectively.

Enclosed is my check or money order for $_____

NAME_____

ADDRESS_____

CITY_____ STATE_____ ZIP_____